D1765037

EDINBURGH NAPIER UNIVERSITY LIBRARY

3 8042 00891 1255

City Branding

City Branding

Theory and Cases

Edited by

Keith Dinnie
Associate Professor of Business, Temple University Japan

CRL
659.2390776 DIN

7dy

Selection and editorial matter © Keith Dinnie 2011
Individual chapters © individual authors 2011
Foreword © Bill Baker 2011

All rights reserved. No reproduction, copy or transmission of this
publication may be made without written permission.

No portion of this publication may be reproduced, copied or transmitted
save with written permission or in accordance with the provisions of the
Copyright, Designs and Patents Act 1988, or under the terms of any licence
permitting limited copying issued by the Copyright Licensing
Agency, Saffron House, 6–10 Kirby Street, London EC1N 8TS.

Any person who does any unauthorized act in relation to this publication
may be liable to criminal prosecution and civil claims for damages.

The authors have asserted their rights to be identified as the authors of this
work in accordance with the Copyright, Designs and Patents Act 1988.

First published 2011 by
PALGRAVE MACMILLAN

Palgrave Macmillan in the UK is an imprint of Macmillan Publishers Limited,
registered in England, company number 785998, of Houndmills, Basingstoke,
Hampshire RG21 6XS.

Palgrave Macmillan in the US is a division of St Martin's Press LLC,
175 Fifth Avenue, New York, NY 10010.

Palgrave Macmillan is the global academic imprint of the above companies
and has companies and representatives throughout the world.

Palgrave® and Macmillan® are registered trademarks in the United States,
the United Kingdom, Europe and other countries.

ISBN 978–0–230–24185–5

This book is printed on paper suitable for recycling and made from fully
managed and sustained forest sources. Logging, pulping and manufacturing
processes are expected to conform to the environmental regulations of the
country of origin.

A catalogue record for this book is available from the British Library.

A catalog record for this book is available from the Library of Congress.

10 9 8 7 6 5 4 3 2
20 19 18 17 16 15 14 13 12

Printed and bound in Great Britain by
CPI Antony Rowe, Chippenham and Eastbourne

Contents

Contents

Contents

Contents

Bill Baker

Cities and mega-cities, rather than countries, are increasingly becoming the principal protagonists between geographical regions. The competition between cities to establish their credentials as the best choice for prospective visitors, investors, business, students and talented people will intensify as places focus on how to convey their competitive edge and relevance.

Following the success of his first book, *Nation Branding – Concepts, Issues, Practice*, it is fitting that Keith Dinnie has turned his focus to the important subject of branding cities. A recent United Nations report titled *Revision of World Urbanization Prospects* has highlighted that for the first time in history half of the world's population of 6.7 billion now live in urbanized settings. The report also predicts that the future growth of the world's population will be concentrated in Asia and Africa, which is where most new cities will develop. This is reinforced by a backdrop of rapid economic growth in many Asian countries where established cities such as Shanghai, Bangalore and Dubai have stepped onto the world stage.

Today, cities of all sizes find themselves competing against places and organizations on the other side of the world. The global search for talented workers, advantageous conditions and access to markets has brought even small cities onto the radar of global corporations. At the same time, international tourists are becoming more discerning and show an increasing inclination to go beyond the traditional gateway cities to lesser known, emerging cities and regions. This new paradigm means that ambitious cities must proactively shape and influence what the world thinks of them and position and market themselves with strategic intent.

Community leaders are increasingly recognizing that there is a direct link between their city's image or reputation and its attractiveness as a place to visit, live, invest, and study. An even greater realization for some is that inaction is not a viable option if they genuinely want to improve local prosperity, build social capital and foster economic growth. Each year, more cities try to penetrate a world that is cluttered with an over-abundance of alternate choices, advertising, media choices, and marketing messages. Not all understand how to cut through this clutter and 'noise' to connect with customers. To succeed, city leaders are now thinking beyond their traditional approaches to embrace branding techniques that were once the domain of commercial products and services.

The thoughts and associations that come to mind when a city's name is heard or read are likely to have huge financial, political, and social value. Too few city leaders think about the number of jobs, businesses, and other organizations that have a stake in their city's image and reputation. Unfortunately, it is a value that often goes largely unrecognized, unappreciated and unmanaged. It rarely gets measured and never appears on a balance sheet or the job evaluation of a Mayor, city manager or elected official. The level of esteem that a city's name evokes has a direct impact on the health of its tourism, economic development, prestige, and respect. With so much riding on its image, it makes sense to have a plan to cultivate, manage, and protect this most valuable of city assets.

The path to revealing a city brand involves a multitude of stakeholders and may depart somewhat from the methodology followed for branding corporate products and services. One reason for the variation is the composite and complex nature of communities that are a compilation of many independent and competing businesses, products, and experiences all of which may be owned and managed by many different organizations with no single management team or brand custodian. Several contributors demonstrate how city brands must withstand a level of political and public debate that consumer brands rarely endure. They show that a city brand must stand the test of time, public debate, political scrutiny, media questions, and the analysis of marketing partners. They explain that the best way to insulate the brand from this scrutiny is to generate community and partner buy-in from the start through an open consultative process.

City Branding – Theory and Cases explores the theory of city branding and provides interesting case studies which illustrate a variety of approaches taken by ambitious cities. The examples reveal the complex, multidimensional elements involved in defining city brands. Importantly, the book's wide range of contributors shine a light not only on those cities which have been successful, but also some that have faltered or failed. Its global perspective and insights make *City Branding – Theory and Cases* a fascinating read and deserving of a place on the bookshelf of all academics and marketing practitioners with an interest in city branding. The book is an invaluable resource for those wishing to deepen their knowledge of branding principles and how such principles apply to cities. Featuring compelling case studies from around the world showcases how the disciplines of branding have been applied in a variety of very different and at times challenging circumstances. There are many salient lessons here for experts as well as newcomers to the discipline.

This book aims to blend the theory and practice of city branding in an accessible and readable fashion that will appeal to policy makers, academics, students, and the interested general reader. The book's wide geographic spread of contributors and cases reflects the global dimension of city branding, including but also transcending the familiar areas of Europe and North America by featuring cases from cities in other parts of the world such as Ahmedabad, Montevideo, Accra, and Chongqing in addition to cases on cities such as Barcelona, Paris and New York.

The globally diverse set of contributors provides a rich array of perspectives on the current state of city branding theory and practice. The contributing authors come from varied professional backgrounds and this provides the basis for many useful insights into the theoretical underpinnings of city branding as well as the practical, day-to-day implementation issues that determine the success or otherwise of any city branding initiative.

This book does not, however, propose a generic template for city branding. On the contrary, by illustrating the wide range of theoretical concepts related to city branding and by analyzing the real life practice of city branding as implemented by cities as different as Budapest, Seoul, Wollongong, Edinburgh, Kuala Lumpur and Sydney amongst many others, the book aims to provide inspiration and ideas for policy makers as they seek to design city branding strategies that truly reflect the unique essence of their individual cities. There is no 'one-size-fits-all' solution to city branding, which is one reason why city branding is such a fascinating topic.

Keith Dinnie
Tokyo

ACKNOWLEDGEMENTS

Editing *City Branding – Theory and Cases* has been an immensely rewarding experience. It has been a pleasure to work with the diverse and highly talented set of contributors who have kindly participated in this project. The contributing authors have shared insights and perspectives on city branding that collectively represent many decades of research, reflection and professional activity in this fascinating domain. I am extremely grateful to all the contributors, and I look forward to working on other collaborative projects with them in the future.

I would also like to express my gratitude to the Palgrave Macmillan team who have so enthusiastically supported this book throughout its gestation. In particular, I thank Stephen Rutt and Eleanor Davey Corrigan for their keen interest in this project and their prompt responsiveness to the editorial queries I sent their way as the book progressed towards publication. Many thanks also to Brenda Rouse at Palgrave Macmillan for encouraging this project and playing such an important role in promoting the field of place branding through publications such as *Journal of Brand Management* and *Place Branding and Public Diplomacy*.

Keith Dinnie
Tokyo

Bill Baker is President of Total Destination Management and is based in Portland, Oregon. He has more than 30 years destination branding and marketing experience in 25 countries. He is recognized internationally for his pioneer work in creating brand strategies for destinations of all sizes, ranging from nations to small cities. His team has developed strategies for over 100 locations in the United States and Australia to advance their tourism and economic development performance. His strategic advice has also been sought by several nations, including Hong Kong, India, Macau, and Saudi Arabia. He is in demand as a conference speaker on destination branding in the United States, Europe and Asia. Bill is the author of the highly acclaimed book, *Destination Branding for Small Cities* (www.DestinationBranding.com).

Juan Carlos Belloso is an expert in corporate and place strategy and branding. He has extensive experience working with companies and places (urban areas, cities, regions and nations) in the areas of strategy, branding, development, marketing and international promotion. He is advisor to the Barcelona City Council in city branding, marketing and development areas as well as to the Strategic Metropolitan Plan of Barcelona (PEMB), a private non-profit association promoted by the Barcelona City Council. He is also advisor to different companies in corporate branding and communications issues. Juan Carlos graduated in Economics and Business Administration at the University of Barcelona with specialization studies in international marketing at New York University, and has been Brand Strategy Services Director at Futurebrand in Madrid, Director of Strategy Consulting Services at Coopers & Lybrand and KPMG and Director of the Catalan International Promotion Agency in New York. He is a frequent speaker as well as author of brand strategy and place branding articles for different journals and magazines. Contact: jcbelloso@valor-demarca.es

Peggy R. Bendel is a globally recognized expert in travel marketing, crisis communications, and destination branding and has worked with clients from Australia to Arizona, California to Chile, South Africa to Sweden. She launched Bendel Communications International (www.BendelCommunicationsIntl.com) in 2009, after heading the Tourism Division of Development Counsellors International since 1985. A principal in the 'I Love New York' campaign, Peggy received a Lifetime Achievement award from the Hospitality Sales and

Marketing Association International. She sits on the Boards of the Association of Travel Marketing Executives and the Public Relations Society of America's Travel and Tourism section, and belongs to the Society of American Travel Writers. A frequent speaker on the topics of branding, crisis communications, marketing and public relations, Peggy is also an experienced media coach. A graduate of Georgian Court College (now University), Peggy also studied at NYU's Graduate School of Public Administration. She lives in Tucson, Arizona and New York with her husband Richard Gussaroff.

Jared Braiterman PhD is a design anthropologist and founder of Tokyo Green Space. His current research examines how bringing nature into the city benefits the environment and people. From 2009 to 2011, Dr Braiterman is a Research Fellow at the Tokyo University of Agriculture, with research funding generously provided by Hitachi and the Council on Foreign Relations. Dr Braiterman helps governments, real estate companies, architects, and corporations create new green spaces. He publishes in a variety of mass media; presents at landscape design, computer, and urban design conferences; and maintains a public blog at: www.tokyogreenspace.com. Previously based in Silicon Valley, Dr Braiterman consulted on business innovation for global corporations, technology startups, and design agencies. His work has appeared at the Centre Pompidou in Paris. Past fellowships include the Fulbright and National Science Foundation. Dr Braiterman received a PhD in Cultural Anthropology from Stanford, and a BA from Harvard.

Keith Dinnie PhD is an Associate Professor of Business at Temple University Japan Campus in Tokyo. He is Director of the Centre for City Branding (www.centreforcitybranding.com). He is the author of the world's first academic textbook on nation branding, *Nation Branding – Concepts, Issues, Practice*, and currently serves as Academic Editor of the journal *Place Branding and Public Diplomacy*. He obtained an MA in French with German from the University of Edinburgh, an MSc in Marketing from the University of Strathclyde, and a PhD from Glasgow Caledonian University. His main research interests are in the branding of cities, regions and nations. He has published in various journals including *International Marketing Review*, *Journal of Services Marketing*, and *Place Branding and Public Diplomacy*, and has delivered seminars, conference speeches, presentations and lectures in the United States, United Kingdom, France, Germany, Portugal, Greece, Iceland, Malaysia, China, Korea and Japan. Contact: keith.dinnie@centreforcitybranding.com

Magdalena Florek is Adjunct Professor at The Poznań University of Economics in Poland and holds a PhD in Marketing. In 2006/2007, Magdalena was

Senior Lecturer in Marketing at the University of Otago in New Zealand. She is the author and co-author of several Polish books on place marketing and various international publications in place marketing applied to locations of varying sizes. She has published in *Place branding and Public Diplomacy*, *Journal of Place Management and Development*, and *Journal of Sport & Tourism*. She is a member of the Editorial Board of *Journal of Town and City Management*. Magdalena has gained experience in place branding and marketing for cities and regions as a member of research and project teams in the United States, Italy, Poland and New Zealand. She is also an Associate Member of the Institute of Place Management (IPM), founder of Place+ consulting company in the place marketing area and co-founder of BestPlace – The European Place Marketing Institute.

Maria Fola (http://mariafola.blogspot.com) is a communications expert. She was part of the Athens 2004 Strategic Communications team between 2001–2005, when she worked with an international team on developing a strategic communications plan for the Olympic Games; contributed to designing and implementing extensive public opinion research; and also worked on developing crisis communications plans for the Games. She studied Mass Media and Communications in Athens, Greece, and holds a Master's Degree in Media and Communications from the London School of Economics. She is a PhD candidate at the University of Crete, focusing on nation branding theories and their current applications. In the past, she has worked as a communications advisor in Brussels and has also advised many large companies in her homeland, Greece, on their communications activities. Maria currently holds a Director position with Burson-Marstellers' affiliate office in Athens, Advocate, focusing on corporate reputation management.

João Ricardo Freire PhD is currently based in Lisbon where he works as a Brand Consultant for Brandia Central. Joao's greatest interest is in branding and, more specifically, place branding. After years of quantitative and qualitative research, Dr Freire has developed new ideas and unique methodologies for place brand identity construction. His research has appeared in several international publications. He is currently the Regional Editor for Europe, Middle East and Africa for the journal *Place Branding and Public Diplomacy* journal. Most recently, Joao developed an innovative project for the Portugal Tourism Board that applies a new managerial tool to measure the attraction of 11 tourism regions of Portugal. Joao's background in economics initially led him to work in the fields of finance and marketing for several multinational companies including Xerox, Saint-Gobain and the Cabot Corporation in Brazil, Portugal and the United Kingdom. He is also the co-founder of two companies, Ecoterra and Epicuspicy, which are specialized in marketing and branding food products. Contact: freire@ecoterra.co.uk

Sicco van Gelder is one of the world's leading brand strategists. He is the author of books on Global Brand Strategy and City Branding, and he has contributed numerous chapters and articles to books and journals on branding. In particular, he has contributed significantly to theory and practice of the emergent field of place branding. Sicco is founder of Placebrands (www.place-brands.net), an international consultancy dedicated to helping cities, regions and countries develop and implement their brand strategies. In this capacity, he has helped form and has worked with city and nation brand partnerships worldwide.

John Glynn PhD is Executive Dean (Business) at the University of Wollongong. In this role he leads the strategy and planning for two faculties – the Faculty of Commerce and the Sydney Business School. Professor Glynn has extensive international experience as both an academic and as a management consultant. His research and teaching interests are mainly in the areas of financial and public sector management, business reorganization and innovation strategy. He has over eighty publications in terms of books, book chapters, and refereed journals articles and conference papers.

Robert Govers is currently serving as Adjunct Associate Professor, holding the Visit Flanders Chair in Tourism Management of the Consortium University of Leuven, Belgium, where he was also Project Manager at the Flemish Centre for Tourism Policy Studies. Besides this, he holds a Visiting Faculty role with The Hotel School, The Hague, Rotterdam School of Management, IULM University in Milan, the University of Turin and several institutes in Dubai. He has co-authored many publications in the field of place branding and image, tourism, hospitality and quality management. As a project manager, Govers has been involved in many consultancy projects for reputable organizations such as IATA, the European Commission, the Flemish Government and various Dutch ministries and tourism promotion boards, and has taught courses on place branding, marketing, services marketing, strategic services management, and research methods (www.rgovers.com).

Pablo Hartmann is Professor of Brand Management at the Ort University of Montevideo, Uruguay where he teaches marketing and advertising. He was previously Associate Professor of Accounting and Auditing at the faculty of Economics at the University of the Republic. He graduated in Finance and Accounting at the University of The Republic in Uruguay and has postgraduate diplomas in International Marketing from Sogesta, Italy and in Corporate Social Responsibility from Universidad de Buenos Aires, Argentina. He is CEO and founder of Marketing Metrix and Associates (www.metrix. com.uy), a marketing and corporate social responsibility consulting firm in Uruguay that serves companies in Uruguay, Argentina, Brazil and Ecuador. Before founding Metrix, Pablo worked as Marketing Manager with Seagram's, Coca-Cola and Santander Funds in Uruguay as well as other local companies.

Gert-Jan Hospers is Professor of City and Region Marketing at Radboud University Nijmegen and teaches Economic Geography at the University of Twente, both in the Netherlands. He is particularly interested in the image, identity and development of old industrial areas and the application of non-marketing theories (for example, behavioral geography and urban planning) to place marketing issues. Over the years, Hospers has regularly published in international journals including *European Planning Studies*, *Tijdschrift voor Economische en Sociale Geografie* and *Place Branding and Public Diplomacy*. Together with Paul Benneworth he edited the book *The Role of Culture in the Economic Development of Old Industrial Regions* (2009).

John P. Houghton is a writer and advisor on cities, housing and regeneration, and a Principal Consultant at Shared Intelligence. He works with private and public sector partners and local people to prepare strategies and deliver programs to tackle deprivation and renew neighborhoods. John is the co-author of *Jigsaw Cities* with Professor Anne Power and writes for a range of publications. He has a BA from Oxford, an MA from the University of London and spent time at the Humphrey Institute of Public Affairs on a Fulbright scholarship researching mixed communities. You can find out more about John's work and read some of his articles at www.metro-politanlines.co.uk. Views are expressed here in a personal capacity.

Bengt-Arne B. F. Hulleman MSc (1978) is currently Protocol Officer of the International Criminal Court. He obtained his Bachelor degree from Hotelschool the Hague in 2001 and did his Masters in Hospitality Management from 2008–2009 at Erasmus University Rotterdam/Hotelschool The Hague. The subject of his thesis was 'The Hague – International City of Peace and Justice, A relational network brand'. From 2002–2008 he was employed as Policy Assistant to the Grand Master and to the Master of Ceremonies of Her Majesty the Queen of the Netherlands. He is a member of the Board of the Hospitality Management Club and member of the Jury for the Gilbert Monod de Froideville Price, the Dutch Protocol Award. He has a son and a daughter.

Andrea Insch PhD is a Senior Lecturer and Researcher at the University of Otago, New Zealand. She has a PhD in International Business and Asian Studies from Griffith University. Her research is focused on place-based marketing and the ways that place identity can create stakeholder value. Andrea is currently working on defining and measuring place brand equity in New Zealand's cities and hopes to extend this research to other countries. Andrea has published work in academic journals including the *British Food Journal*, *Journal of Marketing Communications*, *International Journal of Retail & Distribution Management* and *Journal of Place Management and Development*. In addition, she has written several book chapters, conference papers and invited guest lectures.

Cai Jing is a Lecturer at East China Normal University, Shanghai. She lectures at the Communication College in areas of corporate communications, advertising and marketing. Cai Jing graduated with a Bachelor in Advertising from Soochow University, China in 2006. Following this, she received a Master's degree in Advertising and Marketing from the University of Leeds Business School, United Kingdom. Her research interests are in corporate philanthropy, corporate social responsibility and integrated marketing communication. Some of her current professional activities include working as a part-time lecturer for the Shanghai government charity education training center, and as a volunteer for EXPO 2010, Shanghai, China.

Jean-Noël Kapferer is an international expert on brand management. Professor at HEC Paris, he holds a PhD from the Kellogg School of Management (United States) and is the author of *Strategic Brand Management*, the key reference of international MBA's, now in its fifth edition. He was the first to promote the notion of brand identity as a key concept of brand management. JN Kapferer recently published *The Luxury Strategy: Break the Rules of Marketing to Build Luxury Brands* and is a much sought after speaker all around the world. He regularly teaches in executive seminars in the United States, Japan, China and Korea.

Roland Kelts is a half-Japanese American writer, editor and lecturer who divides his time between New York and Tokyo. He is the author of *Japanamerica: How Japanese Pop Culture has Invaded the US* and the forthcoming novel, *Access*. He is also a contributing editor and writer for *Adbusters* magazine and *A Public Space* literary journal, and a columnist for *The Daily*

Yomiuri. He has taught at New York University, The University of Tokyo and Sophia University, and has delivered public speeches and presentations on contemporary Japanese culture at numerous institutions across the United States, Japan, Australia and the United Kingdom. His writing appears in *Psychology Today*, *Vogue*, *The Japan Times*, *Animation Magazine*, *Bookforum*, *The Village Voice* and many other publications, and he is a contributor to the anthologies and collections *A Wild Haruki Chase, Playboy Fiction, Gamers, Kuhaku, Art Space Tokyo, Zoetrope: All Story* and others. He is the Editor in Chief of the *Anime Masterpieces* screening and discussion series and a frequent contributor to *National Public Radio*.

Greg Kerr DBA has senior management experience in local government in New South Wales. He has contributed to economic development and tourism studies and has researched and published in place marketing. His doctoral thesis examined the process of implementing aspirational place brands. He now lectures in marketing and management at the University of Wollongong and has held governance roles at the university including head of the marketing discipline, member of Academic Senate and is currently Chair of the Commerce and Sydney Business School Alumni.

Peter Eung-Pyo Kim is the Brand Manager in Seoul Metropolitan Government. He is in charge of international branding strategies, media planning and promotion. He has been building up the current international city branding structure and execution system of Seoul. He specializes in international city branding strategies and international media planning. Prior to joining Seoul Metropolitan government, he worked in online media and Korean companies as a marketing manager. He completed his Bachelor and Master degrees at Sogang University Korea, majoring in business administration. He is interested in research on the international branding of destinations and countries.

Kim, You Kyung is a Professor at Hankuk University of Foreign Studies, Seoul. He teaches marketing, communication, advertising and branding. He completed his doctoral degree from New House School of Public Communication at Syracuse University in the United States. He has written several books and articles on subjects including marketing communication, brand management, global brand communication, advertising and related issues. He has also advised many of Korea's leading organizations both in the public and private sectors on brand strategy, global brand management, nation branding, and city branding. He was a former President of the Korea Advertising Society (2008) and is currently a member of the Presidential Council on Nation Branding of Korea.

Freeman Lau is a renowned Hong Kong designer. He achieved one of his milestones by designing the Watson's Water Bottle, which won the international 'BottledWaterWorld Design Awards' in 2004. He created a model of symbiosis among art, culture, design and business acumen that significantly increased the brand's market share. Apart from designing, Freeman works on public art and sculptures which have been collected by museums all over the world. Over the last decade, Freeman has devoted himself to art education and promotion. He takes leading roles in many non-profit making organizations, currently serving as Vice-Chairman of the Board of Directors of the Hong Kong Design Centre and Director of Beijing Creative Centre. In 2006, Freeman was awarded a Bronze Bauhinia Star from the Government of the Hong Kong Special Administrative Region, in appreciation of his efforts in promoting Hong Kong's design industry and arts and design education. Contact: lau@kanandlau.com

Angelica Leung has lived in Canada, France, Singapore and Taiwan and has worked across multiple industries including market research, air transport, design and branding strategy. She is passionate about traditional arts and crafts and often can be found at meditation retreats or seminars on Chinese schools of thought such as Buddhism, Taoism or Legalism. A genuine and enthusiastic people person, Angelica can often be found emceeing at events, or planning her own social activities of varying sizes and themes, where she devotes her energy to creating new synergies through getting people connected. Currently residing in Hong Kong, she dedicates her working hours to promoting her beloved home city, and her non-working hours to her creative pursuits. Contact: angelica.leung@gmail.com

Grace Loo is a freelance reporter based in Hong Kong. She specializes in writing about business and fashion marketing. She also writes case studies for teaching purposes for universities in Hong Kong and China. She holds a BA in International Relations and an MA in Journalism from the United States. She was also a Reuters Fellow at Oxford University in 2001.

Theresa Loo PhD is the National Director of Strategic Planning, Analytics & Insight for MEC China, a media agency under WPP. She started her career in advertising with JWT and O&M respectively. She has also worked in marketing and market research in China. Theresa holds a PhD in Marketing from Manchester Business School and an MBA from the Rotman School of Management, University of Toronto. She is also a Visiting Scholar at East China Normal University and Shanghai International Studies University. She lectures on consumer behavior, integrated marketing communication and new media. Her research interests are in place branding, rural marketing and digital media.

T. C. Melewar (BSc, MBA, PhD) is a Full Professor of Marketing and Strategy at the School of Management and Law, Zurich University of Applied Sciences, Switzerland. He is the Joint Editor-in-Chief of the *Journal of Brand Management*. He has previous experience in the United Kingdom at Brunel University, Warwick Business School, Loughborough University, and De Montfort University, and at MARA Institute of Technology in Malaysia. TC has edited two books: (1) *Facets of Corporate Identity, Communication and Reputation* and (2) *Contemporary Thoughts on Corporate Branding and Corporate Identity Management*. TC's research interests include corporate branding and identity, marketing communications and international marketing strategy. He has published over 50 papers in refereed journals such as the *Journal of International Business Studies*, *International Marketing Review* and *European Journal of Marketing*. TC has taught postgraduate programs in countries such as Sweden, Germany, Russia, Georgia, Moldova, France, Malaysia and Indonesia.

Alan C. Middleton PhD is Executive Director of the Schulich Executive Education Centre and Assistant Professor of Marketing at the Schulich School of Business at York University in Toronto, Canada. He has been involved with brand development both as a practitioner and academic. His 25-year practitioner career includes marketing and advertising roles in the United Kingdom, United States, Norway, Canada and Japan where he was President/CEO of J. Walter Thompson Japan and an Executive Vice-President and Board Director of JWT Worldwide. In the 1990s he commenced his academic career, teaching at Rutgers Graduate School of Business in the United States, business schools in Argentina, China, Russia, and Thailand and then the Schulich School of Business. Alan co-authored the books *Advertising Works II*, and *Ikonica – A Field Guide to Canada's Brandscape*. He has authored book chapters and papers on brand management, integrated marketing communications, marketing communications ROI, client-agency relations and client-agency compensation strategies. In 2005, he was inducted into the Canadian Marketing Hall of Legends in the mentor category.

Ghazali Musa PhD is a qualified medical doctor (MBBS) and has a PhD in Tourism. He is an Associate Professor in the Faculty of Business and Accountancy, University of Malaya, Kuala Lumpur, Malaysia. He has a wide range of interests in tourism research, including scuba diving, health tourism, disabled tourism, tourism for the elderly community, sociocultural impacts of tourism, ecotourism, high altitude tourism, homestay and back-packer tourism.

Satish K. Nair is Assistant Professor at the Institute of Management, Nirma University, Ahmedabad. With an MSc (Physics) and MBA (Marketing Management) and nine years industry experience in front-line selling, logistical operations and retail management, Mr Nair joined the teaching profession at MBA-level in 1998. His areas of interest include strategic management, competitive advantage (especially in the small and medium enterprises context), strategic brand management and strategic marketing. His academic affiliations at the Institute span strategic management and entrepreneurship as well as marketing areas. In the short span of time since joining the Institute in 2005, he has held positions of academic administration such as Chairman, Marketing Area, Chairman, Strategic Management & Entrepreneurship Area and Chairman, MBA (Family Business & Entrepreneurship) program, as well as coordinating an international conference and three Entrepreneurship Conclaves.

Gary Noble PhD is both an Associate Professor and Associate Dean at the Sydney Business School and Faculty of Commerce at the University of Wollongong. Dr Noble teaches and researches in the field of marketing with a specific focus on international marketing and pro-environmental marketing. Prior to becoming an academic, Dr Noble held senior marketing positions with several multinational firms around the world. He is the author of several textbooks on international marketing and his work has been published in leading marketing and management journals.

Can-Seng Ooi PhD is Associate Professor at Copenhagen Business School. A sociologist by training, his research projects are usually comparative in nature, with specific investigation into place branding, tourism strategies and art worlds. His empirical foci are Singapore, Denmark and China. With the support of the Danish Strategic Research Council, he is leading a team of researchers on a project investigating the complex relationships between place branding and the arts and culture. His studies are published in many academic journals and books, including *Place Branding and Public Diplomacy*, *International Journal of Cultural Policy* and *Annals of Tourism Research*. He is the author of *Cultural Tourism and Tourism Cultures*. Information on Ooi is available at http://www.ooi.dk.

Geoff Parmenter was appointed the inaugural Chief Executive Officer of Events NSW in February 2008. Events NSW is the organization tasked with developing and managing the events program for Sydney (and NSW) to drive economic and brand marketing outcomes. Geoff has 20 years of experience in major events, strategy and marketing. Geoff gained significant experience in international events in the United Kingdom and Europe, working on Rugby World Cup 1991, 1995 and Euro 1996 prior to returning to Australia to work for the 2000 Olympic and Paralympic Games. Straight after the Games, Geoff joined the Australian Rugby Union (ARU), initially as General Manager for Rugby World Cup 2003 and later as head of the ARU's new Marketing and Strategy division. In 2004 Geoff took up the role as Head of Marketing, Communications and Strategy for the new Football Federation Australia (FFA) where he had responsibility for developing and driving integrated corporate and brand strategies for FFA, the Socceroos, the A-League and Football in Australia. Geoff is a member of the Brand Sydney Project Team and Director of the Business Events Sydney Board and the Sydney Business Chamber Regional Council.

Saumya Sindhwani PhD holds a Masters Degree from the London School of Economics and Political Science. She holds a PhD from the University of Manchester in the United Kingdom. She is currently a Solution Leader for India & the Middle East at Hewitt Associates in India and has worked on place branding and location attractiveness projects in the South Asian Association for Regional Cooperation (SAARC) countries, North Africa and the Middle East. Recently she was awarded 'Thought Leader' recognition by Hewitt Associates India. She is also Adjunct Professor at the University of Lancaster in India. Prior to Hewitt, she was working with the Manchester Business School. Her interests include music, traveling and trekking.

Anthony Ebow Spio is a lecturer at the Business Administration department of Ashesi University in Ghana. He teaches marketing, services marketing, and strategic brand management at the junior and senior levels. He graduated from the University of Strathclyde in Scotland with an MSc in International Marketing in 1999. He is also a holder of a BA (Hons) in Economics from the University of Ghana, which he obtained in 1987. He is a chartered marketer and member of the Chartered Institute of Marketing, Ghana and the United Kingdom. Anthony has over 19 years of progressive and responsible marketing, communication and business management experience in industry. He served as the General Manager of DiscoveryTel Ghana, an ICT company that provides internet and network solutions to businesses in Ghana. He also worked for Unilever, a multinational company, for 16 years in Ghana and Nigeria. His academic interests include place branding, ethics in business, entrepreneurship and international business.

Andrew Stevens is Deputy Editor of City Mayors (www.citymayors.com) and has written on urbanism and localism for the best part of a decade, both in print and on the web. He is the author of several books and has contributed to others. He has advised local authorities, consulting firms and an embassy.

Gyorgy Szondi PhD is a Senior Lecturer in Public Relations at Leeds Business School, United Kingdom, where he leads the MA International Communication program. His interests and publications include international public relations, communication management, place branding, public diplomacy, risk and crises communication. His articles and book chapters have appeared in the *Journal of Public Affairs; Place Branding and Public Diplomacy; The Routledge Handbook of Public Diplomacy; The Handbook of Global Public Relations*. He has designed and led strategic communication courses and workshops for the School of Government in the United Kingdom, the Government of Estonia, the Estonian Ministry of Social Affairs, and several other governmental and for-profit organizations in Eastern Europe. Prior to academia, Gyorgy worked for international PR consultancy Hill and Knowlton in Budapest and in its international headquarters in London. Recently he has been mentioned among the 50 leading academic experts in the field of communication in Europe. Besides his native Hungarian, he speaks English and Italian and has a good command of German, French, Polish and Estonian. Contact: G.Szondi@leedsmet.ac.uk.

Richard Tellström PhD is a researcher at the Department of Restaurant and Culinary Arts at Örebro University, Sweden. His dissertation project investigated from an ethnological viewpoint how food culture heritage is commercialized and politicized in Sweden and Nordic countries. Important research questions have been to investigate how some parts of food culture are regarded as useful and other parts ignored or 'forgotten'. Richard Tellström is also working as a lecturer at different universities in Sweden and as an adviser to authorities and companies on how food culture can be used as an asset for developing regions suffering from economic regression, and for development of food products and gastronomic tourism.

Kenneth Wardrop BA (Hons), MBA, MTS, MCIM is an economic development and tourism professional with 25 years experience. Kenneth is currently Chief Executive of the Destination Edinburgh Marketing Alliance

(DEMA), Edinburgh's new city promotion body raising the city's international profile as a place to visit, invest, live, work and study. Projects he has led include Edinburgh's Hogmanay and Christmas celebrations, refurbishment of the National Wallace Monument, Stirling Old Town regeneration, visitor center development in Stirling and the Trossachs, and the MTV European Music Awards Edinburgh 2003. He is a Director of the Edinburgh Convention Bureau. A Visiting Research Fellow at Edinburgh's Napier University, he is currently undertaking research on Generation 'Y' as tourism consumers. He is a contributory author to books including *Festival & Special Event Management* (2008) and *Festival and Events Management: An International Arts and Cultural Perspective* (2004). Kenneth is on the Editorial Advisory Board of the *International Journal for Festival and Event Management*.

Opinions expressed in the following chapters are those of the contributing authors only and do not reflect the views of any other individuals or organizations.

PART I

Theory

CHAPTER I

Introduction to the Theory of City Branding

Keith Dinnie

INTRODUCTION

City branding is a topic of significant interest to both academics and policy makers. As cities compete globally to attract tourism, investment and talent, as well as to achieve many other objectives, the concepts of brand strategy are increasingly adopted from the commercial world and applied in pursuit of urban development, regeneration and quality of life. Much of the published research into city branding originates in the disciplines of marketing and urban studies, two fields that have tended to follow parallel rather than interdisciplinary paths. By drawing upon a range of contributors from diverse theoretical backgrounds, the chapters in Part I of the book aim to provide richly differing perspectives on the theory of city branding. This chapter highlights some of the key themes in the city branding literature, provides an overview of the core concepts addressed by the authors of the chapters that appear in Part I of the book, and links these themes and concepts to the examples of city branding practice that appear in Part II.

Interest in city branding may be seen as part of a wider recognition that places of all kinds can benefit from implementing coherent strategies with regard to managing their resources, reputation and image. Recent books on the branding of cities, nations and regions include those by Anholt (2007), Avraham and Ketter (2008), Govers and Go (2009) and Moilanen and Rainisto (2008). Whereas these books encompass the branding of nations and regions as well as cities, a more specific and singular focus on cities can be found in a growing body of journal articles that explore the nature of city branding (De Carlo *et al.*, 2009; Evans, 2003; Gaggiotti *et al.*, 2008; Harmaakorpi *et al.*, 2008; Kavaratzis, 2004; Russell *et al.*, 2009). Parallels between city branding and corporate branding have been drawn by various scholars, who have noted that the branding of cities and corporations share similarities in terms of their complexity and wide range of stakeholders (Hankinson, 2007; Kavaratzis, 2009a; Parkerson and Saunders, 2005; Trueman *et al.*, 2004). Part of the complexity of city brands derives from their obligation to address the needs of a spectrum of fundamentally different target audiences. Any one city brand may target audiences as varied as tourists (Bickford-Smith, 2009), sports fans (Chalip and Costa, 2005), fashion consumers (Martinez, 2007) and current and potential future residents (Greenberg, 2000; Zenker, 2009). The techniques of marketing and branding may also be used in order to combat existing negative perceptions of a city (Paddison, 1993).

A considerable proportion of the city branding literature – particularly in the urban and regional studies domain – is devoted to the concept of the creative city (Bayliss, 2007; Healey, 2004; Hospers, 2003; Ooi, 2008). The popularization of the concept of the creative city owes much to the work of Florida (2003, 2005), who recommends that city policy makers attempt to attract 'the creative class' as residents in order to galvanize local economies. Members of the creative class include scientists, architects, writers, artists and others who create new ideas, technology and creative content. However, Scott (2006) challenges Florida's view and questions whether the mere existence of a creative class within a city automatically leads to the development of a vibrant local economy. Scott emphasizes the importance of sound governance and a holistic approach to urban planning, rather than relying exclusively on the presence of the creative class within a city. Regardless of the relative influence of the creative class upon a city's economic performance, talent attraction remains a key objective for many city branding campaigns. A vibrant cultural life is seen as one prerequisite in branding a city to appeal to the creative class and several cities have made efforts to revitalize their cultural life in this respect (Chang, 2000; Peel and Lloyd, 2008).

In addition to the key themes in the literature identified above, three further core concepts emerge from the chapters in Part I of the book. These are brand architecture and brand attributes; a network approach; and sustainability. Each of these concepts is discussed below.

BRAND ARCHITECTURE AND BRAND ATTRIBUTES

The concept of brand architecture is well established in the branding literature (Aaker and Joachimsthaler, 2000). In the context of corporate brands, Devlin and McKechnie (2008: 654) define brand architecture as 'an organisation's approach to the design and management of its brand portfolio'.

The concept of brand architecture has been applied to the branding of places by Dooley and Bowie (2005) and Dinnie (2008), who examine the ways in which a place brand can organize its many 'sub-brands' in a similar way to that in which corporations manage their portfolio of product or service brands. The key challenge for a city brand revolves around the issue of how to develop a strong 'umbrella' brand that is coherent across a range of different areas of activity with different target audiences, whilst at the same time enabling sector-specific brand communications to be created. Target audiences may be as diverse as a city's residents (Chapters 2 and 9), potential investors (Chapter 3), tourists (Chapters 4 and 8) and internal stakeholders (Chapters 5 and 6). Frequently there is an important relationship between the city brand and the nation brand of the country in which the city is located. This relationship is discussed in the cases on Edinburgh (Chapter 18), Paris (Chapter 25) and Seoul (Chapter 26).

In order to develop a strong brand, policy makers need to identify a clear set of brand attributes that the city possesses and which can form the basis for engendering positive perceptions of the city across multiple audiences. Such attributes are those that the city brand would wish to see evoked when relevant target groups are asked the question, 'What comes to your mind when you think of this city?' The process of identifying and agreeing upon a relevant set of city brand attributes requires stakeholder engagement rather than top-down coercion. Imagination and an open mind are also necessary in the identification and selection of appropriate brand attributes that powerfully express the unique character of the city. Inspiration may, for example, be found in food culture (Chapter 8) or a city's commitment to managing its environment responsibly (Chapter 9). Whatever attributes are selected, they need to be communicated effectively not only through traditional channels but also through the plethora of digital media that are now available (Chapter 10). Example of cities that have attempted to clarify their brand attributes as part of a comprehensive city branding strategy include Accra (Chapter 12), Barcelona (Chapter 15) and Kuala Lumpur (Chapter 21).

A NETWORK APPROACH

A recurring theme in the chapters of Part I of the book is the need for city brands to adopt a network approach rather than to reserve all decision making to a small elite group. This echoes Hankinson's (2004) conceptualization of place brands as relational network brands, a perspective that focuses on the need for a collaborative approach between public and private sector organizations and a distributive approach to the ownership of the city branding strategy. The principles of effective partnerships include inclusiveness and representativeness; long-term commitment; shared vision; sharing responsibility; trusting each other; alignment and engagement; communicating as one; taking 'on-brand' decisions and actions; making 'on-brand' investments; and willingness to evaluate impact and effectiveness (Chapter 5). Inevitably, there will be tensions and challenges inherent in a partnership approach in which a wide range of stakeholders participate, but these challenges should be welcomed and embraced as an essential foundation for creating a sense of buy-in and commitment to the city brand (Chapter 6). Aspects of the network approach to city branding feature in most of the cases in Part II, for example in the context of Ahmedabad where the city and the state in which it is located, Gujarat, benefit mutually from the city and state level brand strategies (Chapter 13); in The Hague, which is analyzed in terms of Hankinson's concept of a relational network brand (Chapter 19); Lisbon, where a key challenge was to define the scope – and by implication the range of stakeholders – of the city brand (Chapter 22); and Wollongong, where a stakeholder approach was required in order to challenge negative perceptions of the city (Chapter 29).

SUSTAINABILITY

Two dimensions of sustainability are evident in the chapters in Part I of the book. The first, more limited, dimension refers to the sustainability of the city brand. The second, wider dimension, refers to the sustainability of the city itself as a living and liveable environment. In terms of the sustainability of the city brand, key preconditions emerge as follows: a long-term commitment to the city brand strategy, rather than a series of short-term, ad hoc campaigns; adequate budget allocation; responsiveness to societal changes; and the need for specific objectives, underpinned by rigorous research (Chapters 5, 6, 7). The importance of research and measurement of city branding strategy is illustrated in the cases on Budapest (Chapter 16), Montevideo (Chapter 23), New York (Chapter 24) and Sydney (Chapter 27).

In terms of the second, and wider, dimension of sustainability there are numerous potential actions that can be taken in order to create a strong city brand through implementing environmentally-friendly measures that benefit residents and visitors to the city. Such measures are based on the concept of creating new green spaces within urban environments and include the role of streets, the beneficial effects of roof gardens and vertical gardens, and recovering rivers and urban bays (Chapter 9). The city of Seoul has been particularly conscious of the need to integrate sustainability into the fabric of its city branding strategy (Chapter 26).

SUMMARY

City branding theory is still in an emergent phase. Over recent years, there has been an increase in the amount of scholarly research published in the domain of city branding. This rise in interest can be expected to continue over the coming years as the competition between cities intensifies for talent attraction, tourism promotion, the hosting of sporting and cultural events, investment attraction, and the many other goals that cities set out to achieve in their quest for urban development and regeneration. In the future a more interdisciplinary approach should become prevalent in the field of city branding, reflecting the need for a diversity of theoretical perspectives in order to capture the full complexity and multidimensional nature of city branding.

CHAPTER 2

Branding the City as an Attractive Place to Live

Andrea Insch

INTRODUCTION

As a sense of urgency grips many city authorities to create a brand for their urban place, the needs, interests and values of important stakeholders might be overlooked. One group is often neglected in the process of building city brands. Undervaluing the stake that residents have in shaping and enhancing a city's brand could undermine the aims and intentions of a city's original brand strategy. While it might be unrealistic to satisfy the demands and desires of all residents, they are instrumental in building the city brand, as they 'live and breathe' the city's brand identity. Residents' attitudes and attachment to the city where they live, work and play can influence the perceptions of tourists and visitors through their recommendations and complaints. Residents' skills, talents and entrepreneurial drive also contribute to the city's and region's growth and prosperity. In these and other ways, residents can add value to the brand equity of the city in which they live.

The purpose of this chapter is therefore to make the case for why residents are critical participants in the co-creation of a credible and enduring city brand. To achieve these objectives, the chapter will first discuss the relevance of city branding to residents. Next, the relationship between resident satisfaction and city branding is explained. The implementation of city branding with the ultimate goal of creating an attractive place to live, work, and play is described. Finally, special considerations are outlined recognizing that a 'one-size-fits-all' approach is not realistic in the process of building a city brand that is attractive to residents.

CITY BRANDING – RELEVANCE TO RESIDENTS

Apart from the economic advantages of urban concentration, cities offer their residents many social and emotional benefits, including opportunities to share information, form close social bonds, and to engage in a range of activities matching their interests. In fact, as O'Flaherty (2005: 12) states, 'cities could persist—as they have for thousands of years—only if their advantages offset the disadvantages'. Opportunities created through cities for individuals – employment, education, housing, social mobility and transportation, and for businesses – reduced costs, financial service provision, educated labor force, proximity to supplies and markets – have supported continued urbanization throughout the 20th century (United Nations, 2005). With concerns that this trend might be unsustainable, there is increasing competition among cities for resources – human, capital, and intellectual – to ensure their health and longevity. As a means to raise the awareness and appeal of a city in competition with others, urban authorities have begun to embrace the branding process as part of city marketing and urban development (Morgan *et al.*, 2002).

Similar to the goals of a product or service brand, the ultimate goal is to create preference and loyalty to the city among the various segments which cities serve. The number of separate, yet overlapping, segments or stakeholder groups with an interest or stake in the city is potentially unlimited. Among the most visible and salient are – business owners, investors, not-for-profit organizations, residents, students, special interest groups, tourists, and visitors. While it is possible to prioritize their competing interests in relation to a specific issue (for example, whether or not to build a new stadium), the brand strategy for a city must appeal to 'outsiders' as well as residents. However, in the race to build a brand that is admired by tourists and other short-term visitors, residents are overlooked, despite their role as loyal supporters and ambassadors of the city brand.

Cities depend on their residents for economic, social, cultural and environmental vibrancy. Maintaining a diverse, skilled, and satisfied residential population is vital for a city since their disenchantment could trigger a vicious downward spiral. Low levels of resident satisfaction are also negatively perceived by potential business migrants who assess residents' well-being and satisfaction compared to rival locations. In addition to the traditional hard factors, quality of life is evaluated by company executives, management and their families in their decision to relocate and invest (Biel, 1993). Furthermore, factors such as quality of life are interrelated with other 'hard' factors considered during this process – human resources, infrastructure, transportation, education and training opportunities (for an extensive list see Kotler *et al.*, 1993). Thus, achieving a desired level of satisfaction among residents should be the ultimate goal of place managers (Guhathakurta and Stimson, 2007; Kotler *et al.*, 1999), as it has the potential to enhance or harm the city brand (Insch and Florek, 2008).

RESIDENT SATISFACTION – THE ULTIMATE OUTCOME OF CITY BRANDING

In addition to the economic benefits of living in cities, individuals derive social and emotional costs and benefits from city life. To attract and retain valued residents, city policy makers and planners must therefore enhance residents' everyday experiences to encourage their long-term commitment. There are basic requirements of living, working and playing in urban communities that most people share – affordable and accessible housing, transport, healthcare, education and training, retail outlets, leisure and recreation facilities, other public amenities, and opportunities for social interaction (Williams *et al.*, 2008). This list may differ depending on an individual's previous experiences that have shaped their expectations, motivations and attitudes towards the place. While the presence of these facilities is highly desirable, there is also a potential danger that cities might become clones with the standardization of certain features. A report entitled 'Clone Town Britain' by the New Economics Foundation (2004) warned of the trend in the United Kingdom whereby the High Street, or other major shopping zones, were becoming dominated by retail chain stores, thus destroying the diversity and unique character of cities and towns.

Similarly, there is growing criticism of the public financing of new sports stadiums, often without residents' support, as a typical solution to urban malaises. According to a review of research, Delaney and Eckstein (2007: 332) summarize that, 'for cities with existing teams (the vast majority), new stadiums provide a short honeymoon period of increased attendance but ultimately very little net increase in consumer spending or government tax revenues from this spending'. Such visible investments do not necessarily enhance residents' welfare or quality of life. Moreover, development projects based on a cookie-cutter commercial strip model that mimic other suburban areas are short-sighted and might destroy the 'diverse urban fabric of neighbourhoods' (Carr and Servon, 2009: 29). Less monumental, quotidian issues such as improved public transportation, schools, public safety and waste services, might be overlooked, yet are a higher priority for residents.

City authorities must consider the motives, expectations and needs of current and prospective residents and ensure their needs are being met (Insch, in press). Various personal and situational factors can also stimulate or trigger this evaluation of the qualities that the place has to offer and the perceived value for money that living in the place provides. If, for example, a resident's evaluation of the city in which he or she lives steadily improves, his or her attachment and commitment to the city is expected to grow. Measuring and monitoring resident place satisfaction is an essential performance indicator for city authorities (for more details see, Insch and Florek, 2008).

IMPLEMENTATION OF CITY BRANDING FOR RESIDENT SATISFACTION

Perhaps the most challenging aspect of city branding is to communicate with the multiple stakeholders or audiences in a way that is relevant, consistent and coherent. To achieve this goal, city brands risk becoming all and nothing, vague, bland, or even meaningless. Cities that try to capture their complexity in a single brand promise often fail. For example, a number of cities have become synonymous with catch-all statements or 'monikers', such as San Francisco, California, which has been associated with the following – Baghdad by the Bay, The City by the Bay, Everybody's Favourite City, Fog City, and The Golden Gate City. At the same time, the city has officially adopted two mottos – 'Only in San Francisco' and 'The City that Knows How'. Alternatively, if the decision is made to appeal to an external audience, such as tourists, the city brand might offend residents and even alienate them. For example, the well recognized Las Vegas motto 'What Happens Here, Stays Here', created much consternation among residents after the decision was made to adopt it in 2001 (Sauer, 2006). In this way, the design and execution of a brand communications campaign cannot proceed without first deciding how to most effectively position the city brand with residents' input and endorsement.

For example, Wellington City in New Zealand aimed to create a positioning statement to serve multiple audiences – domestic and international tourists, event attendees, business and government visitors and residents – which could be adjusted to suit a particular function. For over 15 years, the city's marketing agency invested in an intensive campaign, anchored by the strapline – 'Absolutely, Positively Wellington'. The city is now the number one destination choice for New Zealanders. The city's tourism chief executive, David Perks, credited the successful result to the 'meeting of a city's vision and residents' passion'. As he explains, 'Wellington's gone from being somewhere people couldn't wait to leave to somewhere people can't wait to get to, and that's been a team Wellington effort' (Anon, 2010: 53).

As the quote above mentions, the effectiveness of city brands depends on the support and commitment of local constituents – residents, local business operators and community groups. At the same time, it must also appeal to potential residents who self-identify with the city. Those championing the city brand, typically city authorities, tourism agencies, and chambers of commerce, must engage major stakeholders in developing and implementing the strategy as part of the co-creative process. For example, New York City's official tourism, marketing and partnership organization NYC & Company first launched a campaign in 2007 featuring celebrity residents such as Robert De Niro, Julianne Moore, Sean 'Diddy' Combs, and Kevin Bacon named 'Just Ask the Locals'. The campaign aimed to encourage New Yorkers to welcome visitors and share their expert tips and insider knowledge about best late-night eats, great bargains and liveliest flea markets in the city (Illroots, 2008).

Since residents are the lifeblood of the community they should be involved in determining the city's long-term economic, social and environmental direction. Articulating a shared vision for the city's future is the starting point for crafting the city brand strategy. However, city authorities often become fixated with the visual aspects of the branding process, such as logos and slogans, since these are perceived to be the easiest to create and control. Consequently, cities spend much time, money and effort in transmitting a one-dimensional campaign, based on a particular phrase and logo that is not perceived to be credible, memorable, distinctive or sustainable, either by residents or external audiences. Through engaging residents, a city's formal marketing agency can collaborate to capture the city's identity and distil this to produce the essence of the brand. In addition to the specific decisions and associated tasks in executing a brand strategy (see Figure 2.1), consideration must be given to how the branding process can co-create desired outcomes for residents including enhancing their satisfaction with city life and attachment to the city (Insch and Florek, 2010).

Encouraging and enabling residents to share their ideas and thoughts on the future of the city in general and the brand strategy in particular, is influenced by the existing sense of community, trust and participation in public and community issues (Holman, 2008; Morton *et al.*, 2008). Therefore, overcoming residents' and community groups' mistrust and perception of indifference to their views is paramount to fostering participation and support in city branding initiatives. Previous research on community participation and engagement suggests that local residents and community groups can enhance the ability for their 'voices to be heard' and their ideas to be influential through understanding the network structure of local government agencies and decision makers (see, for example, Holman, 2008).

FIGURE 2.1 | **Key Questions for Developing a City Brand Strategy**

Identity

Who are we?

What do we stand for?

Community assesses its shared assets, personality ,desirable attributes and so on and selectively emphasizes aspects of the city's place identity. Mechanisms and environment must be conducive to encourage community participation and support of the brand strategy.

Nominated outcomes

What do we want to achieve?

Who do we want to attract?

How do we measure progress?

Integration and consistency of brand essence with city's development goals. Definition of segments the city is aiming to attract and appeal to. Selection of appropriate measures to monitor progress and assess return on investment. Resident participation in the selection of indicators is vital.

Communication

How do we reach, and interact with our audiences in a creative and convincing way? How do we tell the story of our city with credibility?

Brand communications are no longer transmitting a message to a passive audience. Messages cannot be controlled. Consideration must be given to how selected audiences can be reached and invited to participate in a dialogue about the city and its offerings. In addition to traditional media channels, there is increasing use of interactive social media for building the city brand.

Coherence

How do we organize programmes and actions to achieve consistency and uniformity in communications?

A major part of implementation is to decide who will drive specific initiatives. Consideration must also be given to the big picture, that is, how consistent particular action items and activities are.

In particular, groups can identify and connect with important strategic links in the network, thus overcoming an elitist, exclusionist, top-down approach to city branding. Urban economic development projects emphasizing a neighborhood's local heritage and culture are likely to be successful if local residents and community organizations play a key role at all stages. Further, this process involves residents having ownership in local businesses and their own homes to benefit economically as well as socially from their investment (Carr and Servon, 2009). Opportunities for residents to participate in their city's economic and identity development projects fosters a climate in which civic community thrives, enhancing their well-being and in turn their attachment to the place where they live, work and play.

SUMMARY

Residents embody a city's local culture, own and operate local businesses, and represent the personality of the place. As Hayden (1997: 15) explains, 'indigenous residents as well as colonizers, ditchdiggers as well as architects, migrant workers as well as mayors, housewives as well as housing inspectors, are all active in shaping the urban landscape'. These groups and other stakeholders each have an interest in preserving aspects of their city they value and making their cities more appealing and viable places to live. A city's richness and diversity, a source of inspiration for its branding strategy, may also present challenges and complexity. Thus, a one-size-fits-all approach is misguided and impractical. Among the specific factors that combine to construct a city's distinctiveness are scale, personality, history, values, residential composition and urban assets. In this way, each city is a multiplex system and its components penetrate and overlap each other and are reflected in the image of that place (Florek *et al.*, 2006). Cities must identify these components, or features, and how they are interrelated and structured to preserve their uniqueness and to communicate them to new and existing residents, as well as the array of audiences a city, or even a neighborhood within it seeks to serve. Furthermore, residents must be engaged in the process of co-creating their city's brand in order to build an identity that is credible, compelling and sustainable in the minds of the stakeholders it serves.

CHAPTER 3

City Branding and Inward Investment

Alan C. Middleton

INTRODUCTION

In a world where cities and regions aggressively compete for investment from public and private sectors, brand reputation is critical. The brand is both a lens through which information is viewed and a decision criterion.

Branding a city is more complex than branding a product or service. The stakeholders and target groups are broader – including citizens, tourists, and public and private sector organization decision makers – and each is looking for different benefits. Yet if the city lets its brand develop separately for each group, it loses much, if not most, of the value of active branding.

To succeed, the city administration must complete a strategic examination of trends in the social and economic environments; determine where the opportunities, skills, resources, and capabilities lie within the city; what core values, attitudes, behaviors, and characteristics have enabled the city to achieve these; and then figure out what combination of these provides a differentiated appeal to its various target groups. Based on this examination, an integrated brand strategy and execution must be developed and, from these, an integrated brand communications strategy and execution: one brand position based on the city's core values, attitudes, behaviors, and characteristics. Administrators can then look at this and identify the best blend of those skills, resources, and capabilities that can be expressed as relevant benefits to each of the targeted groups.

Avoiding an integrated approach to city brand communication weakens the brand, as does failing to engage in an active city branding process. Toronto, Canada, is an example of a city with great skills, resources, and capabilities that is in need of an integrated city brand communications approach.

CITIES AS BRANDS

'What is a city, but the people.'

— Sicinius in Shakespeare's *Coriolanus*, Act III, Scene I

Cities have always been hubs of activity and change. And now urbanization is truly universal: in 1925, only 25 per cent of the global population lived in cities, but by 2025, it is estimated that this figure will rise to 75 per cent. In all aspects of economic, environmental, political, social, and business analysis, there are critical clusters to understand.

It has been noted by place branding authorities such as Simon Anholt and Keith Dinnie that branding a place is more complex than branding a commercial product or service. Anholt (2007: xii) states that the branding of places 'covers some of the hardest philosophical questions one can tackle: the nature of perception and reality, the relationship between objects and their representation, the phenomena of mass psychology, the mysteries of national identity, leadership, culture and social cohesion, and much more besides'. If this is indeed so and the challenge is so great, why try? What is the real value?

A nation brand has been defined as 'the unique multidimensional blend of elements that provide the nation with culturally grounded differentiation and relevance for all of its target audiences' (Dinnie, 2008: 15). By replacing the word *nation* with the word *city*, we have a serviceable definition of a city brand.

Anholt (2004), Clark (2007), Dinnie (2008), Temporal (2001), and others have emphasized the value of building a positive brand for a nation. Adaptation of this thinking works for cities and includes:

- attraction of inbound investment

- attraction of inbound tourism

- credibility and confidence by investors

- increase of political influence internally (national) and externally (multi-national)

- better and more productive global partnerships with other cities, public or private research and university institutions, and private sector organizations

- 'city of origin' effect on products or services

- civic pride: ability to focus local harmony, confidence, and resolve

To this list, I would add two additional benefits that derive from building a powerful place brand: first, planning process advantage, and second, execution advantage. Planning process advantage refers to the clarity of what the city brand is and what it stands for. This clarity is helpful in focusing strategy. Brands exclude associations and activity as much as they include them. As strategy is the allocation of scarce resources to areas with the highest likelihood of return, so too is a city's brand an expression of its strategy.

Execution advantage flows from this clarity of what the city brand is and encourages greater coordination and communication of activity, which is what those in commercial branding have identified as the path of brand success, that is, establishing the relevant differences of the city brand from its competitors that, over time, result in an increase in awareness and esteem, provided that the brand is appropriately managed.

Some might argue that because city target groups are so different, from tourists to businesses seeking suitable headquarters, a singular brand stance is neither possible nor useful. While there is some validity in this view, the conclusion is at fault. Great brands are like great people. Certain characteristics are consistent, as in, for example, Winston Churchill's eloquence, John F. Kennedy's youthful dynamism and optimism, Nelson Mandela's wisdom, courage, and tolerance, and Margaret Thatcher's stubborn determination. These traits do not define the whole person and – depending on people's viewpoints – other aspects may also come to mind. However, few would disagree with these defining characteristics.

Equally, commercial brands often cover a wide range of products and services, yet with strong brands, there are certain core characteristics that transcend the particular product or service. IBM, GE, Louis Vitton, and Sony are brands that are ranked as some of the world's most valuable (Interbrand, 2009), possessing powerful core characteristics.

Either the corporate brand model (such as IBM and GE) or an ingredient brand model (such as Intel) may represent an appropriate model for cities. The key is to identify and build on the core values and activities. Core values, attitudes, behaviors, and characteristics mark the essence of a brand – not necessarily the product, service, features, or, in a city's case, its activities. World alpha cities New York and London share a focus on entertainment, financial services, and tourism, yet no one would describe their brand persona as either restricted to any one of these, or – because their foci are similar – as the same. New York has an entrepreneurial, worldly, aggressively opportunistic, individualistic brand persona, whereas London is as lively and worldly yet with a touch of British historical 'class'. The effect of branding a city has been described as telling the story of the city to the world (Clark, 2007). And it needs to be a differentiated story (Markusen and Schrock, 2006).

BRAND ROLE IN ATTRACTING INWARD INVESTMENT

There is aggressive global and national competition between cities for investment. Clark (2007) suggests that the role of cities is to be investable and investment-ready. Investment creates jobs, expands the tax base, helps manage budgets and credit ratings, and funds education, infrastructure, and services. Regions and cities are active promoters of their benefits. In two business magazines during a single two-week period, the following advertising appeared:

- 'Jalisco – Mexico's innovation capital', (*Fortune*, 2009)

- 'The Madrid region concentrated 82% of foreign direct investment into Spain during 2008. Do you want to know why?', (*Business Week*, 2009a)

- 'Japan regional initiative – food industry Saitama-Shizuoka: a mouth-watering opportunity', (*Business Week*, 2009b)

- 'The Kyrgyz Republic looks ahead', (*Business Week*, 2009c)

A city's brand reputation and image remains a decision criterion and a lens through which investment-related information is viewed. Recent work by Florida (2003, 2005), Markusen (2006), and others has emphasized the importance of the totality of a city's activity in attracting economic investment, talent, and investment in that talent – especially in a so-called knowledge economy. According to Clark (2007), three tiers of activity are critical for economic competitiveness.

- Tier 1 *economic factors* includes innovation/creativity, investment, human capital, and connectedness (real and virtual transportation and communication)

- Tier 2 *socio-political factors* includes economic diversity, quality of life, decision making, and governance

- Tier 3 *infrastructural factors* includes quality of place (for example, educational quality and availability); the range, quality, and affordability of housing; parks and green spaces; safety and 'walk ability'. It also includes location factors such as culture, education, and how easy or difficult the city administration makes it to invest there

In the same way, these factors combine to enable the attraction of economic investment, so the city brand must integrate the essence of the city's distinctiveness. The strategic plan and the brand plan must determine which activities are supported and – like a commercial brand – these activities should be tested against several relevant criteria, as follows:

- What, for example, are the megatrends in the global, national, and regional economies; environment; society; and technology that will impact the city in its medium-term future?

- Based on the current skills, resources, and competencies of the city, what emerging opportunities can be a point of focus?

- Based on megatrends, what city skills, resources, and competencies could, with the right transitional programs, be city capabilities?

- How unique or distinctive are those skills, resources, and competencies?

- Are there any broader regional or national initiatives that could be developed through effective joint strategies and action?

- How can the current activities that have major current economic value be balanced against those activities that represent a degree of distinctiveness and could be developed further?

Answers to these questions should determine what changes need to be made to tax codes, incentive plans, infrastructural development, private-public partnerships, and so on. The activity must also be communicated to the relevant target groups.

In many city administrations, the brand communications role is misunderstood. These misunderstandings take many forms. For example, brand communications is often seen as a marketing communications role only, separate from the main strategy/brand activity. Likewise, brand communications is frequently viewed as a series of separate activities depending on the organizational silo and specific target group. While any brand's communication should be tailored to deliver target group-specific, benefit-based communication, the essence of the brand must be consistent and clear.

Another way in which many city administrations are deficient in their use of brand communications is that such communications too often ignore local decision makers, decision influencers, and citizenry. Recently, private-sector brand marketers have begun to recognize the power of employee branding and regard it as an essential part of total brand communications. Internet communications and social marketing need not be expensive. To effectively communicate with and persuade external target audiences, internal ones must be addressed first.

Furthermore, a common misperception occurs when marketing communications is seen solely as advertising, with slogans as the most important communication. On the contrary, good marketing communications integrates advertising, public relations, direct marketing, promotion activity (including sponsorships), and social network marketing in order to achieve its strategic objectives. Advertising alone can have but a limited impact unless supported by other elements of the brand communications mix.

Before adaptation of the brand concept is made to fit the specific communication needs of external businesses (to encourage investment), current businesses (to encourage expansion), or tourism businesses (to increase convention activity), the core brand stance and platform needs to be determined.

The ingredients for great city branding can be summarized thus:

- embody a clear, distinctive, ambitious yet realistic brand position and persona

- base the brand positioning on the population's values, attitudes, behaviors, and characteristics

- reflect a clear city strategy and its points of emphasis regarding skills, resources, and capabilities

- adapt effectively to deliver benefits to target groups

- communicate successfully to internal key influencers

- integrate efficiently across various marketing communications media

- be consistent over time

TORONTO, CANADA – 'NEW YORK RUN BY THE SWISS'

Let us examine a work in progress as an evocation of these principles. Peter Ustinov coined the phrase 'New York run by the Swiss' in an August 1987 interview (The Globe and Mail, 1987), when Toronto was emerging as Canada's primary city, overtaking Montreal in population and business importance. The City of Toronto is now the fifth largest city in North America with a population of 2.6 million (and a total of 5.5 million in the immediate area). Toronto is a focal point for immigration into Canada with 40 per cent of all immigrants stopping there, and it is one of the world's most multicultural cities with 46 per cent of the population born outside of Canada and speaking 100 languages and dialects. No one ethnic group is dominant. This balance of ethnicity and multiculturalism has resulted in Toronto's attraction as a cosmopolitan, safe, and liveable city with extensive business and employment opportunities. Rankings by organizations such as EIU, Forbes, KPMG, and Mercer consistently place Toronto in the top 15 cities in the world for culture, economic development, and liveability.

TORONTO'S ECONOMY

The City of Toronto alone is estimated to generate about 10 per cent of Canada's GDP ($140 billion) and the Toronto region about 20 per cent ($269 billion). Toronto is home to 40 per cent of the nation's business head-quarters with 174 of Canada's top 800 corporations located there.

According to the Globalization and World City Research Network (GaWC) 2008, and based on the provision of 'advanced producer services' such as accountancy, advertising, finance, and law, Toronto ranks in the Alpha City category with an A rating, the third highest, a group that includes the likes of Milan, Madrid, Seoul, Brussels, Mumbai, Buenos Aires, and Kuala Lumpur. *Foreign Policy* magazine and A. T. Kearney's Global City 2008 Index rates business activity, human capital, information exchange, cultural experience, and political engagement, and Toronto ranked tenth after cities like New York, London, Paris, Hong Kong, Los Angeles, and Seoul.

Toronto's business base

The financial, insurance, and real estate sector is estimated, at around 26 per cent, to be the largest GDP contributor to the Toronto region. Toronto has approximately 250,000 highly skilled employees, and many of the corporate global players are headquartered there: three of the world's 25 largest banks and all of Canada's five largest; two of the largest ten global life insurers; three of the top 50 global pension funds; 38 foreign bank subsidiaries; and 119 securities firms. All the world's top accounting organizations have extensive practices in Toronto. The Toronto Stock Exchange (TSX) is seventh in the world based on market capitalization and one of the world's largest mining and resource exchanges. This makes Toronto the third-largest financial center in North America after New York and Chicago and, according to the London-based Global Financial Centres Index, thirteenth in the world in 2009.

Other sectors with strong clusters in Toronto and its immediate area include:

- automotive: there are six major assembly plants in the immediate Toronto area, as well as the Canadian headquarters of Chrysler, Ford, GM, Honda, Hyundai, and Toyota, plus many Tier I suppliers such as Magna

- creative industries: Toronto is the center of English-speaking Canada's cultural sector, be it advertising and design, theater, movies, publishing, or recording, and it is a major center for outsourced Hollywood movie locations

- food and beverage: food processing employs approximately 50,000 people and generates approximately $20 billion in sales

- green industry: this industry includes more than 1,000 companies, 20,000 jobs, and $2 billion in sales

- information and communications technology: with the headquarters of Bell and Rogers, two of Canada's communications leaders, in Toronto and RIM in Waterloo less than an hour's drive away, this sector has over 300 foreign corporations and generates approximately $33 billion in sales

- manufacturing: this general sector represents the historical strength of the Toronto area. Accounting for approximately 20 per cent of the Toronto region's GDP, the largest sub-sectors are those in decline, such as metal industries, the chemical industry, machinery, furniture, printing, and plastics. Sub-sectors such as transportation, food and beverage, and IT represent the growth opportunities

- health, medical, and biotech: Toronto is home to some of Canada's leading hospitals and medical schools, and this category includes pharmaceutical companies and a research sector handling approximately $1 billion in research

- tourism: each year, some 26 million visitors come to Toronto and spend approximately $5 billion

The key ingredient: A diverse, educated workforce

One of the primary ingredients for Toronto's success is its labor force. First, 52 per cent of Toronto's population is of working age – a very high proportion. This is partially a result of the immigrant advantage, as most are younger. Second, Toronto has a well-educated working population: over 32 per cent are university graduates. Toronto is home to two strong universities with top global business faculties (Schulich School of Business and Rotman School of Management) as well as to a number of highly rated colleges. One of the world's top technology universities is in Waterloo and the campuses of Sheridan College, a top animation and broadcast production school, are in the western suburbs of Toronto. Third,

the diversity and multinational background of the immigrant population aids not only established organizations but also the entrepreneurial
community.

INVESTMENT IN TORONTO

In addition to domestic public and private investment, Canada is a major
recipient of foreign direct investment. Toronto obviously wishes to attract
federal and provincial government investment, domestic private sector investment, and foreign direct investment. To do this, it needs to be seen as a suitable destination for risk-acceptable return, requiring the fact and reputation
of an attractive brand.

The phrase 'New York run by the Swiss' captured the dynamic, business-
oriented North American orientation of the city combined with the Swiss
sense of reserve and respect for order and privacy. In terms of effective
brand communications, the Toronto picture is no less positive. Despite
all the positive rankings, Toronto is in danger of losing its attractiveness for business due to stiff competition. This is primarily due to the
decline in the manufacturing sector and some identified labor productivity issues. As a result, in 2009, two new corporations were established with board members from both the public and private sectors,
reporting to the City of Toronto Council. These corporations are Build
Toronto and Invest Toronto. The role of Build Toronto is to engage
private and public partners in the developing of underutilized city real
estate to generate new revenue, stimulate the creation of desirable jobs,
and regenerate neighborhoods. The role of Invest Toronto is to engage
the private sector in promoting Toronto as an investment opportunity
through marketing, conducting trade missions, and coordinating with
other governments and businesses.

The City of Toronto continues promotional activity in its Department
of Economic Development, Culture and Tourism. Other groups engaged in
promotion are:

- Toronto Economic Development Corporation (TEDCO): transferred its
  general urban development responsibilities to Build Toronto and evolved
  into the Toronto Port Lands Authority to manage Toronto's waterfront in
  2009

- Toronto Financial Services Alliance (TFSA): manages a public-private
  partnership between the province of Ontario, the City of Toronto, and

the financial services private sector to promote Toronto's financial services

■ Tourism Toronto: an industry association that works in partnership with the City of Toronto and the Province of Ontario

These groups undertake an extensive range of activities. They review administrative procedures to make investment easier; review business and residential taxes and tax incentives; encourage development of city-owned land and resources; develop private-public partnerships to promote specific sectors and activity in those sectors, such as innovation; gain private-public cooperation in identifying, attracting, and training labor market skills needed for key sectors; improve infrastructure, especially transportation; and they promote Toronto and its attractions, both internally and externally.

While much of this work is in progress, the branding of the activity – and especially the communications activity – has been weak. In fact, Toronto's current position seems to be a micro-version of Canada in that it boasts many strong features but lacks a coordinated brand plan or communication strategy. While all the background research on city branding and key Toronto working papers and presentations (such as Clark in 2007) recommend a central city brand communications strategy, there does not yet seem to be one, and each of the major groups (Build Toronto, Invest Toronto, Toronto Tourism, and TFSA) are developing their own communications plans.

Part of the reticence may be due to the hostile response to a high-profile attempt to brand Toronto in 2004–2005. Tourism Toronto, the City of Toronto, the Toronto City Summit Alliance, and the Ontario Ministry of Tourism & Recreation formed the Toronto Branding Project, which worked with advertising agencies to develop an advertising campaign with a new logo and the slogan 'Toronto Unlimited'. It attempted to express the diversity, multiculturalism, and range of Toronto's attractions. But it failed to connect with locals and was ridiculed in the media. In hindsight, while some of the strategic thinking was sound, the creative execution was weak. In addition, the campaign focused too much on the advertising and was insufficiently directed to the development and execution of a strategic plan.

What should be learned from this experience is that a clear strategy and actions for the city need to be determined first; then, based on those conclusions, as well as on good research among key target groups, a revised brand communications strategy and creative platform should be developed, tested, and modified accordingly.

SUMMARY

In terms of attracting inward investment, several key lessons from theory and Toronto practice may be drawn.

In a highly competitive world for investment, major national and global organizations seek the most favorable locations for their activities. While rigorous evaluation is usual in these decisions, brand impressions play a major role in determining an initial shortlist and final selection.

Successful brands follow a progression of creating a distinctive appeal (versus competitive cities/regions) and then building awareness and esteem based on that appeal. This distinctive appeal comes from an understanding of how core values, attitudes, behaviors, and characteristics have developed into special skills, resources, and competencies of the city, and how these fit with emerging trends in economic, environmental, social, and technological developments. This appeal only evolves into a powerful brand if a coherent strategic plan is acted upon and if that plan is consistently communicated to its target audiences. A strong city brand relies on more than just its communications: the city must take action as part of its strategic plan.

Even though cities have several different target audiences and brand communications must be adapted to meet their needs, the core brand stance must be consistent. One city, one brand. A helpful approach is to think of a city as a corporate brand such as IBM or GE, striving to please a range of customers and stakeholders. When a city has a number of points of credibility for investment, it needs an ongoing and consistent commitment to external brand communications. Toronto has many globally competitive assets that it has not effectively communicated to key target groups. External brand communications strategy and execution should use marketing communications media mixes that best fit the target groups and, when chosen, should convey an integrated, consistent message.

Internal brand communications is a critical first step to succeeding externally. As Toronto discovered with an aborted attempt at a monolithic brand, the opinions of key internal stakeholders and decision influencers in the community are critical for success.

Progress should be regularly tracked and compared to competitors. Assessment via the established ranking measures is a necessary but not complete evaluation. Progress should be widely disseminated, internally and externally. Putting data on a city website does not classify as effective communication unless there is a strong campaign to draw people there. In this era of social marketing, creating a buzz is critical.

ACKNOWLEDGEMENTS

My thanks to the following for their time and cooperation:

Ms Janet Ecker, President, Toronto Financial Services Alliance

Mr Peter Finestone, Film Commissioner, City of Toronto

Mr Carl Knipfel, Marketing Manager, Economic Development, Culture & Tourism, City of Toronto

Mr John MacIntyre, Senior Vice-President Corporate Affairs, Build Toronto

Ms Terrie O'Leary, Executive Vice-President Operations, Invest Toronto

Mr Joel Peters, Senior Vice-President & Chief Marketing Officer, Tourism Toronto

Ms Christine Raissis, Director of Economic Research and Business Information, City of Toronto

Mr Peter Viducis, Manager Economic Research, Economic Development, Culture & Tourism, City of Toronto

Mr Michael Williams, General Manager, Economic Development, Culture & Tourism City of Toronto

CHAPTER 4

City Branding and the Tourist Gaze

Gert-Jan Hospers

INTRODUCTION

Urban tourism is a fast growing segment in the worldwide tourism market. Thanks to the growth of easyJet, Ryanair and a number of other low cost carriers, city trips have become increasingly popular. To be sure, Dutch couples and families still take the car or train to Amsterdam for a week-end break. For the same amount of money, however, they can book an all inclusive cheap flight to Valencia. Planning a city trip has become easy: nowadays, more than half of European consumers arrange their holidays on their personal computer. Not surprisingly, competition between cities for tourists has intensified (Selby, 2004).

Against this background, more and more cities invest in city branding. The branding strategies employed are usually twofold (Jansson and Power, 2006): cities emphasize either material characteristics of the place such as buildings and events, or its immaterial aspects, for example, stories, slogans and logos. In this way, cities hope to differentiate themselves from the competition and attract tourists. Indeed, city branding can be a useful method to build a touristic image. But how does this image building work? What can cities do to attract attention? Why is, for instance, Venice a tourist magnet? In this chapter we approach these and related questions by using the theory of 'the tourist gaze' (Urry, 1990). We discuss, complement and illustrate the theory in order to draw lessons for city branders.

CITIES AND THE TOURIST GAZE

In his book *The Tourist Gaze* (1990), the British sociologist John Urry develops a theory on why people travel for leisure and why they visit certain places. Urry argues that tourism involves going away to search for visual experiences that we normally do not see at home or at work. The main activity of tourists is 'gazing at signs': they look at particular features of a place, such as a famous cathedral, beautiful landscape or another attraction. Take the example of New York: most visitors want to see the Statue of Liberty, Wall Street and Little Italy. As tourists we usually look for different things in a place than its inhabitants; we adopt a 'tourist gaze'.

Places gazed upon are not randomly chosen; the tourist gaze varies by society and is always socially constructed. Chinese tourists, for example, prefer the skyscrapers of Frankfurt am Main above the ancient heritage of Rome – something Europeans find hard to understand (Hospers, 2009a). In turn, American tourists would not visit the Italian town of Pisa and its Leaning Tower of their own accord. They do so because they have been manipulated by a variety of media channels constructing that gaze. Travel guides, newspaper articles, adverts and stories in magazines, promotional brochures, television documentaries, postcards, websites, blogs and public photo sharing sites enable us to form an image of what to expect when visiting a place. Thus, in Urry's view, both tourists and attractions are manipulated: the gaze falls upon exactly those features of a place that are already anticipated. Or, as Urry (2002: 3) puts it: 'When tourists see two people kissing in Paris what they are gazing upon is "timeless, romantic Paris"'.

This theory is supported by the rise of mass tourism since the second half of the 19th century. Right from its invention photography started to accompany tourism, which was the same time that organized tours and travel guides emerged. In fact, the growth of tourism closely followed the development of photography. By taking pictures of places that were no longer used, 'sites' were turned into 'sights': tourists started to visit churches, not to pray, but to photograph them (MacCannell, 1999). This 'site sacralisation' was the engine behind tourism. In an attempt to become what places are expected to be, the tourist industry has produced a lot of 'pseudo-authentic attractions' (Osborne, 2000). Quintessential Dutch cities like Delft and Gouda, for instance, reinforce stereotypes of 'Dutchness' and have invented spots, events and souvenirs suggesting to foreign tourists that they have found 'the real Holland'.

Clearly, not all tourists are of the same type, as Urry (1995) rightly notes. Tourists with a 'collective' gaze feel safe in following the herd and usually book organized trips to visit tourist magnets. More and more tourists, however, develop an individual, 'romantic' gaze and search for authenticity. Think of students that are looking for adventure and follow 'insider tips' (see for example the website www.spottedbylocals.com). Over the years, however, Urry has observed the emergence of the 'post mass tourist' for whom being at a historic spot with a real story is as valid as gazing upon Las Vegas and Eurodisney. The post mass tourist knows that most places are pseudo-attractions anyway, but still can find pleasure in visiting them.

Urry is a sociologist and did not develop his theory in the context of city branding. The notion of the tourist gaze, however, is relevant for cities that want to build an image and attract tourists. After all, if we mainly visit places because we know them from photographic images, then city branding can help in providing and distributing these pictures. Even more, cities are largely free to highlight some of their signs. Thus, city branders can manipulate the gaze of possible visitors. From this perspective, city branding is a powerful tool to construct the tourist gaze. Cities do not have to offer an authentic experience as such, but rather make sure that they provide an experience that resembles the images used in their branding. Clearly, this pragmatic view can be criticized for historical and social-cultural reasons (Morgan, 2004). At the same time, it offers hope for every place, even for localities that suffer from offering nothing special. Ystad in the south of Sweden is a telling example: the town is the setting for the Wallander detective television series and takes advantage of this by organizing Wallander tours. Likewise, the Spanish village of Buñol has developed a reputation with a photogenic attraction: at the annual Tomatino festival the villagers throw tomatoes at each other – coloring the streets of Buñol entirely red.

A CITY'S IMAGE CARRIERS

Which signs of a city lend themselves best to photography, city branding and the tourist gaze? As a matter of fact, anything that is somehow special in a city might attract tourists. The most popular objects gazed upon are different from what people usually encounter at home or work – they are different in terms of scale, meaning or experience. This explains, for example, why the Coliseum (Rome), the spot where President Kennedy was murdered (Dallas) and the Oktober Fest (Munich) have become tourist magnets. In the literature, three main categories of urban image carriers have been identified: the built environment, hallmark events and famous personalities (Lynch, 1960; OECD, 2005; Ashworth, 2009). Below they will be discussed.

First, tourists visit a city to gaze upon objects in the built environment. Based on extensive empirical research in American and European cities, Lynch (1960) and his followers argued that most individuals perceive a city predominantly as a set of built objects. In particular, five physical elements play a role in constituting people's image of a city:

- **Paths**: the streets, rail lines, trails and other channels along which people move. Examples are Berlin's Kurfürstendamm and the Champs-Elysées in Paris.

- **Edges**: clear transition zones and linear boundaries, for example, waterfronts and green zones. Illustrations are the boulevard in Nice and the Quayside in Newcastle.

- **Districts**: quarters, neighbourhoods and other sections of the city with a distinctive character, such as London's Soho and Toronto's Chinatown.

- **Nodes**: strategic meeting points, such as squares, junctions or train stations. Examples are the Dam in Amsterdam and the Plaza Mayor in Madrid.

- **Landmarks**: physical objects that serve as public reference points, like Bilbao's Guggenheim Museum and Malmö's Turning Torso.

Interestingly, Lynch and his colleagues found that because of their differing 'imageability' – that is, the ease with which parts of a city make a strong mental impression on people – some cities stick better in our minds than others. For tourists in particular, edges and landmarks function as image carriers, because they can easily be identified, recognized and remembered.

Tourists also direct their gaze to hallmark events taking place in a city. Some events recur every year, while others are one-off happenings. A city can not only identify with the activities organized during the event (for example, music, art or sports), but also demonstrate its organizing capacity by hosting it. Although the benefits of hallmark events for the local economy are mostly overestimated, their impact on local image can be considerable (OECD, 2005). Well-known recurring city events are the annual film festival in Cannes, the Salzburg Festival and Copenhagen's Fashion Week. Good examples of one-off mega-events that contributed to image building were the Summer Olympics of Barcelona (1992) and Lille European City of Culture 2004.

Tourists may visit a city because they associate it with a personality, such as a famous painter, musician or writer. Often, the claim of a place to have a special link with a named individual is the result of city branding. Therefore, Ashworth (2009) calls this branding technique the 'Gaudí gambit' after the successful personality branding of Barcelona with the architect and designer Gaudí. Painters and musicians are suitable icons for a city, even if they are not exclusively linked to the place in question. Cases in point are as diverse as Vermeer (Delft), Hundertwasser (Vienna), Mackintosh (Glasgow), Bach (Eisenach), The Beatles (Liverpool) and Kraftwerk (Hamburg). For the image of cities historical figures can also be important, such as Vasco da Gama (Lisbon) or Anne Frank (Amsterdam).

In practice, image carriers often overlap. For example, in cities with a flagship building by Calatrava (Valencia, Liège), Foster (London, Berlin) or Koolhaas (Rotterdam, Essen), the architect is as renowned as the object he created. Obviously, cities might have more image carriers than the three types mentioned (Hospers, 2009a). Some cities are in the public imagination because of their important position in history. By way of illustration, think of Athens (antiquity), Rīga (Hanseatic League) or Berlin (Cold War). Finally, places might have a reputation related to aspects of the local economy, such as crafts, products or companies. Such a 'city-of-origin effect' can be observed in Parma (Parma ham), Eindhoven (Philips) and Wolfsburg (Volkswagen).

LESSONS FOR CITY BRANDERS

With the theory of the tourist gaze and urban image carriers in mind it is not hard to explain why, for example, Venice attracts 12 million tourists a year. Few cities have a visual impact with the same power as Venice: the city is spread over 117 islands, linked by over 400 bridges and split by 150 canals (Reader, 2004). Besides these numerous edges the city has many landmarks (churches and palazzos) and nodes (piazzas). The Venice Carnival and Biennale are recurring hallmark events, while figures like Marco Polo, Casanova and Vivaldi are local heroes. Due to these strong image carriers Venice has been the stage for many novels, paintings, plays and movies. In this way, the image of the city as an extraordinary place has been reproduced over the years. The ironic result of this accumulative process is that more and more young Venetians are leaving the city now, because they cannot find a job outside the local tourism industry.

The popularity of Venice is an example of the 'Matthew effect' that is named after Matthew 25:29: 'For to all those who have, more will be given, and they will have an abundance; but from those who have nothing, even what they have will be taken away' (Merton, 1968). Apparently, cities that are already in the public eye attract more attention than unknown places – they have an accumulated advantage. The emergence of digital photography and the internet has made the Matthew effect even more relevant. An analysis of 35 million images on flickr.com – a popular public photo sharing site – suggests that its users take pictures of exactly those spots that have been photographed the most before. The study finds that the Eiffel Tower in Paris is the object that has been reproduced most frequently (Crandall *et al.*, 2009). Paradoxically, as tourists we are not looking for surprises: with our cameras we take pictures confirming what we were expecting to see.

Cities can easily account for these notions in their branding strategies. Branding professionals can easily check the imageability of their city. To what extent does the city stick in people's minds? What edges, landmarks or other distinctive physical objects does the city have – if any? What are the buildings, events, personalities or products that can be put on a picture postcard or a website? The Hague has the Peace Palace, Dublin has the writer James Joyce and Havana has its cigars, but it is less clear what the image carriers of Oslo, Southampton and Toulouse are. The theory of the tourist gaze suggests how important it is to identify urban signs that can be photographed, multiplied and distributed. More and more cities seem to realize this and set up an online database with pictures of the city's highlights that can be downloaded for free.

If a city does not have imageable and scenic features, it will generally be hard to brand it. Brussels is an example of a city that lacks clear highlights that can be used to tell the city's story as 'the European village'. When asked for spontaneous associations with the Belgian capital, international respondents mention the little statue Manneken Pis twenty times more than the headquarters of the European Commission or the Expo 1958 monument Atomium (Anholt, 2008). At the same time, the image of some cities (for example, Copenhagen and London) has been blurred due to an overinvestment in impressive buildings and events that can be gazed upon. Therefore, it makes sense for local authorities to explore whether the urban narrative they want to communicate can be visually symbolized on one spot or a limited number of spots in the city.

From this perspective, investments in public art, a city quarter, a harbor area or a recurring city festival can have intrinsic, symbolic and promotional value. Anholt (2008) recognizes the importance of such 'symbolic actions' by the local government, but stresses that they always should have substance and be part of a long-term strategy. Indeed, only with substantial, strategically informed symbolic actions can city governments create 'an unbroken chain of proof' (Anholt, 2008) that improves the photographic qualities of the city and the tourist gaze.

HELSINKI AND BARCELONA

Let us explore how the theoretical notions discussed thus far can be used to analyze the practice of city branding in two European cities: Helsinki and Barcelona. First, we discuss the imageability of Helsinki. After that, we turn to the tourist gaze on Barcelona.

The imageability of Helsinki

Traditionally, Helsinki has branded itself as the visiting card of Finland. Over the years, city branders have emphasized beautiful nature, welfare state values and advanced high-tech – thus the story of Finland rather than Helsinki. Also the images used in tourist brochures and websites stress the position of Helsinki as a capital city: more than half of the pictures depict the Senate Square of Helsinki, which is seen as a strong symbol for both the city and the nation (Vanolo, 2008; Winter, 2009). To be sure, on this very spot the most important public institutions of Finland and Helsinki are located – the national government, the university, the cathedral and the City of Helsinki. In addition, the square is a photogenic object for the tourist gaze, because it is – in terms of Lynch (1960) – a 'node' that hosts some distinct 'landmarks'.

The imageability of Helsinki, however, is not limited to the Senate Square. Take the Eteläsatama harbor around which the city center is built: it is a scenic 'edge' where city and water meet. More importantly, Helsinki is a hot spot of architecture. Tourists can find many architectural landmarks here, although they are located throughout the city (Jansson and Power, 2006). Examples are the Finlandia Hall and Academic Bookstore by Aalto, the Stockman Department Store by Frosterus and the main railway station by Saarinen. Last but not least, Helsinki has accomplished much in the field of modern design. The city has a strong Design District, well-known design companies like Nokia, Kone and Marikemekko, events like the Helsinki Design week and a link with famous designers such as Saarinen and Aalto. In 2009, the city was even appointed World Design Capital 2012. It is time for the city branders to select new pictures for Helsinki's tourist brochures – the city has far more icons than the Senate Square. In short, it might be useful to map a city's image carriers and examine whether they are fully exploited for the purposes of city branding.

The tourist gaze on Barcelona

The Spanish metropolis of Barcelona is a tourist magnet. Since the early 1990s the city has pursued an effective re-imaging strategy, starting with the 1992 Olympic Games. This event and the associated branding efforts were followed by 'symbolic actions' by the city government: the restoration of Barcelona's architectural heritage and the 'monumentalization' of the city with the help of modern 'imageable' buildings (Balibrea, 2001). Examples are public investments to restore Gaudí's Sagrada Familia and Park Guell and the erection of the Communication Towers (Calatrava and Foster) and the Fish Sculpture (Gehry). All of these photogenic buildings benefit from the reputation of 'starchitects', generate a lot of free publicity in the international media and thus attract an increasing number of tourists from all over the globe (Smith, 2005).

Usually, Barcelona is seen as a best practice of city branding. But there are also some problematic issues. Smith (2005: 414) rightly notes that 'the critical mass of iconic edifices now present in Barcelona may be beginning to confuse the city's image, rather than enhance it'. Or, to put it in Urry's terms: how many signs can a tourist handle? Are there limits to the tourist gaze? Is Barcelona running the risk of 'architectural fatigue' and a visual overload? Another problem in Barcelona has to do with its re-imaging success. The city is crowded with visitors and has developed into a destination for mass tourism (Marshall, 2004). In Barcelona the 'collective' gaze is starting to dominate, which is gradually keeping visitors with a 'romantic' gaze away. It must be said, however, that the city of Barcelona is aware of this development. Recently, the municipal promotion office has been trying to attract tourists who are searching for more authentic experiences. This is done, for example, by offering guided tours along spots in the city that formed the stage of the bestseller *The Shadow of the Wind* by the Spanish writer Zafón.

SUMMARY

Tourists are an attractive target group for city branders. Urban tourism is a growth market, while tourists are quite responsive to branding techniques. Urry's theory of the tourist gaze suggests that people mainly visit a city to 'gaze at signs': they look for those features in the urban landscape that they already know from pictures, for example, Copenhagen's Little Mermaid and the Eiffel Tower in Paris. From this perspective, city branding is a powerful tool to construct the tourist gaze. It involves the selection of photogenic signs in a city and the reproduction of these signs in images via media channels such as newspapers and websites. At least three types of image carriers in a city are suitable for the tourist gaze: the built environment, hallmark events and famous personalities. Examples are a waterfront, recurring festival, or a link with a renowned architect.

This theory can explain the self-reinforcing 'Matthew effect' in tourist magnets like Venice and Amsterdam: imageable cities that are already in the public eye attract even more attention – they are famous for being famous. There is hope, however, for every city. As the cases of Helsinki and Barcelona make clear, cities can easily identify their image carriers, trace and possibly construct new ones and thus improve the imageability of the place. At the same time, they should prevent the emergence of a visual overload for the tourist gaze. All in all, if cities want to build a stronger touristic image, they should literally start with building images.

CHAPTER 5

City Brand Partnerships

Sicco van Gelder

INTRODUCTION

For a city brand to be effective it needs to represent all of its key stakeholders and it needs to remain viable and relevant over time. City branding is different from traditional location and destination marketing and investment promotion in that it drives and inspires consistent and on-brand behavior by all of its stakeholders, rather than just those organizations responsible for sending out marketing messages – messages which may or may not be supported by the reality of the place. Engaging and connecting key stakeholders in the development and implementation of a city brand strategy strengthens the brand beyond what the stakeholders could achieve individually.

Effective city branding requires a clear vision for the future of the place and a coherent strategy for brand development, as well as effective policy implementation and the communication of progress, for external and internal audiences. To be successful, it is also necessary to introduce and combine new leadership and partnership practices with an imaginative approach to city brand leadership, policy making and public involvement and consultation. Such an approach will enable the place to build on all of its strengths and to align and involve all of the stakeholders in its city brand development. The importance of a collaborative stakeholder approach has been acknowledged in the context of companies (Mitchell *et al.*, 1997; Parent and Deephouse, 2007) and has now also been recognized as fundamental to the successful branding of places (Hankinson, 2009; Skinner, 2005).

INVOLVING THE STAKEHOLDERS

A key element of city branding is the need to involve all of the key stakeholders who can help shape the future of the place. The investments that they make in the development of the place, the actions they take and the communications they put out are all vital elements of how the story of the place will be told. The principle channels through which places such as nations and cities communicate are their tourism, their private sector, their foreign and domestic policy, investment and immigration, their culture and education, and their people.

Tourism

The policies of the relevant public authorities on, and the investment made by the private sector in, tourism facilities, attractions and its workforce communicate powerful messages about the place to potential visitors about how the place operates. The scale and nature of investment in tourism, in culture, the arts, and heritage, says a great deal about the place and how well it caters for and cares for its visitors.

Private Sector

Brands that are exported from the place say a great deal about their origin, about its ability to produce world-class products and services. It can also demonstrate things to the world about other aspects of the place such as its private sector's regard for sustainable development, its treatment of natural and human resources, its respect for its arts, culture and heritage.

Government Policy

How the city conducts its business and its relations with other places and (inter)national bodies communicates much about its values and its leaders that can create distinct impressions in people's minds. Similarly, international perceptions of the city can be altered by the way the city's leadership treats its own citizens through their education, training, housing, social security, cultural and environmental policies and programs.

Investment and Immigration

The pattern, scale and nature of investment in the city, by the government and by the private sector sends messages to potential investors and immigrants, especially to people with the talents and competences that the place needs.

Culture and Education

The culture of the city communicates a great deal about its values its arts, literature, traditions and heritage. Its heritage and how it is valued communicates how the population values its past. Investment in education and training says a great deal about how a city values its people as does the extent of private sector investment in the development of the workforce.

The People

The way the population of the city behaves and communicates is key to demonstrating the city brand in action. The interactions with ordinary citizens can have a strong influence on the credibility of the city brand. If the locals do not believe in the brand then why should an outsider?

The basis for successful city branding is some form of joint responsibility between the key stakeholders of the city. No one stakeholder has the ability and capacity to develop and implement a brand strategy on its own. Many of the problems that arise during city branding exercises are due to flawed relationships between the city's key stakeholders. Governments often consider themselves to be the 'owners' of the city brand and concentrate their efforts on getting their departments aligned first. This leads to situations whereby other key stakeholders are only consulted (if that) and are left feeling out of the loop and uncertain about what to do with brand books, brand guidelines, marketing materials, and communications guidelines that are foisted upon them. In other cases, various stakeholders may take it upon themselves to define their particular brand for the place, in which cases the city ends up with various and unaligned (sectoral) brands: a tourism brand, an investment brand, a cultural brand and so on.

At best, these kinds of situations lead to confusion and to contradictory signals about the city being sent to the local community and the outside world. At worst, everyone decides to ignore whatever has been developed and precious resources will have been wasted.

In this chapter we focus on what constitutes an effective city brand partnership and how that can be organized in such a way that key stakeholders take joint responsibility for the development and implementation of the city brand.

THE PRINCIPLES OF EFFECTIVE PARTNERSHIP

City branding requires partnership between key stakeholders who can effectively shape and, more importantly, implement a brand strategy. There are plenty of examples of dysfunctional partnerships in the areas of city branding and city marketing that have been formed in order to give the impression of unity while being stripped of any real influence or denied the means of effective implementation.

We believe that a brand partnership should be taken seriously as the main body that is tasked with developing, implementing and managing the brand of an area, a city, a region or a country. When this is the case, it is essential that the partnership is effective and does not waste time infighting with other institutions or plastering the city with logos or slogans. Based on our experiences with partnerships, we have formulated the following ten principles for effective partnership working.

1. Inclusive and representative

A city brand partnership must include all the key stakeholders of the city. The key stakeholders are those that can significantly contribute to shaping the future of the city through their policies, investments, actions, behavior and communications. The key stakeholders must also meaningfully represent their constituencies. The brand partners must also accept each other as equals and regard the task of branding their place as a truly joint initiative. Partnerships that are dominated by political or financial heavyweights are likely to be ineffective, as they do not take into account the meaningful roles of partners with less clout but with great (potential) value to the brand of the city, for example, culture, education and sports. Also, government representatives tend to change every number of years. Making a city branding process dependent on electoral cycles makes for a very fragile situation. When government is one of the partners in a partnership of equals, then political changes do not affect the functioning of the partnership. A city brand partnership should be open to newcomers. As the city develops, new members should be invited that can contribute meaningfully to the place's brand.

2. Long-term commitment

The development and implementation of a city brand is a strategic endeavor that requires the partners to commit their efforts and resources towards changing people's minds about their city through a progression of activities that will take years to complete and even longer before they fully bear fruit. This commitment needs to come from the partner organizations rather than just from the individuals that represent them, as the latter will regularly join and leave the partnership throughout the years. The commitment can be formalized in a contract between the partners. However, it is more important that the commitment is acknowledged by the partners through their activities, such as joint public appearances, joint investments, joint events, and the like.

3. Shared vision

The brand partners need to agree on a shared vision for the future of their city. This vision needs to be of a higher order than their individual visions. Most places do not have such an overarching vision for their future, but often have formulated separate visions for business, culture, education, healthcare, housing and such. Taken together these individual visions seldom add up to more than statements of intent and do not form a coherent view of the future of the city.

4. Sharing responsibility

Not only must the partners decide how they envisage the future of their city, they also need to agree on taking shared responsibility for making that future a reality. This means taking decisions together as well as taking responsibility for the actions that follow on those decisions. It also means that partners will be jointly responsible for actions that one or several of the partners take even when they do not have direct authority over those organizations.

5. Trusting each other

From the start, it must be clear between the city brand partners what it is that each partner expects from the city branding process. Each organization's agenda must be tabled, and expectations and objectives must not remain hidden. Hidden agendas will destroy trust within a partnership and will hinder the ability of the partners to work together effectively. Partners who know each others' goals will help each other achieve those goals, as long as they are beneficial to the partnership as a whole. Developing a city brand together requires trust because no one knows at the outset of the process what the brand will be or what the necessary actions will be to make it a reality. All that the brand partners can know at the outset is that they are coming together to ensure that their place will be able to compete in the future for those things it wants and needs. That in itself should be motivation enough for most brand partners to start the work together.

6. Aligned and engaged

A brand partnership is not a committee. Although the brand partners regularly come together for meetings, their work on the brand continues in between meetings and they work together in small subgroups on specific projects. Meetings are aimed at discussing new initiatives, taking decisions on projects prepared by subgroups and evaluating activities. In addition, a brand partnership is aligned to one purpose, namely to develop and implement a brand strategy for their place. Once the brand is agreed between the partners, it becomes the guiding principle for the partnership.

7.   Communicating as one

One of the great strengths of a city brand partnership is its ability to speak for all of its partners and each of its partners to speak for it. This seamlessness of communications between the members and the entire partnership is possible once the brand has been agreed and every partner has the same understanding of what the place's promise of value is. Although each partner will often communicate about the brand from their own perspective, they know how this fits with the other partners' perspectives. Having a highly visible unified brand partnership sends out strong signals to both local audiences as well as outsiders. In our experience, an active brand partnership can generate as much positive media attention for a city as any investment in infrastructure, education, healthcare or advertising. This is due to the fact that the city shows that it has its act together, which is exactly one of the major issues facing many towns, cities, regions and countries.

8.   Taking 'on-brand' decisions and actions

With an agreed brand, the brand partners must start taking decisions and action that will turn the brand into reality. Obviously, what these decisions and actions are will differ from one city to another. Such decisions and actions may have to do with urban planning and architecture, economic, social and cultural policies, attracting major events, stimulating local entrepreneurship, attracting specific industries, showcasing local traditions or striking up alliances. Whatever they are, it is important that the people making the decisions and those carrying out the work are fully steeped in the brand so as to be able to determine whether what they are doing is actually 'on-brand'.

9.   Making 'on-brand' investments

The same goes for investments that have a major impact on how the place functions, what it produces, how it services the needs of its citizens, businesses and institutions, and how it deals with the outside world. Sometimes, investments that have already been allocated can be 'tweaked' to become 'on-brand'. For example, planned upgrades for airports and railway stations can be used to ensure that this is done in an 'on-brand' manner: in architectural style and the facilities offered. This usually does not require any additional budget, but only extra attention to how the upgrade is designed and executed.

10.   Willingness to evaluate impact and effectiveness

Finally, a city brand partnership must be willing to assess what it has done right and what not, what was successful and what has failed, and what was and was not carried out in accordance with its plans. It is important that the partners, before starting implementation work on the brand, agree what their measures of success will be. This at least allows the partnership to determine whether activities met their expectations and to establish the reasons for their success or failure.

CREATING THE CITY BRAND PARTNERSHIP

Effective partnership working cannot be taken for granted and has to be worked at. Every partnership has its own particular personality and approach, largely created by the mix of partners and the task they come together to undertake and achieve. However, despite their differences, the majority of partnerships face common problems and challenges and have common development needs. Chiefly these are:

- The need to agree what it is that unites the partners, in this case the vision for a city and the creation of its brand.

- The values of the partnership in relation to its purpose; what it stands for and believes to be important.

- The way it will operate to achieve its purpose – its *modus operandi*.

- The way the partner's staffs deal with each other and how they operate jointly towards a common purpose.

- The style of leadership it will adopt and who will lead the partnership.

- The allocation of responsibilities for leading on the work to be undertaken.

- The way it will communicate internally and with its partner's staffs and externally to the communities the partners represent, to key target audiences, and how it will involve, align with and work through the media.

During the entire brand development process, the brand partners develop the following aspects of their shared leadership and teamwork capabilities:

- Establishing individual, organizational and collective interest. It is important to make sure that these are aligned and reinforce each other.

- Gaining clarity on shared purpose by combining individual views and lifting these on to a high collective plane.

- Defining shared aspirations to ensure that everyone is striving to create that same future for the place.

- Defining shared values and team culture to facilitate discussions, decision making and negotiations.

- Defining the role and remit of the team to ensure that everyone is clear as to what the partnership is tasked to do.

- Defining critical success factors so it is clear from the outset what it is that the partnership wishes to achieve and to be able to determine later on the process what has been successful and what has not.

- Clarifying the resources available to the team to ensure that strategies, plans and initiatives can realistically be achieved.

- Communicating effectively within the team, with other stakeholders and with target audiences.

SUMMARY

Places are set to change the way they operate in order to compete, solve their problems and innovate more effectively. The involvement of groups of citizens, businesses and institutions in doing so should be applauded because it turns them from passive consumers of policies, decisions and public services into producers who can better deal with their place's issues and shape its future. This will also help to develop more closely knit communities in a time when these are more and more fleeting.

For city branding to be successful, it is necessary for its key stakeholder organizations to come together in partnership. This is not your usual public-private partnership or a committee of wise men and women. This is a formal or informal body in which the key stakeholders jointly develop, create and lead on the implementation of the brand of the place, under shared responsibility.

City brand partnerships are not like central government departments, or local government or private companies or voluntary, community and charitable organizations. They are a hybrid form of organization. Their characteristics are determined by those who set them up, the purpose for which they were created and by those who lead the work of the partnership. The form of partnership organization and operation is rarely a given. It has to be negotiated and agreed upon by those who are going to be involved.

The representatives of the stakeholder organizations that constitute the partnership have their own agendas and motivations for participating, as well as their own ways of working, of making decisions and of getting things done. They need to devise a whole new way of working together to reconcile their goals and practices and to make the partnership an effective vehicle for enhancing their place's competitiveness, taking the lead on finding or creating the resources required.

The members of the brand partnership need to understand and reconcile differing policies and strategies, decide on what the future of their city will look like, what it will offer of value to consumers, how it will be experienced and what it is they can jointly do to make that future a reality. This requires a willingness to come together and work through these matters even when that may be difficult due to conflicts of interest, different opinions, differing timescales and sometimes even personal dislikes. All of this is for one common cause: to make the city better able to compete for the things that will make it a better, a more sustainable and a more competitive place.

Once the city brand strategy has been agreed by the partnership, its task changes to ensuring that the right actions are taken to make the brand come alive. This requires decisions on how best to manage the city brand, taking into account that the required actions, policy changes, investments, attraction programs, events and the like will be the responsibility of various city stakeholders, some of whom may not even have been represented on the original brand partnership and now need to be brought on board.

CHAPTER 6

City Branding and Stakeholder Engagement

John P. Houghton and Andrew Stevens

INTRODUCTION

This chapter sets out a simple but challenging proposition: stakeholder engagement is crucial to the success of any city branding strategy, but doing it effectively requires an approach that is more democratic and exploratory than much standard practice.

It is a regrettable fact that many city branding strategies fail, occasionally with a bang, more often with a whimper. A key reason for failure here is the absence or inadequacy of a program for engaging and energizing local people, businesses and community groups in shaping, articulating and conveying the brand. More often that not, the branding team opts for limited consultation or validation from external partners, preferring immediate buy-in and co-option over meaningful dialogue and challenge.

The participatory and iterative approach to city branding we set out is designed to generate and support a greater sense of ownership, which is a crucial ingredient in any branding initiative. If the range of partners in a place feels that they have been involved in shaping the message, the more likely they are to vocalize and embody it.

The first part of this chapter explains why stakeholder engagement is integral to the success of city branding strategies and, more broadly, to the emerging discipline of city branding as a whole. The second sets out some of the key elements of successful stakeholder engagement. The third explores some of the common tensions and challenges which need to be addressed and worked through as part of an effective branding or rebranding strategy.

WHY STAKEHOLDER ENGAGEMENT MATTERS

Stakeholder engagement is a relatively under-explored aspect of the literature on city branding. Kavaratzis and Ashworth (2006) argue that there is a gap in the literature with regard to the branding process of cities in general. This chapter draws on the available literature on city branding (for an overview of the topic see for example Hankinson, 2001; Trueman *et al.*, 2004; Kavaratzis, 2009a), analysis of a number of areas in the United Kingdom that are working to brand themselves, and evidence and experience from stakeholder engagement techniques in related disciplines such as place visioning and scenario planning.

Stakeholder engagement (Greenley and Foxall, 1997; Mitchell *et al.*, 1997; Parent and Deephouse, 2007) matters to city branding on two levels. First, there is growing evidence that the most effective city branding initiatives involve and energize a wide range of local players to craft and convey the new message about the place. Equally, there is a weight of evidence that initiatives which do not engage, and in some cases alienate, local stakeholders are almost always destined to fail. Second, effective stakeholder engagement is crucial to the acceptance of city branding as an important and respected discipline within modern urban development and management. The more people are engaged in effective and productive city branding strategies, the more the scepticism and suspicion that surrounds it can be countered.

To explore the first argument in more detail, part of the skepticism around city branding stems from the way in which many strategies have been developed and executed. Public bodies can struggle to engage their partners and citizens in their core areas of work. So it is of little surprise when they find it hard to involve people in a new and unfamiliar task like city branding.

As a result, there are many examples of city branding strategies which have been developed by a small group of people, supported by external experts who understand branding techniques but lack a rich or rounded understanding of the place. These strategies can make sense on paper or sound plausible on a flipchart, but gain little traction in the real world. The failure to engage is particularly problematic given the emphasis that so many areas now place on nurturing local creativity as the source of their new identity.

An effective city brand has to be both intelligible and credible to local people, effectively the owners if not the managers of the brand, who should be engaged at each stage of the branding process. Stakeholder engagement enriches and deepens the quality of the branding discussion, introducing new opinions, ideas and perspectives. Some of those opinions might be difficult to hear, and the discussion usually requires structure and neutral facilitation, but it is ultimately more helpful to any city's branding process to listen to and address concerns at the beginning and throughout the process, than allow them to fester.

Stakeholder engagement introduces a level of invaluable 'real world' testing. Ideas that do not make sense, that seem too abstract or superficial, that are too far away from the reality of the place, will quickly be challenged. City branding consultant Bill Baker's practitioner perspective highlights the value of engagement in 'a community-based brand' (Baker, 2007: 166), noting that city brands fail when they have been developed behind closed doors by agencies which do not reach out to the required range of stakeholders. In contrast, a brand that has been developed with stakeholders is, according to Baker, able to stand the test of time because it has generated adequate buy-in during the brand development phase. A further longer-term benefit of stakeholder engagement is that the process of engagement itself helps to create a cadre of informed advocates who are willing to promulgate the message later on. This can include those who were previously skeptical but were won over, and who can proselytize with the zeal of the convert for the new brand.

After several underwhelming attempts, Liverpool began to rebrand itself around its successful 2008 Capital of Culture program. A key part of the process was a fairly extensive program of consultation and listening to local people and 'outsiders'. The resultant 'brand personality' plays on some of the city's traditional brand strengths, like its down-to-earth character – 'the only front here is the waterfront' – while stressing its dynamism and diversity. A team of brand advocates were recruited to promote these new messages, and local people were given a prominent role in many Capital of Culture activities.

The second reason why stakeholder engagement matters is that it will help counter the skepticism around city branding as a discipline. City branding is a new venture for many places. It is a little ironic that branding itself should have such poor associations in the minds of so many people – lending itself to impressions of superficiality and 'spin'. This latent hostility to branding is further sharpened in the case of city branding because it deals with people's homes and neighborhoods, and therefore invites reactions of defensiveness and bruised civic pride. The only way to counter this hostility is by engaging people and demonstrating how effective and beneficial city branding can be. The more people are involved in effective and productive city branding initiatives, the better informed the discipline as a whole. If more people can see that city branding is not about trashing the existing image of a place or pedalling a false message, the more city leaders will see it is a valid, if not vital, part of modern urban development.

HOW TO ENGAGE STAKEHOLDERS SUCCESSFULLY

We will now look at the city branding activities of a number of areas in the United Kingdom in order to explore some of the key ways to engage stakeholders successfully. There is no off the peg or set approach. Each area has to develop a tailored program that reflects the branding challenge, the range and accessibility of different stakeholders and other unique factors. There are, however, some basic starting points for engaging stakeholders successfully, drawn from practical experience of city branding and related place visioning and scenario planning work.

First, it is crucial to understand and work with the diversity of stakeholders in a place. Stakeholders are not a discrete and tidy group. The term describes the mixture of people, groups and organizations that have an interest in the future of the city. This ranges from individual citizens, through local businesses and groups representing communities of identity, interest and place, to national and international agencies which have a presence or strong interest in the area. These groups need to be engaged proactively and in different ways. Proactive engagement, going out and asking for people's views and input rather than waiting for them to come forward, matters for a number of reasons. There are always some groups, often described as 'hard to reach' or 'hard to hear', who require particular effort to be engaged effectively.

As more and more areas stress their diversity as a key element of their appeal, so it becomes ever more important to ensure that the brand reflects the strengths of that difference. Tapping into the diversity of perspectives and interests can also aid the development of a sophisticated city brand which, like a highly developed product brand, can project nuanced messages to different target audiences.

Second, an additional basic starting point is to engage stakeholders from the beginning of the branding process. Local stakeholders cannot be treated like participants in a focus group discussing options for an advertising campaign. They have to live with the results of the branding effort, and their knowledge needs to be harnessed from the start in any preliminary discussion about the strengths and weaknesses, opportunities and challenges facing the place. Effective branding strategies therefore seek out and utilize the people who make the place work, from recognized civic, community and business leaders through to taxi drivers, hairdressers and all those others who play unrecognized but vital public-facing contact roles in the area. This approach takes longer than simply signing up the local burghers but, as set out above, brings a range of perspectives to the process and helps to ensure that the branding strategy has been tested before implementation.

Third, stakeholders need to be engaged on the basis of evidence. City branding does not start with a blank slate. Cities are already branded, whether or not they realize or acknowledge the fact, and it is very difficult to erase or amend the associations which people attach to them. The starting point for an effective and inclusive branding strategy, therefore, is to take a critical look at what the city has to offer to current and potential residents, visitors and investors; what unique assets and strengths can be developed and emphasized; and what flaws and weaknesses need to be addressed.

Exemplifying an inclusive approach to its branding is the seaside town of Margate in Kent, England, which is in the middle phase of a longer-term process of regeneration and redevelopment. It declined in the latter half of the last century as the traditional seaside holiday industry, the mainstay of the local economy, lost out to the continental package holiday. This was a common story for many seaside towns in the United Kingdom and other parts of Europe.

Margate has eschewed a major rebranding campaign in favor of a more organic approach. Each housing redevelopment, hotel renovation and new amenity, including the major new Turner Contemporary Gallery which is funded through the regeneration program, is designed to build the new picture of Margate as a traditional seaside resort with a contemporary cultural offer. To underpin the regeneration program, the local council and its partners, including regional and central government, commissioned detailed studies of deprivation, housing and labor market conditions and dynamics, potential investment sources, demographic trends and more. This took time and resources to assemble, but has paid off in terms of visioning what each actor involved in the process can do to bring about the town's revival in a realistic and sustainable way.

At each stage, partners in Margate have been able to root their thinking around promotion and perception in a rich and detailed profile of the challenges and opportunities facing the town. This has been crucial to developing a regeneration strategy that will deliver what the promotion promises.

The fourth and final element of success is the importance of challenge. Effective teams often disagree, but can do so in a constructive and deliberative way that leads to better outcomes. Branding teams need to be prepared to challenge the assumptions and preconceptions of partners who do not see the need to rebrand or recognize the scale of the task. This need to be done sensitively, and be well evidenced, but is important for creating an open dialogue.

To return to the example of Liverpool, that city's branding attempts prior to the Capital of Culture campaign were often criticized for trading on over-familiar symbols – most commonly football and The Beatles – which had been sadly overtaken by more recent negative associations such as crime, unemployment, political militancy, and the 'scally' culture. The Capital of Culture program was important to the city's confidence because it allowed local people and civic leaders to recognize that their global image had been seriously damaged, to debate new directions and images, and to put forward an assured and endearing new face (that barely included the Beatles or football). Ultimately, the city's leaders felt that the brand value accrued under the Capital of Culture period had created a momentum that required a vehicle to carry it forward beyond the event, which led to the creation of a durable Liverpool City Brand Partnership. This responsive way of working does not come naturally to many public services, but is increasingly important to new policy imperatives such as the branding of places (Trueman *et al.*, 2008).

TENSIONS AND CHALLENGES

We now turn to some of the most common challenges and tensions in city branding, and look at what different areas have done to address and resolve them.

Perhaps the most common tension is that some stakeholders will be uneasy and perhaps resentful at the prospect of rebranding. In part this reflects the latent hostility to the general notion of branding and stems from a combination of civic pride, the fear of change and an understandable resistance toward perceived external criticism of the place that people call home. In some cases, there is a more rational cause for rejecting branding if, for example, the strategy is premised on attracting new kinds of investment or visitor groups which may not benefit some existing businesses. Whatever the cause, it is usually the case that some stakeholders will see little value and even some threat in city branding. This is especially true of areas which have been criticized and made the butt of jokes; places which are in greatest need of help with rebranding, but most resistant to it, because it implies further criticism.

Middlesbrough is one town which has suffered at the hands of its poor national reputation, culminating in being dubbed as 'officially' the 'worst place to live' in the United Kingdom, according to research by the popular British property television show *Location Location Location*. The town has responded by investing in the already internationally acclaimed Middles-brough Institute of Modern Art (mima) as the centerpiece of a strategy to not only capitalize on the North East region of England's night-time economy but also to develop an attractive and hitherto unknown creative hub in the aspirant city based around existing academic excellence in the computer gaming sector.

This strategy has, however, been challenged by some local stakeholders (including opposition councillors) on the grounds that it represents an elitist attempt to change what the town is about and is, in essence, a rejection of the 'real Middlesbrough'. Civic leaders have responded by recognizing the 'concentric' nature of the town's audiences, moving from local taxpayers, through regional investors to national and international visitors, and pitching the benefits of mima and other developments to those different groups.

The second common tension is the confusion between branding and promotion, and how that affects the role of stakeholders. In some cases, stakeholders are keen to promote the positive elements of the place and expect branding to do that for them. When it becomes clear that the process of branding is much more critical and exploratory than simply promotion via marketing communications, the result can often be confusion and frustration. To avoid this tension, it is important to be clear from the outset that branding is quite different from promotion, and requires a more open and critical debate about the place and what it has to offer, now and in the future.

As in Middlesbrough, the branding strategy for East London has also been contested and argued over on several fronts and epitomizes the tension between branding and promotion. In spite of the opportunities afforded by the 2012 Olympic Games, the post-industrial area of East London remains in need of regeneration and economic stabilization through attracting diverse new businesses and talent. The traditional brand of the Brick Lane area is precariously balanced: world famous and associated with London's vibrancy and multiculturalism, but increasingly regarded within London as a variable-quality tourist destination.

The new strategy for East London links its traditional association with vibrancy and diversity to a new emphasis on new media, fashion (although this was previously very closely associated with East London) and creativity. Some of the tension underpinning this strategy was exposed by local residents' protests at the filming of the novel *Brick Lane*. The film was seen by local and regional agencies as a welcome opportunity to showcase East London to a global audience, but by some residents as a controversial insult to the values of the local Bangladeshi community.

Edinburgh Napier
University Library

The final challenge relates to the nature of leadership and partnership working in relation to city branding. In his writing on place branding, van Gelder (2008) stresses the importance of working in open and fluid partnerships, focused on a common goal but open and willing to accommodate divergent styles and ways of working. More democratic forms of city branding utilize the leadership of different players, each of whom can convince different internal and external audiences.

The rebranding of Manchester offers a powerful example of cross-sector partnership working. An element of the city's traditional 'brand personality' is its history of can-do innovation and make-do self reliance, from the Rochdale pioneers and 'the first industrial city' to Factory Records and the reinvention of East Manchester as a sports, media and culture hub, spurred by the hosting of the 2002 Commonwealth Games. The city council recognized early on that it could achieve more by 'steering rather than rowing'; setting the overall direction of the brand and the overarching framework for development, but drawing on other sectors and partners to provide much of the energy and expertise, including the vibrant music and arts industry. As the partnership has developed, the interaction between different sectors has increased and the city has become increasingly regarded as a cultural hotbed. In 2003, Manchester topped a list of British cities with the greatest creative potential – 'the UK's answer to San Francisco' – according to a newly created 'Boho Britain' index (Demos, 2003).

What these challenges demonstrate is that stakeholder engagement is not an easy or straightforward task. Like consultation or public engagement more widely, it is sometimes treated as a soft or fluffy exercise, but branding teams that rush into stakeholder engagement (if they do so at all) with a blasé attitude can very quickly run into conflict. Stakeholder engagement is valuable precisely because it is difficult and challenging, because it generates disagreement and debate, and from that new perspectives and ideas. There is no way of avoiding these tensions, but respecting the diversity of stakeholders and engaging them from the start in open and evidenced discussions can help to ensure that debate and disagreement is creative and productive.

SUMMARY

City branding is an old art, but a new science. For centuries, city leaders have recognized the need to project a unique and powerful image to the rest of the world. Yet it is only in the past few decades that city branding has begun to be recognized as a distinct discipline. Even more recently, city branding practitioners have developed a specific set of tools and skills to engage stakeholders. The application of these new tools is sometimes blunt, but the continued refinement of effective and inclusive stakeholder engagement techniques benefits not only cities working to rebrand themselves, but also the discipline of city branding as a whole.

This chapter has demonstrated that stakeholder engagement is crucial to the success of any city branding strategy, but achieving such engagement requires an approach that is more in line with partnership working rather than with traditional brand strategy imposed from above. The participatory and iterative approach to city branding set out in this chapter is designed to generate and support a greater sense of ownership amongst the broadest possible range of stakeholders, which represents a crucial ingredient in any city branding initiative. If the range of partners in a place feel that they have been involved in shaping the message, they are more likely to vocalize and embody it.

CHAPTER 7

Paradoxes of City Branding and Societal Changes

Can-Seng Ooi

INTRODUCTION

The 2009 United Nations Climate Summit (COP15) attracted more than 45,000 people to Copenhagen. The world watched the unfolding of the two-week conference. With international attention and the hope of finding an agreement on managing global warming, the event was a city branding scoop for the Danish capital. The summit started with optimism; the Copenhagen local authorities dubbed the city as Hopenhagen. At the end of the summit, the resulting so-called Copenhagen Accord was not legally binding and thus toothless. World leaders, including United States President Barack Obama and China Premier Wen Jiabao, failed to engineer a firm global commitment on tackling climate change. The summit was subsequently dubbed 'Brokenhagen', 'Nopenhagen' and 'No Hopenhagen' in international media reports.

Copenhagen city authorities were disappointed with this feeble outcome but they remained excited by the extensive positive international publicity for the city (Astrup, 2009). For example, Tom Chesshyre (2009) of *The Times* described Copenhagen as 'Europe's greenest city'. Tom Zeller, Jr (2009) published a feature in the *New York Times* on how New York City Mayor Bloomberg was impressed by the use of renewal energy in the Danish capital. The high profile United Nations summit increased the international awareness of Copenhagen. The world also saw the city beyond its historical sights (for example, the statue of the Little Mermaid, castles and churches) and its famed social openness. The Copenhagen portrayed through COP15 was a modern green city. Although the Danish host was partly to blame for the failure of the summit, BBC reporter Richard Black

(2009) summed up the ambivalence by stating that '[we] will remember the city and people of Copenhagen with some affection. But it is likely that history will judge that the government's political handling of the summit covered the prime minister in something markedly less fragrant than glory'.

Hosting big events is one of many strategies of branding and promoting a city (Brown *et al.*, 2002; Burgan and Mules, 1992; Green and Chalip, 1998; Smith, 2004). As the opening COP15 example shows, hosting internationally significant and popular events draws attention to the place and provides an opportunity for the host city to showcase its strengths and uniqueness. Davos is an example of a city branded literally by a series of annual events, the World Economic Forum meetings. Cannes is best known for its film festival.

A city may also be branded by being the finest and best in certain dimensions. London and New York are financial centers, boasting intense business activities there. Cities are thus branded for the types of activities they are good at. Along the same lines, city branding authorities refer to global ranking surveys such as the *Economist*'s 'liveability' index (*Economist*, 2009) to brand their metropolises. Relatively small cities like Vancouver, Vienna and Melbourne are ranked high in the liveability index. Besides recreational and cultural activities, other factors such as crime rate, threat from instability and terrorism, healthcare and education availability, state of transport and communications infrastructure are included in this ranking.

In conjunction with other city branding strategies, a branded city also has a slogan or catchphrase, such as 'I amsterdam', 'I ♥ NY' and 'Your-Singapore'. These brands contain messages and stories to describe and portray their respective cities. The brand stories highlight the uniqueness of the city and also provide frameworks to understand these cities. Reflecting the hope for a more sustainable global environment and that Copenhagen leads not only in green living but also in drafting a global agreement on the environment, 'Hopenhagen' was to encapsulate these messages during COP15.

The myriad strategies are well discussed in the literature, including the chapters in this volume. There is, however, a dearth of research on the evolving relationships between city branding campaigns and the changing society. Branding a city is an ongoing exercise. In the case of COP15, the Copenhagen authorities used the United Nations summit to renew and update the world's image of an emerging green Copenhagen. Cities evolve and new realities emerge. The relationship between city brand and the city is multifaceted. When a city changes, its brand images may not move with the city's emerging reality. On the other hand, a new brand may have moved too fast; the new brand stories are aspirations that have yet to be realized.

The perception of the city by the outside world may also have changed, while the official brand slides behind public perception. A city brand may also provide the impetus for the place to change in a desired direction. This chapter looks at issues such as these pertaining to city branding and societal changes.

CITY BRANDING AND SOCIETAL CHANGES

Cities are, by definition, relatively large, densely populated and socially heterogeneous. They conjure up images of vibrancy. These images contrast against the idyll of the countryside and the coziness of villages. Many cities are also considered social, cultural, economic and political centers. New social practices and trends often emerge in cities and spread to other places. As spaces for diverse interaction and trend setting, a city is a crucible for social changes. Some changes take time to be entrenched, for example, the evolution of a local dialect. Other changes may come about more quickly, for example, the making of Dubai into a world city. Dubai's progress is now symbolized by the world's tallest building, the Burj Khalifa. The building has not only shaped the skyline of Dubai, it has also become the brand icon of Dubai's aspirations to be an ultra modern global business center.

Despite the many strategies used in city branding, a city branding exercise works within a set of inter-related parameters. These parameters, as will be elaborated later, place paradoxical demands when societal changes are considered. The first parameter is that the city brand will always present only positive aspects of the place. A city brand selectively frames the metropolis and draws people's attention to positive images of the urban milieu. There are many aspects of the city that are ignored because these aspects are not considered attractive or interesting by the branding authorities, for example, smog, organized crime and ghettos. Similarly, appropriate traditions and history are often roped into branding the society while more negative aspects of the past are ignored. For instance, the historical Forbidden City and Tiananmen Square are sites that have come to characterize Beijing. They are constantly featured in branding and city promotional materials. Despite making great strides in political openness in China, the 1989 demonstrations and subsequent massacre at Tiananmen Square are ignored in branding Beijing.

The city brand explicitly aims to modify public perceptions (Andersen *et al.*, 1997; Kleppe *et al.*, 2002; McCleary and Whitney, 1994; Richards, 1992). This is the second city branding parameter. A city branding exercise is about shaping people's perception of the location. For example, staying with Beijing, the 2008 Beijing Olympics branded the Chinese capital. In challenging perceptions that Beijing is the political center of a polluted and backward authoritarian state, the opening ceremony of the games reminded the world of the four great Chinese inventions – paper, compass, printing and gunpowder. With the successful hosting of the games, Beijing is now to be seen as modern, efficient and yet traditionally Chinese. It is debatable if the world's perception of Beijing has changed but the games and spectacular opening and closing ceremonies wowed Chinese and foreigners alike.

The third parameter deals with the tacit link between the city brand and the city identity. Despite the fact that the city brand is selectively constructed, the brand is also the identity statement of the city. The brand is a summary that captures the truthful story and uniqueness of the place. For instance, the Danish city of Aarhus is branded as 'Denmark's second largest city, where the pulse beats, but never too fast for the heart to enjoy it' (Visit Aarhus, 2010). This tagline highlights Aarhus as a relatively small city that does not overwhelm visitors and residents with too much hustle and bustle. The tagline gives a snapshot of the city and aspires to give an honest image of the place.

The last parameter highlights the ability of the city brand to affect people's interpretation of the location. A successful city branding campaign, among other things, will provide a framework for locals and non-residents to imagine and experience the place (Moscardo, 1996; Ooi, 2007; Prentice and Andersen, 2007; Waller and Lea, 1999). For instance, in the branding of Singapore as a destination, the 'YourSingapore' brand suggests how people should understand and interpret the city-state as a smorgasbord of different cultures and attractions, through which a visitor can pick and choose what he or she likes to experience. Singapore is a modern Asian society that blends cultures from the East and the West, the modern and the traditional (Ooi, 2007). Many modern skyscrapers in Singapore can also be appreciated through *feng shui* principles or traditional Chinese geomancy. Without the 'YourSingapore' gaze lens, foreigners could see the tall buildings in the city-state as just modern structures and/or as manifestations of centuries-old cultural practices. 'YourSingapore' tells of the diversity and possibilities in the island-state.

These multiple parameters give rise to a number of challenges to any city branding exercise, in the context of societal changes. A city branding process is ongoing. It is not static. Neither is society. I would like to highlight these challenges as paradoxes.

PARADOX I – BEING EQUALLY SPECIAL

A city brand presents a picture and packages the place. The brand package accentuates the uniqueness of the city, so as to stand out in the competition.

The city branding process is also an ongoing one. Over time, a city changes and the city brand updated. Paradoxically then, as cities develop, they also become more alike, particularly when authorities learn from other cities on attracting investors and tourists. For example, as mentioned before, there are a number of surveys that rank cities. These rankings, among other things, brand cities. Besides the already mentioned *Economist*'s liveability index, there is Anholt's city ranking (2006a) in which Paris, London and New York are rated highly because of these cities' vitality, their people and facilities. Florida (2003) offers yet another way of ranking cities through his Creativity Index. Florida focuses on three different criteria: technology, talent, and tolerance. Urban places are ranked on the number of patents per head, the density of the population of 'bohemians' and gay people, the proportion of immigrants and the number of so called 'knowledge workers' (Florida, 2003; Peck, 2005).

Many city branding authorities refer to selected indexes, pointing out their cities' high rankings. Just as importantly, these surveys have also become frameworks for authorities to organize and manage their cities. For instance, Singapore, in wanting to attract more skilled labor, investments and tourists, has invoked Florida's arguments by loosening up the cultural scene in the island-state and informing the public that the government has no more qualms about employing self-professed homosexuals. When conservative voices rise, the authorities justify the changes by saying that these moves are part of the signalling and branding process of a tolerant, open and creative Singapore (Ooi, 2007). With the same goals and branding aims, cities drive forward by using the ranking criteria as benchmarks. Such rankings are then tools for cities to learn from one another, and as a result, many cities become equally special. They are also then branded similarly.

PARADOX 2 – THE BOTTOM-UP AND TOP-DOWN TENSION

In the branding literature, there is much emphasis on taking the interests of different stakeholders into consideration, in particular, local communities and residents. Respecting stakeholders is not only necessary to ensure the success of a branding campaign, it is also ethical. Consultation shows respect and courtesy. Surely, city brands must reflect the different interests in society. The brand must be developed and promoted from the grassroots. Therefore studies of place branding have moved beyond treating place branding as merely marketing exercises and into aspects of place management. The branding process requires mobilizing and garnering local support, enhancing public-private collaboration and engaging with audiences around the world (Mossberg and Getz, 2006; Nilsson, 2007; Tatevossian,

2008; Therkelsen and Halkier, 2008; Vasudevan, 2008). Cities, for instance, are not only enhancing their images through advertising, they are also increasing more activities and events for visitors and residents. Besides beautifying the city through urban planning, city authorities are also enlivening their cities' cultural scenes, nightlife and the celebration of diversity. The enlivening processes would benefit both residents and visitors. Different stakeholders benefit from these strategies (Brown *et al.*, 2002; Florida, 2003; Harmaakorpi *et al.*, 2008; Smith, 2004). But bringing the interests of residents and outsiders together through a city branding exercise can generate yet another paradox.

As mentioned, city brands are also brand identities. Identities are supposed to reflect and describe the place. It would otherwise not be sincere and authentic. While the city brand aims to tell a story of the society from the bottom-up, when the brand is 'fixed', it also imposes an image on the place. As gaze lenses, the brand story affects how we interpret the place. In other words, the city brand, inadvertently or otherwise, becomes a visionary exercise for the place branding authorities to imagine and reflect on how different their city is from other cities. The crystallized public image may be introduced to the native population for it to recognize itself (Lanfant, 1995; Leonard, 1997; Oakes, 1993; Ooi, 2005). The city brand then brings about societal changes in a particular direction. Let me elaborate.

The city branding campaign may destroy the original spirit of the place. For instance, popular local places may become expatriates' and tourists' haunts when such places are promoted via the city brand; the social make-up of the place would change and may lose its local appeal. For instance, Chinatown in Singapore is promoted in the destination brand story. It has been spruced up and now attracts expatriates, tourists and yuppies. Bars and cafes have sprung up to cater to new wealthy visitors. As a result, many locals find Chinatown expensive and most shops no longer cater to them. To residents, the traditional Chinatown spirit has disappeared. Ironically, Chinatown was promoted in the city brand because of the local atmosphere. The authorities took the next step of 'enhancing' the atmosphere by renovating the area.

On the other hand, city branding can bring about societal change that is appreciated by locals. Shanghai is no longer a fishing village or a colonial outpost of the 1930s. Today, it is a booming metropolis with more than 23 million people. The city is modern. The famous skyscrapers have come to characterize the city. While the city is searching for its soul amidst the tall buildings, highways and shopping malls, the authorities have decided to conserve parts of old Shanghai. The neo-classical colonialist buildings along the Bund have been listed. Yu Gardens – a landscaped traditional

Chinese park – and its surrounding area, have been locally dubbed as 'Chinatown'. Newly built traditionally Chinese-looking houses and shops clutter the area outside the gardens. In this case, the branding of the city, with the support of urban planning, has maintained and reinvented aspects of old Shanghai. Residents shop there and they have come to accept the spruced up Yu Gardens as quintessentially Shanghai. In other words, while a city brand identity is supposed to reflect society, it also brings about and shapes society – top-down.

PARADOX 3 – DIFFERING RESIDENTS' AND NON-RESIDENTS' INTERPRETATIONS

City branding messages that resonate with locals may not resonate with outsiders. One aim of a city brand is to shape people's perception. The brand messages must be attractive and authentic. The authenticity of the message may be compromised if the message is geared largely towards foreigners; it may then sound too simplified and commercial for local residents. On the other hand, while appreciated by locals, a sophisticated and convoluted brand message is not attractive to non-residents. For example, food is often used in city branding. Many non-Chinese do not differentiate between the cuisines of Shanghai and Hong Kong. *Xiao long bao* is a Shanghai specialty. It is a type of steamed dumpling. *Dim sum* (in Cantonese) is a range of steamed dumplings from Cantonese cuisine. To many Chinese, they make a distinction between *xiao long bao* and *dim sum*. And thanks to cultural movements, *xiao long bao* and *dim sum* are found in these two cities (and other parts of the world). Dishes travel and add to the variety of cuisines found in cities. Regardless, to enjoy local cuisines as part of the city brand experience, one should enjoy *xiao long bao* in Shanghai and enjoy *dim sum* in Hong Kong. Changes in society have made it difficult for non-Chinese to know what is historically local and what is not. Making such differentiation can be considered pedantic and uninteresting for foreigners, although locals will find the differentiation more accurate and sophisticated. City branding authorities do not make such deep demarcation in their promotional materials. To many locals, lumping *xiao long bao* and *dim sum* together as just part of Chinese cuisine erodes the authenticity of the local cuisine brand. Time will tell if the lack of reiteration that *xiao long bao* and *dim sum* do not come from the same Chinese kitchens will erode local cuisine identities. The attractiveness and authenticity demands of the brand messages may contradict one another. Complex messages of history and societal changes are often ignored, to the chagrin of some locals. To non-locals, a simple city brand message is beautiful. A new authenticity may emerge (Cohen, 1988; Ooi and Stöber, 2010).

SUMMARY

The opening example of the local authorities of Copenhagen of using COP15 to tell the world that the Danish capital is modern and green, is an aspiration and a reality. 'Hopenhagen' tells how the city authorities want the Danish capital to change. Many residents share the same vision and imagination of the city. The world should see Copenhagen and Denmark in that light. In the Environmental Performance Index 2010, Denmark was ranked 32 out of 163 countries, behind countries such as Iceland, Albania and Peru (Yale Center for Environmental Law and Policy, and Center for International Earth Science Information Network 2010). The brand message, the public imagination and the reality may not meet.

Societal changes are often not discussed in the literature of city branding. The time element is very important because it highlights the fluctuating reality of society. The city brand message freezes the place but in fact, the city branding exercise is a continuous process. Society emerges too. City brands are supposed to accentuate the uniqueness of the city, be built from the bottom-up and reflect the city's identity. As the three paradoxes indicate, city branding processes can make cities more alike, bring about societal changes and forge new city identities. City branding exercises affect society, just as the city shapes how it should be branded.

CHAPTER 8

City Branding through Food Culture: Insights from the Regional Branding Level

Richard Tellström

INTRODUCTION

Food culture is not an easily defined concept. It deals with categories as diverse as the raw ingredients, such as the salmon swimming in cold ocean waters, and the little canapé with cold smoked salmon we put in our mouths during an evening reception. The process of defining food actually starts even before we have a raw ingredient to work with. It starts during the intellectual and reflective phase in which plants and animals are culturally, socially and politically defined as edible or non-edible, like a festive salmon or a non-edible salmon. Food culture is a process that transforms the edible raw ingredient into a more advanced and value-added product and eating situation.

Food culture, along with harvesting, cooking and serving, is a tool for making a group gather around the same values and expressions that make the group into a group and hold it together. It is also an easy and visible way of excluding others, for example, those who eat things we do not, or of separating the snake-eaters from the frog-eaters or the fermented fish-eaters, those who eat with their fingers, those who start the meal with cheese and those who finish the meal with cheese, and so on. So, to be frank – food has nothing to do with food. Instead, a food's value extends beyond its nutritional value and is one of the oldest tools and most concrete cultural expressions which state who we are and to what we wish to belong.

The practice of using food and beverages as an explicit branding tool for a region or nation extends back 150 years or so to the time of the Great Exhibition in London in 1851 and to the industrialization era. Over the past few decades in the Western world and in Sweden in particular, which will be a focal point in this chapter, the emphasized origins of food have come into widespread use.

THE OLD AND THE NEW RELATIONSHIP BETWEEN PLACE AND FOOD

A food's values can be transferred not only to other objects, but also to areas to which we want to give a particular value. It is also possible to transfer values in the opposite direction. An area's reputation can add value to a food product even if we do not know much about the food product itself (Bell and Valentine, 1997). There have been links between marketed food products and places throughout history, for example, Stilton cheese, a cheese produced in the Stilton area and sold in the village of Stilton (Tregear, 2003) or between food products and an area or town, for example, Krakow sausage, which has been known since Medieval times (Yoder, 1981). The phenomenon of geographic names or areas being linked to food and wines can probably be traced back in time for as long as food products have been sold at markets, where it has long been used as a way of categorizing products.

One theoretical perspective concerning the link between area and product is the concept of country-of-origin and its relationship to marketing (Papadopoulos and Heslop, 1993; Peterson and Jolibert, 1995; Verlegh and Steenkamp, 1999). The perceived relationship between a country and food quality is well known, as in the case of France and its excellent reputation for food. Country-of-origin can be understood as the mental representations of a country's people, products, culture and national symbols (Askegaard and Ger, 1998). One conclusion therefore is that food has always had a market value and has been the conduit for ideas that a buyer is searching for, as the purpose of consuming a food product is to make use of its value in a meal situation. It is probably impossible to think of food products without also thinking of their origin or relationship to places, people or other status-related definitions. This links food and place, forming the basis for an experience that is integrated within the contemporary development of the experience economy (Pine and Gilmore, 1999), and a new use of the landscape is visible.

POLITICAL FOOD BRANDING

Food with an emphasized origin has become a political tool to promote economic and rural growth in regions suffering from recession (OECD,

1995; Kneafsey, 2000; Tregear, 2003; Nordic Council, 2005), and to create new businesses at the intersection between food and tourism and the experience of a particular place (Long, 2004; Trubek, 2008). Since the early 1970s, it has been a goal for the European Union (EU) to strengthen its member states' regions in order to prevent the European nations from going to war against each other because of economic inequality. The EU has developed financial aid schemes based on the existence of regions, and the value for the various EU nations of having many regions is that they can apply for different kinds of regional EU aid.

Some regional food cultures have been used as a concept in political projects since the 1990s (Delanty, 1998; Ilbery and Kneafsey, 2000), underlining the economic-political use of food culture emphasized by the EU. This has also been expressed through protective legislation from the EU concerning the origin of food products, and there are also EU programs for rural development such as artisan food production (Tregear, 1998), visible as an aestheticization of the rural, which in turn is further developed by non-governmental food organizations such as the Slow Food movement (Miele and Murdoch, 2002).

The EU's regional projects have been of various types, including agricultural support and innovative entrepreneur projects aimed at creating economic growth. An important target group has been those whose aim has been either to create regions which have not previously existed, or to lift regions which lost their regional profile during the national identity-building projects in the national unification process of the late 19th and early 20th centuries. In 1998, a major new region was established in Sweden, the region of Västra Götaland, following the merger of three counties. As part of the information initiative for the inhabitants of this large new county, a recipe book on the food culture of the new region was produced, entitled *The Governor's Residence Cookery Book* (1999). This politically-encouraged food culture initiative was also used to brand the region in order to attract investors to the area and to promote tourism and other visitor-related businesses. This relationship between food and tourism is well known, with many examples not only from Provence and Tuscany but also from California and South Africa (Hall *et al.*, 2003; Wolf 2006).

One example during the first decade of the 21st century of a regional EU project aimed at economically promoting the archipelago between Sweden and Finland is the food branding project entitled, 'A taste of the archipelago'. This defined and named archipelago region is new and has been defined in the context of the EU Interreg program for cross-border development within the EU (Heldt-Cassel, 2003). This branding process is twofold, as it both creates and markets a regional identity, and encourages small-scale entrepreneurs to make use of the branding expression when they market their food products or tourist services using the project logos. However, not all representations of the archipelago are useful, for example, those representations which can be found in other areas and which are already used there, or contradictory food culture representations of socially stigmatized groups, people living at the periphery of society, or the food culture of immigrants now living in the branded area. A brand profile is simple and positive, not contradictory and negative.

The greater importance of regional profile strategies can be seen as part of a societal development where places, region or cities compete with each other in a global market whose purpose is to create regions that are both units for economic growth and the basis for identity and culture (Heldt-Cassel, 2003). The projects all make use of the idea that a region has a certain flavor and that you can experience the area more closely by using food's visual impact and the signals you receive through the taste receptors in the mouth and nose. The stimulation of the senses is an important factor, not only in attracting capital to a region and encouraging tourists to travel, but also in making people proud of the area in which they live. This type of branded food project makes use of a postmodern search for authenticity but with a contemporary twist, and in the branding work the endeavors of both traditional and contemporary chefs to develop new flavors and dishes can become very useful in achieving the political and economic aims of the project.

Since 2006, the Nordic Council of Ministries has been running a food project entitled 'New Nordic Food', which aims to make people in the Nordic Countries proud of their Nordic origin and identity by upgrading their attitude towards Nordic food products and Nordic food culture. The political support of Nordic food has also been a tool to develop sparsely populated areas and districts suffering from a lack of economic progress. This project will continue over the coming years. National food projects have also been launched. The government initiative entitled 'Sweden – Land of Food' in 2008 aims to enhance the experiences of tourists and to stimulate food tourism which can promote economic development in the rural areas of Sweden as well as doubling food exports within ten years. Branding Sweden as a country with interesting food products and food experiences is a tool in this project and the Minister of Agriculture says that his vision is for Sweden to be known for having the best gastronomy in Europe and that 'we should be known as a better food country than France' (Svenska Livsmedel, 2009).

The civil servants responsible for managing the food projects are tasked with monitoring how the selected food profile is perceived and ensuring that the projects match the ideas of political leaders as regards how a region should be perceived compared with other regions throughout Europe. Branding a region with food is also a question of branding politicians with the right food profile.

COMMERCIAL USE OF BRANDED REGIONS

Many food companies benefit from a marked branded regional expression and two types of company in particular can be noted – restaurants that profile themselves as attached to a particular region and food producers that express their market profile with the aid of the values associated with a particular region. Both of these types of enterprise mix facts concerning regionality, food culture and historical background, but in combination with market messages which may make them historically inaccurate. Instead, it becomes a mixture of selected elements emphasized as being the single and unique characteristics of the region, and contradictory and pluralistic expressions are under-communicated or not mentioned at all. This is, however, often of lesser importance to the enterprises and their customers. However, if an authentic template is not available, an illusion can be used when food culture is used to brand products or areas (Tellström *et al.*, 2006). The only important consideration for them is that the commercialized regional profile is perceived as being trustworthy at the point of consumption.

A branded food culture acts as a manuscript for the production of a food product or food service profile and has many similarities with the work associated with manuscripts in literature, film and other art forms. Branded food culture can therefore be understood as fiction and the manuscript work is especially visible when traditional regional food culture is revitalized with the aim of creating emotions or affection towards a regional identity and has been discussed by many researchers (for example, Salomonsson, 1984). In a reworking of the concept of invented tradition, food researchers have added concepts such as 'invention', 'innovation' and 'retraditionalized' to describe the process whereby traditional food culture is commercialized with the aim of creating an emotion when bought and consumed, which underlines the economic value of cultural expressions in a postmodern society (Urry, 1990; Boissevain, 1992).

Restaurants in rural areas that profile themselves with a regional food culture they consider as their own work use one of two major strategies to attract their different target groups (Tellström *et al.*, 2005). The first group, comprising tourists on holiday or travelers who have a particular profiled restaurant as the destination for their journey, is often searching for food experiences that match their idea of the region. They often visit during a short period in the summer. This group has previously encountered the region through marketing or branding messages in advertisements, on television, in travel books and in recipe books, concerning the food that can be found or 'what the region tastes like', and is now searching to experience the food culture they have heard about. They are open to the idea of eating foods from the food culture they associate the region with, although this perception can include food from a much larger area than the region itself.

A region's size will vary according to who is doing the defining and the definitions that already exist. A restaurant in northern Sweden which is located in a traditional northern farming district is often visited by guests who consider this part of Sweden to be arctic and alpine, and therefore accept reindeer as a local meat, which historically it has not been. However, the restaurant does not argue with its guests over this geographical and historical misunderstanding and instead offers a variety of reindeer dishes on the menu and sells a lot of them (Tellström et al., 2005). The only saleable regional food culture on a restaurant's menu is based on the guest's ideas of the region rather than the correct historical facts, and for the customer it does not matter that the food has been taken out of its true context, as long as it feels authentic.

The locals living close to this northern profiled restaurant look for another kind of authenticity and visit the establishment in order to celebrate a family occasion or to eat something other than the dishes they normally eat from their daily regional food culture. This creates a demand for fancy restaurant dishes but not the dishes that are found regionally, as this food type often forms part of the daily diet at home. The idea of eating at a restaurant is to encounter a different cuisine compared with the one you have at home. This local customer group is, however, of major importance as it generates out-of-season income. A rural restaurant that benefits from a branded regional profile during part of every year must have another menu when the group that travels in response to the branded regional message has gone home and the locals express their own, different demand. The restaurant referred to here has solved the diverging demands by serving a regional fish, white fish, to the restaurant guests in two styles: tourists buy the white fish smoked or grilled which the locals eat at home, while the locals buy the white fish at the restaurant as fillets served with a French white wine sauce, a fancy restaurant format that they do not eat at home.

City tourist boards must take into account the fact that they have at least two target groups for their marketing messages: domestic tourists and international tourists. The City of Stockholm markets itself differently according to whether the language in the tourist booklets is Swedish or English, and presents two different food profiles depending on whether the target group is international (in which case the menu features smoked herring and scrambled egg) or domestic (in which case the menu features sushi).

Food producers can make use of the consumers' interest in food that is associated with a regional profile in different ways, either by producing a product in the geographic region itself or by using an expression that creates an emotion of regional feelings. For example, this may be done by underlining an old-fashioned preparation method or some other production circumstances that create a sense of authenticity. There are many examples of this. In Sweden, a brewery has developed an entire regional profile around a beer brand called Mariestad's beer, by mentioning the former production plant in the rural city of Mariestad. However, in the early 1970s, the historical brewery was closed and the recipes sold to the brewery that produces the beer today. The beer is produced at two production plants situated over 200 miles from the city of Mariestad. These manuscript settings can create feelings of authenticity which are a desired expression in contemporary consumption. Bell and Valentine (1997) have concluded that communicated cognitive meanings such as a product's local association, have a greater value to the consumer than a product lacking this association.

These examples underline the fact that branding linked to a place, region or city is a work of fiction in which certain elements are undercommunicated and other elements are emphasized, particularly those elements which the entrepreneur considers to be relevant for the consumer.

CULTURAL USE OF POLITICAL AND COMMERCIAL BRANDING

In food culture, values are added and removed in different sequences, altering how we perceive a food product and the context in which we can use it. According to Metzger (2005), the transformation of food from being everyday food products and dishes into cultural icons and authentic representatives of an era, time or geography is the result of a selection process in several steps, in which food that has a blurred expression is of no use. The food product that remains after the selection process is representative of a thought and a value, rather than the food culture of a region or place.

Food culture has a value in itself as a means to develop a tourist destination, as a tool for regional development or for marketing a region, and also as an expressive instrument for urban intellectual ideas and values, for example, going to farmers' markets or travelling to a rural restaurant as a weekend event. The similarity between these uses is that food is used beyond its nutritional function. The use also emphasizes the fact that food can carry values and as such support commercial targets and matching contemporary consumer ideas concerning authenticity, as well as political goals such as regional development or identity purposes.

The multicultural values in food cultures are seldom projected when food is used to profile areas and regions. Often the opposite is apparent as stereotypical food profiles are highlighted, the food preferences of society's leading groups are emphasized, and contemporary industrialized food production is rejected. According to branding logic, food products and dishes which in terms of market communication are recognized as cultural icons, as representatives of a geography, or expressive in another context, must not be found anywhere else, in order to maintain their exclusive appeal.

SUMMARY

Origin and authenticity are important considerations when we select food to buy and eat. It is a signal to us that confirms that the food fits into our culture and matches our own ideals and identity expressions, and we select the food with values that we like and respect. However, not all food products or food ideas are useful in a political or commercial branding perspective. Uniqueness is an essential factor in creating authenticity. In this process, similarities with other regions, products or situations can be a blurring factor, and values that do not support the goal are actively removed from the branding profile. Branding an area with food should therefore be understood in the same way as branding with other art forms such as books, films or dramas; it is a question of creating a story about who we think we are, where we come from and, more importantly, who we want to be.

CHAPTER 9

City Branding through New Green Spaces

Jared Braiterman

INTRODUCTION

Now is the time for cities to take bold action and to exponentially increase green spaces. Faced with an ageing 20th century urban infrastructure and the emergence of many new cities, there is an increasing recognition that plant life and new public spaces are central to the vitality of global cities. Industrial era urban design banished nature to the outskirts of cities or contained nature within strictly defined parks. Recently, local government and private sector urban leaders have been creating interconnected green spaces that transform the urban fabric for human and environmental benefit. Green infrastructure and new forms of urban living provide functional benefits, including clean air and water, and improve quality of life, as new public spaces allow inhabitants to connect with each other and with nature.

Cities with abundant green spaces hold a competitive advantage in a global economy with increasingly mobile corporations and workforces. Both mature and emerging cities can support low-cost and high-return initiatives that promote job growth, reduce the cost of infrastructure maintenance, and attract creative residents as well as national and international visitors.

Two Asian cities convey the increasing role of the urban environment as a key driver of economic growth and the potential costs of failure. Over the past ten years, Hong Kong's air pollution has reached disturbingly high levels, prompting chief executives and other business leaders to warn of the danger of multinational corporations leaving Hong Kong or declining to locate there. In addition to the threat of losing jobs and educated workers, air pollution causes hospital admissions and lost productivity estimated at

HK$21.2 billion per year (Pesek, 2006). In contrast, Seoul's mayor Oh Se-hoon has promoted a range of green city initiatives, from electric buses to 'daylighting' a central river that had been covered by pavement and a highway (Choe, 2010). These actions raise urban real estate values, promote South Korean clean technology companies, increase job growth, and attract people and corporations to reconsider Seoul as an Asian regional business headquarters location.

For generations, affluent city workers lived in leafy suburbs to combine the benefits of urban work opportunities with the pleasure of access to nature. In an era of peak oil and climate change, we are now seeing urban cores attracting highly skilled workers who want to live in close proximity to work, shopping, education, and cultural activities. These highly desirable city residents are no longer satisfied with the old divisions between city life and nature, work and residential zones, commerce and food production, private and shared resources.

Nature is returning to the city, including trees, flowers, wildlife, clean water, and agriculture. Cities are now central to visions of a sustainable post-industrial era that supports population growth and a high quality of life. Instead of choosing one or the other, biodiversity (Braiterman and Takahashi, 2010) and urban forests can thrive with concrete and people. In cities throughout the world, new technology and new visions are creating vital green spaces in the densest cities as we increase our understanding

FIGURE 9.1 ▌ Benefits of City Plants

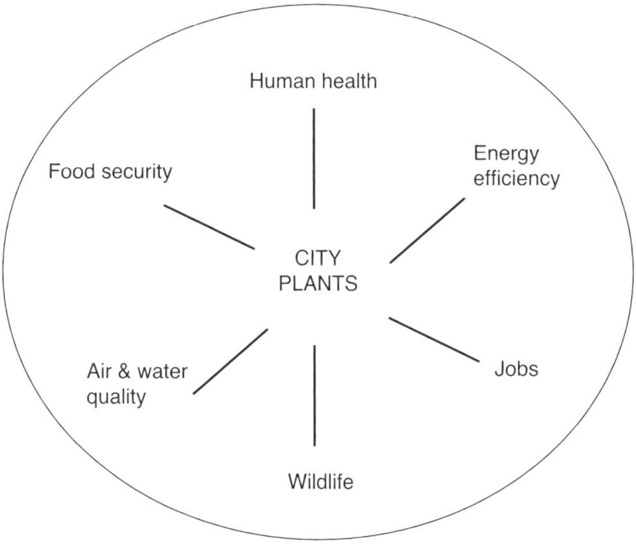

of what is and can be usable urban space. Making our cities more liveable for people and hospitable to nature directly impacts air and water quality, carbon emissions, food security, public health, community bonds, crime reduction, wildlife habitat, energy independence, historical preservation, tourism, and job creation (see Figure 9.1).

This chapter outlines some of the ways that cities, both mature and emerging, can brand themselves with green space by making better use of material and human resources that already exist. These initiatives connect innovative landscaping with transportation, power generation, recreational facilities, and water systems. Reversing industrial age policies, cities are beginning to promote liveable streets and urban food production for energy efficiency, human health, and environmental promotion. Green spaces can be low-cost and high-impact by involving ordinary residents in transforming the daily life of the world's most vital cities (Hestor, 2006).

CONTEXT

Already more than half of the world's population lives in cities and this majority will grow substantially in the next decades. Creating cities that benefit people and the environment involves retrofitting ageing cities in Europe, the Americas, and Japan, and designing new urban models for emerging cities in Africa and Asia. According to the United Nations Population Fund (2007), the urban populations of Asia and Africa will double between 2000 and 2030. Out of a total global population of 5 billion urban dwellers in 2030, 81 per cent will be living in the developing world.

The other context driving sustainable cities is the combination of climate change and peak oil. Twentieth century models of the automobile city continue to be exported to the developing world, yet these resource choices are unsustainable given the unprecedented numbers of new global city residents, the limited quantities of fossil fuel, and a dangerously warming earth. China has already become the world's largest consumer of automobiles, and it is quickly expanding its networks of intra and inter-urban highways. Since Chinese automobile companies are state-owned in part or in whole, local governments have an added incentive to promote residential sprawl and traffic congestion. Privately owned cars still signify modernity for many developing nations, and this pattern of increasing urban spaces that are devoted and dependent on cars repeats itself throughout the developing world. Emerging technology solutions such as electric vehicles respond to the high cost of fossil fuels, yet ultimately do not address systematic energy efficiency or land-use planning.

Dense cities offer the potential for the highest quality of life and low emissions by sharing resources such as transit, recreational and green space. Green corridors and parks can connect urban dwellers with nature and the surrounding region by supporting wildlife including fish and birds. Urban farms – on roofs, empty lots and walls – offer fresh food close to consumers, create community with neighbors and co-workers, and educate children and adults about healthy eating.

Exponentially increasing plant mass on public and privately owned land and buildings will make cities more functional and more enjoyable. There is an unquantifiable pleasure when human activities are integrated with natural cycles. The historically recent dichotomy between urban life and nature has negatively impacted human health and the environment and is not an inevitable result of urbanization (Brown, 2010).

We know much more now than we did before about how to design future cities that are sustainable, enjoyable and healthy. But what about cities that are already built-out? Some might say that crowded cities have no room for nature. Cities like Tokyo grew rapidly in the 20th century, and there remains little conventional open space. Many other cities experienced

FIGURE 9.2 ▌ **A Tokyo river covered by elevated freeway reduces natural environment and land use values**

similar natural and man-made calamities, and developed by prioritizing buildings and roads over planning and open space.

Even these built-out cities can be revitalized by using common urban spaces that have been long ignored: city streets and walls, as well as rivers and waterways that were buried under a web of elevated freeways and hard surfaces (see Figure 9.2). Awareness, experimentation, and imagination are required to identify and transform underutilized urban space. The process of retrofitting mature cities also provides new ideas for the design of new and emerging cities.

THE ROLE OF STREETS

From the world's newest cities to its oldest cities, streets have become a vital indicator of environmental health and urban liveability. Up to 25 per cent of urban space is devoted to pavement, including streets and car parking. Every city has more street space than parks or gardens, and yet until recently this public space was not considered suitable for anything but vehicle traffic.

Streets remain a largely underutilized resource for cities that are already completely built-out. For streets to become truly useful, two shifts must occur: first, a reduction in urban driving and an increase in higher use values for this abundant space, including biking, walking, public transit, gardening, and farming; and second, the creation of new public places where people can encounter each other and nature. To get a sense of the economic cost of car-focused cities, CEOs for Cities (2010) published an analysis of what they call New York's 'green dividend'. New Yorkers save $19 billion per year because of their low rates of private automobiles and high rates of transit, walking and biking. In addition to avoiding 23 million carbon tons of emissions, the money that New Yorkers save on transportation directly increases their purchasing power for other goods and services. Even though New York's housing costs are higher, combining housing and transportation costs produces a lower cost of living for urban versus suburban dwellers.

Green space in relation to paved and built space offers a compelling new way to imagine how future cities will compete. The CEO for Cities report concludes that if New Yorkers drove as much as the average American, the city would require a parking lot the size of Manhattan to store the cars. Given the limited space in any city, a reevaluation of transportation choices and street usage is long overdue.

New York and San Francisco have begun 'pavement to park' programs with new mini-parks replacing automobile traffic, including on Broadway at Times Square. This concept dates back to 1976 when Bogota, Columbia pioneered the 'ciclovía' program where main streets are closed to automobiles every Sunday and holidays. During street closures, a city-wide network of connected open space is devoted to bicyclists, runners, skaters, walkers, yoga practitioners, and other recreation. It is estimated that two million Bogota residents, 30 per cent of the population, use the 120 kilometers of car-free streets (Hernandez, 2008). The cost to create this gigantic network of public space is zero.

FROM ROOF GARDENS TO VERTICAL GARDENS

Many cities have recognized the potential of roof gardens for cleaning the air, lowering summer temperatures, insulating buildings, and even protecting building integrity during earthquakes. New York architect Vanessa Keith (2010) makes a convincing argument that cities have far more surfaces available for greening, farming, and energy creation than is generally acknowledged. Keith's term 'usable surface area' includes not only roofs but also the vertical walls of the built city. Walls remain vastly underused

FIGURE 9.3 | An example of a Tokyo vertical garden, where lack of horizontal space does not prevent a lush garden with individual and social benefits

and unimagined resources. Walls can be planted or used to collect energy from sun, wind, and water. Keith makes an interesting calculation. If a typical six-storey building occupies a footprint of 2,100 square feet, there are 12,000 square feet of vertical surface on free-standing buildings, and 3,600 square feet on in-fill buildings. Considering how unproductive most building walls are, the potential far exceeds existing parks and urban green space. Including roof and walls, buildings provide two to six times the usable surface area of the land on which they rest (Keith, 2010). Figure 9.3 shows an example of a Tokyo vertical garden.

Suginami, one of Tokyo's 23 wards, introduced summer-time 'green curtains' made of climbing vines, plastic planter buckets, and net. Using their eight-storey local government office as a demonstration project, Suginami ward built the world's largest green curtain rising nearly 30 meters tall and running the width of their south-facing office wall. Plants include ornamentals and food-producing vines such as morning glory, cucumber, loofah, and bitter melon. Throughout Tokyo many urban residents now cover their balconies with one- and two-storey green curtains that reduce summer heat and air conditioning costs, clean the air, and offer gardens for even those with no ground soil for planting.

Governments play a critical role in public demonstration of new ideas for urban greenery. By seeing the spectacular ward office, or participating in a municipal workshop, or reading about green curtains in the media, citizens learn how to create vertical urban gardens that require minimal space and produce social benefits such as energy efficiency and air quality improvement.

RECOVERING RIVERS AND URBAN BAYS

Industrial era cities frequently directed sewage and industrial pollution to their bays and rivers. In many cases, city governments buried the very water that gave rise to human settlement and connected the original towns with resources and regional commerce. A variety of techniques are now being used to restore the health of rivers and bays, and to integrate them into the life of the city. Elevated freeways and pavement are being removed from large rivers and small creeks (Kajikawa *et al.*, 2005). Abandoned port areas are being developed into open space amenities. Street landscaping and roof catchment systems are lowering the burdens of water treatment and raising water quality.

Healthy rivers and bays provide habitat for wildlife and recreational areas for city inhabitants and visitors. What was once marginal and polluted land gets greater usage and a higher monetary value as parks replace pavement and people replace vehicles. Restoring rivers connects cities with their regions, and economic growth with history and heritage. Revitalized urban waterways can again provide food for people and wildlife. Rivers play a central role in urban biodiversity, a key indicator for the health of urban environments. In one small section of Tokyo's Kanda River, the Tokyo Metropolitan Government's 2001 survey documented 260 plant species, 42 riverbed species, nine types of fish, 291 types of insects, 30 bird species, two reptile species, and three mammal species (Puntigam *et al.*, 2010).

Seoul in South Korea recreated a central river called the Cheong-gyecheon that had been buried under pavement and freeways. Prompted by earthquake damage to its port-side freeway, San Francisco in the United States opened its bay to the city, creating new parks, office, and cultural spaces. Paris is now considering a bold plan to reconnect the River Seine with the city by replacing a riverside highway with parks and people (Kazis, 2010). Urban planners in Tokyo have proposed restoring its historic rivers and canals for heritage, tourism, recreation, and higher land values (Mishima *et al.*, 2010). New York's Brooklyn Bridge Park is being built in stages and the 85 acre waterfront park will become the most significant new urban park in Brooklyn since Prospect Park was built 135 years ago; it will feature floating pathways, fishing piers, canals, and restored wetlands.

HOW TO MAKE GREEN SPACE A COMPETITIVE URBAN ADVANTAGE

Green spaces connect the growth of cities with the expansion of natural habitat. Even in the densest cities, there is plentiful space to exponentially increase plant life and public spaces. Ideas that were considered impossible, if not inconceivable, just ten years ago are becoming a reality in cities around the world. Branding cities with green space relies upon community support and participation to create vibrant new public places.

Set ambitious goals

With green spaces of all sizes sprouting in world cities, branding a city as green requires bold actions. Local governments will have to approach transit, infrastructure, public health, and life design in new ways that marshal support across city departments and with civil society and community groups. Improved air quality, reduced infrastructure spending, waste reduction and access to green space are all green city goals. Green space metrics include doubling the tree canopy, composting all food waste, planting fruit trees in every neighborhood, removing pavement, and increasing indicator wildlife species. City landmarks draw special attention as representing the city, and there are many opportunities to improve how municipal buildings, schools, streets, and offices use energy and relate to their surroundings and regions.

These green city goals are achievable when matched to local communities and passions. Individuals, nonprofits, and corporations have launched urban farming and gardening projects in cities across the world. Making the goal and the process tangible to residents motivates participation, increases experimentation, and spreads successful ideas.

Take the park outside the gate

Experiencing the benefits of parks should not be restricted to the inside of the park's gate. Open space and access to nature should not be a special destination but a constant experience, part of mobile, work, and home life. By removing pavement, urban soil can be revived with benefits ranging from reducing the stress on ageing water treatment facilities to providing new green spaces in every neighborhood. From anonymous residents to globally acclaimed gardener Patrick Blanc, there are many examples of vertical gardens in city centers. De-paving roads and paths could exponentially increase the potential for trees and plants that offer shade, beauty, clean air, and natural filtration for storm water.

One of the most remarkable visions of a new urban forest comes from Japanese animator Miyazaki Hayao's 1991 book *Totoro no sumu ie* (The place where Totoro lives). The illustrated book is inspired by his movie and the neighborhoods of western Tokyo. Since the anime character Totoro lives in a tree in the Japanese countryside, Miyzaki's urban vision is a complete remaking of the spaces between buildings to create an urban forest that shelters nature, mystery, and magic. Reducing pavement in half allows for the diffusion and growth of trees, bushes, and moss. Miyazaki's new city benefits existing residents and relies on community participation to create a new balance between city and nature.

San Francisco began six-month experiments in 2009 installing 'pavement to park' projects throughout the city. Wasted street spaces are transformed quickly and at low cost into new public plazas and parks. Landscaping, seating, and tables replace streets and create new pedestrian-friendly and inviting places. Built with lightweight materials, these projects are meant as experiments that can be removed or changed later. With public acceptance and participation, successful parklets can be modified and expanded. This model, too, depends on community and business stewards.

San Francisco's local government program is rooted in a community art and planning experience. 'Park(ing) day' started in 2005 as a one day per year event promoted online and on the streets by a collective named

REBAR. The collective and then those who heard about the idea were invited to convert metered parking spaces into mini-parks, allowing for unexpected green spaces throughout the city. Videos and stories quickly spread this idea to global cities and transformed commercial corridors, residential neighborhoods, retail spaces, and offices. Within several years, the idea of reclaiming street space for plants and people became municipal policy promoted and funded by local government.

Build zero waste government buildings and streets

Cities and local government are often their area's single largest property owner and manager. Along with city streets, local government offices and buildings can be sites of environmental innovation and experimentation. City governments can partner with universities, nonprofits, and businesses to host the latest technologies for energy generation. Under-utilized space can become edible school yards, rainwater harvesting locations, bee farms, healing gardens, and habitat for butterflies and birds.

Government buildings, no different than ageing private sector buildings, were not built for maximizing use value and resource conservation. Inviting non-governmental expertise and participation will generate new ideas and the passion to make them a reality. In turn, government facilities serve to educate residents who experience green space projects at city landmarks, neighborhood streets, and government offices. Examples include Chicago City Hall's green roof, Suginami, Tokyo's giant green curtain, and the edible schoolyard movement begun by Berkeley, California's Alice Waters.

Support residents and non-governmental entities

Innovation in urban green space ideas increasingly comes from the private sector and includes people who have not previously been considered stake-holders in urban design, including cooks, farmers, entrepreneurs, corporations and artists. In earlier times, master plans organized the flow and growth of cities. As a way to accomplish more despite budget constraints, local governments are increasingly turning to the private sector and the talents of its residents for material and creative resources. A multitude of approaches and distributed implementation are more likely to create green space solutions that thrive and spread.

City-wide goals need the support of the widest possible base to make ambitious change possible. Neighborhood gardeners, amateur and professional naturalists, and plant entrepreneurs have knowledge and experience with city farming, tree planting and maintenance, and monitoring and promoting city wildlife. Green space interest spans ages and backgrounds, including seniors, school children, birdwatchers, and cooks. Local governments can brand their cities by recognizing and publicizing the diverse city people who are bringing nature back to the city.

In New York City, a community of amateur naturalists track wildlife in Central Park after dark, observing nesting, sleeping, and migrating patterns of hawks, owls, and even coyotes (Winn, 2008). In Tokyo, a construction company is considering the incidence of Japanese pygmy woodpeckers as an indicator of urban health (Kumagai and Yamada, 2008). In San Francisco, a utility company and a university have joined efforts to webcast a falcon nest on top of the utility's downtown office tower. Guerrilla gardeners are planting public and private land that is temporarily available or ignored. In Tokyo's Ginza, an urban farming entrepreneur built a temporary rice field that attracted regular visits from shop clerks, office workers, construction workers, neighbors, and passers-by.

Local government support can include zoning changes, tax incentives, street lab experiments, and public contests to find and spread the best green space ideas. With the rise of new media, there are many new opportunities for people to learn from other communities and for quick adaptations, variations, and disbursement across the world.

SUMMARY

Unique green space relates to local resources and culture. The opportunities for branding cities with green space are growing with peoples' expectations for everyday experiences and quality of life. Reclaiming abandoned and underutilized resources enables the creation of new green spaces that connect people with nature and with each other. Ideas for remaking urban spaces are still emerging and no single model will fit all cities. A rice paddy in London would not have the same meaning as in Tokyo. Environmental challenges are global: from the colony collapse disorder affecting bees worldwide, to peak oil and climate change. Yet the solutions will need to be a mix of globally shared ideas such as city farming, to locally created innovations that respond to specific places, climates, and cultures.

The best solutions take full advantage of local human and material resources. Cities can draw upon their heritage and unique resources to create a new balance between the built environment and nature. Urban planning mistakes of the 20th century can now be viewed in the context of the resiliency of cities and of nature. Despite overwhelming natural disaster and wartime devastation, cities like Tokyo revived with land use patterns that reveal continuity over centuries (Jinnai, 1995). And while we see our concrete, bridges, and skyscrapers as permanent, we have recently learned how quickly nature would reclaim the built environment without our constant efforts to control and tame it (Weisman, 2007).

Increasing plant biomass and building new public spaces will make cities more liveable and attractive for businesses, residents, and visitors. We are entering a new era where urban life is reconnecting with the natural world. With the full participation of civil society, there are limitless opportunities to brand cities with green space. By re-imagining cities as natural habitat, cities can compete in terms of human health, quality of life, job creation, and environmental innovations.

CHAPTER 10

Online City Branding

Magdalena Florek

INTRODUCTION

Much discussion in the branding literature has focused on whether the Web will change the ways in which branding and brand management are conducted (see for example Sterne, 1999; Ind and Riondino, 2001; Lindstrom, 2001; de Chernatony and Christodoulides, 2004). From a marketing perspective, the internet provides companies with new channels for advertising, selling, direct distribution and support channels for customer feedback. Many organizations now recognize the need for integrated marketing communications across offline and online channels in today's digital world.

The development of the internet and its tools has also changed the ways that cities can and should communicate and build their local brands. However, as Rowley (2004: 138) argues, 'online environments are by their nature information-based service environments. Conceptualizations of brand as experience emphasize at the very least that brand is built not by what an organization says, as by what it does, and further, by how the user experiences what it does'. This is a particular challenge for branding places, where physical presence is necessary to experience a place and the place brand promise communicated online can far exceed the reality of the place itself. The challenge is ever greater because the number of internet users and simultaneously potential city audiences is rising dramatically.

Not only has the number of internet users grown, but the time spent online is longer and longer each year (Harrisinteractive.com, 2009). As a result, the internet has made worldwide branding more possible than ever before. Two dominant directions in online branding can be discerned: first, the promotion and communication of brand values, identity and personality; and second, the creation of online communities associated with the brand. Some argue that with the wealth of information on the Web, users will no longer rely on the shorthand of brand. Instead they will gather detailed information on products and services and make their own judgments (Rowley, 2004). Therefore, brand managers have to implement new tools to build and communicate their brands. What is more, they have to follow dynamic changes in the virtual environment of what has become known as Web 2.0, since it is continuously undergoing further revolutions. The term Web 2.0 is commonly associated with applications that facilitate interactive information sharing, interoperability, user-centered design, and collaboration on the World Wide Web. Examples of Web 2.0 include web-based communities, hosted services, web applications, social-networking sites, video-sharing sites, wikis, and blogs. In other words, Web 2.0 provides services that invite users to engage in direct and strong participation.

As a consequence, we are witnessing a new model of communication. Nowadays, in order to say something about themselves, cities do not have to count solely on journalists. Today, everyone has become not only the receiver but also the sender of messages. In addition, the cost of sending messages has dropped to a minimum and the tools to do so are widely available. Consequently, everyone creates a parallel circulation of information. Indicative of this phenomenon is the appearance of 'prosumers' – a segment of users midway between consumers and professionals – as active participants taking up a dialogue with the city, which has changed communication strategies and their associated tools. Prosumers search for more and more information, are present in virtual reality, exchange opinions, files and personal profiles, participate in discussions, and watch and post videos. Gerhardt (2008) has shown that because of their complex lifestyle, which combines a demanding workload and an active family life, prosumers are eager adopters of Web 2.0 products and services who typically embrace Web 2.0 technologies such as social networking (Facebook, MySpace), blogging, video on demand (VoD), podcasting, VoDcasting, virtual realities (Second Life, There.com), mobile communications, and other internet-based technologies and services that allow people to stay connected whenever and wherever they desire.

One of the most important features of Web 2.0 applications is the rich wealth of user- generated content. With the advent of user-generated content, any individual might potentially influence the way that a city is perceived and evaluated. Everyone can easily access and share information regardless of content managed by official city sources. As a result, the opportunities that Web 2.0 offers may become either a source of added value or a source of negative publicity for a city. In light of the trends and influential power of Web 2.0, city managers are forced to take advantage of what it offers. Cities need to be active participants in this environment as well as be aware of the independent and uncontrolled role of such online environments in shaping city perceptions. As Miguéns *et al.* (2008: 2) state, the virtual environment 'can prove highly influential in directing tourists' choices, but can be also of extreme value for the comprehension of preferences, needs and reactions which can (or should) inform many decisions from a management point of view'.

Among the range of existing online tools, the most popular and already used by cities to communicate their brands' characteristics include websites, the blogosphere, social networks, virtual realities and email. These tools and their potential uses in a city branding context are discussed in the following sections.

WEBSITES AS COMMUNICATORS OF CITY BRAND IDENTITY

Websites are the primary, the most popular, and nowadays obligatory tool in branding places. A website helps to increase place awareness, familiarity, and finally to shape its image. The essential role of the website is therefore to communicate the city brand identity through passing on relevant information. This communication might take the form of passive transmission of information, for example, general information, picture gallery, brochures, city council projects and plans, as well as interactive communication such as customized information, consultations, feedback, events calendar, interactive maps, virtual sightseeing, and accommodation booking (Florek *et al.*, 2006). As a relatively passive medium, websites are capable of transmitting an unlimited amount of information to all potential audiences (Sharp, 2001) controlled exclusively by the senders themselves (White and Raman, 1999). On the other hand, owing to technological progress, it is possible to send more and more sophisticated and attractive forms of messages. Consequently, unlike traditional mass media, the website content can be tailored to target different audiences through customizable settings to create a favorable image of the place. What is more, websites enable cities to learn more about their audience by including interactive features on their websites to encourage visitors to enter into a dialogue with the city in the same way that companies enter into a dialogue with their consumers (Hurme, 2001).

Typically, via websites, cities can develop their brands by presenting the system of identification or brand design (logos, slogans, coats of arms, flags, characteristic colors, and so on), the city's offer (packages for target markets, lists of attractions, calendar of events, picture gallery, maps, folders, webcam), behavior (news, projects, plans, policies, reports, bylaws, details of local authorities, sister city relationships), as well as interacting with city target audiences via online forums, feedbacks, newsletters, and comments. All the items should be integrated to achieve a unique picture of the city. The holistic approach, distinctive features and tools must be applied in order to distinguish the website itself and consequently the city that it is portraying. As Palmer (2002) concludes, to have an electronic presence is not adequate in itself; a strategy is necessary to bring that presence close to potential customers.

CITY BRANDING VIA THE BLOGOSPHERE

A blog is a type of website, usually maintained by an individual with regular entries of commentary, descriptions of events, or other material such as graphics or video. Many blogs provide commentary or news on a particular subject, whilst others function as more personal diaries. A typical blog combines text, images, and links to other blogs, web pages, and other media related to its topic. The blogosphere is made up of all blogs and their interconnections. On average the number of blog posts in a 24 hour period is around 900,000, and 77 per cent of active internet users read blogs (Futurebuzz.com, 2009). The rapid growth of the blogosphere has resulted in a perception of blogs as one of the most credible and objective information sources. Consequently, bloggers are becoming the new leaders of opinion with strong influential power. This power may include the ability to shape perceptions of cities.

Blog creators as well as blog readers include city residents, former and potential tourists, students, and investors. In the case of cities, people write and read about tourist attractions, different types of events, the quality of life in the city, social issues, politics, art and culture, studies, sports, and so on. For example BlogTO (http://www.blogto.com/about/) is a website about Toronto written by residents of Toronto – 'a group of obsessed artists, musicians, photographers, politicos, advertising and media types, dancers, tech geeks, food lovers, aspiring film directors, fashionistas and people for the ethical treatment of animals'. It presents the essence of city life and is therefore very useful for city residents as well as tourists. Another interesting example can be found on www.newyorkology.com, where 'hall-of-fame dive bars, Brooklyn pizza tours and double-chocolate pedicures are all part of freelance writer Amy Langfield's blogging beat. Lifestyle categories are broken down into drinks, food, shops, sights and travel' (Forbes.com, 2009). Such information can have enormous reach as everybody in the world who has got an internet connection can read blogs.

Travel blogs are one of the most popular type of blogs. Generally in diary form, a travel blog contains descriptions of the traveler's experiences. For other tourists and visitors, travel blogs are a priceless source of information.

These blogs need to be monitored by city marketing managers, especially those blogs with a strong tourism focus as they may influence city perceptions in terms of the tangible as well as intangible components of the city brand. In addition, these bloggers themselves might become a target group of high significance.

Therefore it is necessary to build relations and to collaborate with bloggers, to encourage important and active opinion leaders to write positively about the city. In other words, to make them city allies. What is more, from blogs, especially those written by city residents, it is possible to derive inspiration for future publicity campaigns. Cities and tourism organizations have gradually begun to notice the growing impact of the blogosphere and have started to organize special conferences and meetings with bloggers. Such meetings are, for example, regularly organized by the Caribbean Tourism Organization. In February 2006, for the first time, the organization invited to New York well-known and recognized bloggers who write about tourism and travelling. The United States is the main target market for the Caribbean tourism industry. The leitmotif of the conference, organized together with the International Association of Online Communicators, was 'What's New and Hot in the Caribbean'. The main purpose of the meeting was to encourage American bloggers to take up the topics related to the promotion of tourism to the Caribbean islands and to establish relationships and cooperation by providing news and information that bloggers could write about. The bloggers were also invited to discuss the future of this sector with representatives of Caribbean tourism institutions.

Similarly, in July 2008, Greater Philadelphian Tourism Marketing Corporation (GPTMC), responsible for the promotion of the city and region of Philadelphia, organized a conference called 'Blog Philadelphia Social Media Unconference' to which hundreds of bloggers from the United States were invited. GPTMC presented how to use Web 2.0 communication tools via special city internet service such as videocasts, podcasts, and articles about the city and region. In addition, the intention of the meeting was to build closer relations with bloggers' society, to encourage them to write and read about Philadelphia as well as to educate them on how to use the available tools of social media.

Together with the development of the blogosphere, journalists' attitudes towards blogs have changed. In the past, journalists considered blogs to be unreliable as a source of information. Recently, however, journalists have been adopting social media tools at a steady rate. The number of journalists reading blogs and RSS feeds increases every year. A survey by Brodeur conducted among a random sample of North American reporters and editors found that blogs are having a significant impact on journalists' story ideas, angles and insights. Over 75 per cent of reporters see blogs as helpful in giving them story ideas; 70 per cent of reporters check a blog list on a regular basis; and 21 per cent of reporters spend over an hour per day reading blogs. Journalists are also increasingly active participants in the blogosphere – 28 per cent of reporters have their own blogs (O'Keefe, 2008).

In addition to monitoring activities by the most influential and opinion-leading bloggers, city managers have to think about creating their own blogs, including blogs of city authorities and leaders. For example, the Miami Mayor's blog (http://mayormannydiaz.blogspot.com/) provides a daily summary of issues that his office is working on. For the internal market, such tools enable the building of relationships with city residents and help to create support amongst the local people for local activities, including brand-related initiatives.

Another phenomenon in the blogosphere is micro-blogging. Micro-blogs are short textual comments usually delivered to a network of associates. Micro-blogging and Twittering (from the application, Twitter, by far the most popular micro-blogging application in this sector) are the act of posting micro-blogs. This is a form that allows users to send brief text updates or micromedia such as photos or audio clips and publish them, either to be viewed by anyone or by a restricted group which can be chosen by the user. The content of a micro-blog differs from a traditional blog in that it is typically smaller in size. Twitter, launched in July 2006, is the most popular of an estimated 100 websites that offer micro-blogging. Twitter forecasts that it will have 350 million users by the end of 2011 (Thetourismcompany.com, 2009). With this profile and the potential of micro-blogging as an online branding tool, it is not surprising that a number of tourism enterprises and destinations are already using micro-blogs and a much larger number are actively considering using them.

Although there has been little research to date into the effectiveness of micro-blogs as a branding tool for destinations, one way to measure their usefulness is to look at how many people choose to follow the micro-blog feeds of destinations. For example, VisitBritain has 5,369 followers; VisitScotland 1,378; and VisitWales 1,402. It is also important to look at the growth rate of followers, the number of interactions with visitors, and the number of clicks-through from posted Tweets to destination web-pages (Thetourismcompany.com, 2009).

SOCIAL NETWORKS AND INTERACTIVE CITY BRAND-BUILDING

Social networks are online communities of people who share common interests and activities. They provide a user with a collection of various interaction possibilities, ranging from simple chat to multiple video conferences, and from the exchange of plain email messages to participation in blogs and discussion groups. Online social networks may also contain categorized relationships (for example, former classmates), means to connect with friends, or recommendation systems for some kind of objects or activities (Miguéns *et al.*, 2008). From a branding perspective, due to interactions between consumers and building a friendly online community, marketers can track consumer perceptions about and feelings toward the brand. As McWilliam (2000: 45) has pointed out, 'In the traditional brand relationship, communication flows between the vendor and the consumer. Brand-based online communities have demonstrated the potential benefits of dialogue flowing between consumers'.

Some of the most widely attended online social networks are systems such as FaceBook, MySpace, Orkut and LinkedIn. The number of social network users has encouraged companies – and more recently cities – to focus on their online presence and to create and design creative, motivating and effective branding campaigns using social media. Place marketers who are aware of the possibilities that such a medium provides, include social network sites such as Facebook in their branding activities. For example, on Michigan's official travel and tourism site (http://www.michigan.org/Default.aspx) one can find links to Facebook. Other important social networks for destinations are TripAdvisor and WAYN. TripAdvisor is a website based on the idea that travelers rely on other travelers' reviews to plan their trips, or at least can be satisfactorily helped in their decisions by them. At the time of writing, TripAdvisor contains ten million travel reviews and opinions written by five million registered members and counts 25 million visitors per month. It was founded in 2000 and currently covers 212,000 hotels, over 30,000 destinations, and 74,000 attractions worldwide. WAYN.com (an acronym for 'Where are you now') is a travel and lifestyle social networking website whose goal is to unite travelers from around the world. WAYN is present in 251 countries and membership has grown from 45,000 users in March 2005 to over 15 million today.

The travel social networks are therefore increasingly a subject of interest in the process of creating city brands. For example, Johannesburg Tourism Company decided in 2008 to partner with WAYN to develop a campaign intended to both change perceptions and to create endorsement for Johannesburg as a major international traveler destination. The strapline was 'Joburg – a world class African city'. By building a profile on WAYN, Johannesburg Tourism Company was able to interact with a worldwide audience of 14 million people across 193 countries in a fun and dynamic way. Key elements included member surveys, a holiday prize competition, newsfeeds about

Miss World, banner ads, a newsletter and internal communications. Pre- and post-survey results showed that over a period of seven weeks a significant change appeared in terms of highly positive perceptions of the city and it became a top destination of choice (Travolution.co.uk, 2009).

With the increasing choice of social networks, city managers have to integrate adequate channels that are appropriate for building city brand image and also analyze their online target markets. City managers must also stay continuously and proactively involved in conversations, posts, chats, and forums. Running a brand community requires offering a sense of involvement and even ownership. Communities require a bottom-up view of brand-building, whereby the customers create the content and are in a sense responsible for the brand (McWilliam, 2000).

PLACE BRANDING IN THREE-DIMENSIONAL VIRTUAL ENVIRONMENTS

Second Life, established in 2003, is the most famous and widely used three-dimensional virtual environment. Second Life is free, allowing anyone with internet access easy access to the Second Life environment. It has its own internal market with the Linden dollar as the currency. Second Life has over 20 million unique avatars and over 40,000 people online at any one time. There are many communities in Second Life, which allow people to interact and communicate with others of similar interests, persuasions and nationalities.

Already many places have located themselves in the virtual reality of Second Life in order to influence the way their destinations are perceived. One of the first ever marketing campaigns launched by a destination or tourist board in a virtual world was conducted in October 2007 by Tourism Ireland in Second Life. According to Tourism Ireland (Tourismireland.com 2007), in 2007 60 per cent of Second Life's users came from Ireland's four biggest tourist markets: Great Britain, United States, Germany, and France. Half of them were aged over 30 which was a key demographic for the island's tourism. As part of the marketing campaign, Tourism Ireland sponsored a range of events and activities including St Patrick's Day 2008 in Second Life's replica city of Dublin. According to a statement by Tourism Ireland's Director of Central Marketing from the year 2007, 'the organisation has already doubled its digital marketing spend over the past three years, to 14 per cent of all marketing activity – an investment of €6.5 million last year. Tourism Ireland plans to spend close to a quarter of its entire marketing budget online in 2008' (Tourismireland.com 2007). Cities, as well as countries, are expected to make increasing use of the brand-building potential of three-dimensional virtual environments such as Second Life and others.

EMAIL AS A COMPONENT OF CITY BRAND STRATEGY

Along the spectrum of Web 2.0 possibilities, one should not neglect the most popular and direct form of online communication – email. Aimed directly at the target market, email is still a valuable form of contact and tool for city branding. The Monaco Convention Bureau, for example, implemented an email marketing strategy in late 2007. The main objective of The Monaco Convention Bureau is to offer advice regarding technical and economic amenities to organizers of congresses, seminars, exhibitions and trade shows. Within one month, the Monaco Convention Bureau had designed and sent the first email to over 6,000 recipients, including meeting and incentive agencies and corporations. Subject areas change from month to month and include venue of the month, event of the month, forthcoming events, latest news, a 'Did you know?' section, and testimonials. The monthly email represents the development of a trusted and regular communication channel with key decision makers (dottourism.com, 2010).

SUMMARY

The Web 2.0 environment is predicted to continue to grow. As a consequence, it has to be monitored by city managers and included in the city branding tool kit. In particular, online communities have proved to have a strong influence on consumer behavior and decisions, and on the way that cities are perceived. City managers need therefore to acknowledge the role of online interactive technologies and embrace these as an integral component of their city branding strategies. Given the diversity of Web 2.0 platforms, the simplicity of creating new blogs and the quick adoption of technology by its users, it is a considerable challenge for city managers to choose the most viable online media to communicate the city brand image. But city managers need to take on that challenge in order to derive the benefits that can flow from a synergistic approach to city brand-building, in which city officials and members of the public collaborate in the process of city image formation. At the same time, cities need to be ready for the next online wave – Web 3.0 – and its implications for city branding.

PART II

Cases

CHAPTER 11

Introduction to the Practice of City Branding

Keith Dinnie

INTRODUCTION

The chapters in Part II describe, analyze and critique the city branding practices of 18 cities across the world. These cities have been selected as cases because of their geographic, economic and cultural heterogeneity. A holistic understanding of city branding requires such an examination of diversity rather than a limited focus on any one particular country or continent. The cases in Part II feature cities that range in size from Wollongong with its population of 200,000 to the immense megalopolises of Seoul, Chongqing and Tokyo. The case cities are spread throughout Europe, Asia, Africa, Australasia, and North and South America. Despite their differences, a number of common issues can be detected in the city branding activities conducted by these cities, as follows: addressing the challenges that city brands face; clarifying identity and image; the importance of tangible evidence; hosting events; partnership working; creativity, innovation and boldness; and repositioning the city brand. These issues are discussed in the sections below.

ADDRESSING THE CHALLENGES THAT CITY BRANDS FACE

City brands face numerous challenges. As Anthony Ebow Spio describes in the case on Accra (Chapter 12), two of the key hurdles that may need to be overcome are over-stretched and inadequate facilities, as well as limited financial resources. The rapid population growth being experienced by Accra and by other cities around the world puts huge pressures on road networks, electricity and water supplies, and housing supply. These fundamental issues need to be resolved if a city brand is to make credible claims in terms of promoting itself as an attractive place to live in, visit or invest in. The challenge of limited financial resources also restricts efforts to develop a strong city brand. In many cities, the municipal coffers are bare and the need to brand the city is given low, if any, priority. However, some cities have allocated significant budgets to their city branding strategy and have obtained demonstrable benefits from doing so. In their case on Seoul (Chapter 26), You Kyung Kim and Peter Eung-Pyo Kim highlight the historic increase in Seoul's marketing budget that occurred in 2008 and the focus that was placed by Seoul Metropolitan Government on boosting tourism to the city as a means of economic revitalization.

A different kind of challenge faced by city brands relates to the skepticism towards brands and branding that is harbored by many policy makers. Gyorgy Szondi describes how the branding of Budapest has evolved in the face of considerable resistance to the very concept of branding (Chapter 16). Szondi suggests that in order to counter this type of brand skepticism, it is necessary to emphasize that the branding concept is an intellectual and interdisciplinary process rather than a simple promotional or marketing campaign.

CLARIFYING IDENTITY AND IMAGE

A further issue that is discussed in the case of Accra also features prominently in the cases on Lisbon (Chapter 22), Montevideo (Chapter 23) and Paris (Chapter 25), namely the need for city brands to clarify their identity and image. What is the essence of the city and how does it wish to be perceived? Without a reasonable degree of clarity at this initial stage of brand development, the likelihood is that there will be no clear city brand but rather an incoherent set of fragmented sub-brands each delivering its own messaging, or worse still, no conscious branding at all, in which case the city's reputation is completely at the mercy of a hostile or indifferent world. João Ricardo Freire examines the identity-image question in the context of Lisbon, showing that it is crucial for policy makers to define the scope of the entity which they intend to brand. If the brand is limited to the city itself, then that will influence strategic branding decisions differently than would be the case if the city-region (a broader entity with more stakeholders and a wider range of attributes) is to be the subject of the brand development.

In the case on Montevideo, Pablo Hartmann describes how local and national policy makers have attempted to close the gap between the city's identity and its image. An analysis of Montevideo's strengths reveals many positive points such as its good quality cultural, leisure and recreation options; its status as a capital city; and its high level of safety. However, these strengths are not widely perceived and the city is committed to a plan of action to counter its weak image, particularly in terms of tourism. Another perspective on the identity-image issue is provided by Jean-Noël Kapferer's discussion of the relationship between country image and city image, specifically in the case of Paris. Kapferer notes that regardless of the country brand's image and performance, the city brand has its own momentum. This raises interesting questions related to brand architecture. Should a city brand itself as a standalone brand, with no reference to its country brand, or should the country brand act as an overarching umbrella brand under which the city brand is positioned? Some cities position themselves as standalone brands, with no explicit reference to their country in their brand tagline, for example, 'The Hague, International City of Peace and Justice'. Other cities make a different strategic choice and consciously draw upon the country brand equity of their nation by including both the country name and the city name in their tagline, for example, 'Edinburgh: Scotland's Inspiring Capital' or 'Glasgow: Scotland with Style'.

THE IMPORTANCE OF TANGIBLE EVIDENCE

A city brand needs to be rooted in reality, rather than a delusion peddled by mendacious marketers. Making exaggerated claims for a city will backfire as soon as target audiences realize that they have been misled. Therefore cities need to ensure that they have got the tangible evidence to back up their proclaimed strengths. In his case on the Indian city of Ahmedabad (Chapter 13), Satish K. Nair usefully demonstrates this point by detailing the specific developments that the city has recently undertaken. These significant developments include the launch of the city's Bus Rapid Transit System (BRTS) and the Sabarmati Riverfront Project. Both projects not only enhance the quality of life of Ahmedabad's citizens, they also promote an evidence-based image of the city as environmentally responsible and committed to real improvements to the city's infrastructure.

The importance of tangible evidence is also stressed by Juan Carlos Belloso in his examination of Barcelona's city branding (Chapter 15). Belloso shows how the branding of Barcelona is to a large extent grounded in a profound transformation of the city and notes that a city brand is not built in the short term but rather it requires many years of sustained initiatives and commitment. The creation of new transport infrastructure, the establishment of more universities and the modernization of the public health and education systems are among the important initiatives undertaken by Barcelona's city authorities over recent years. In their analysis of Kuala Lumpur's city branding (Chapter 21), Ghazali Musa and T. C. Melewar also highlight the need for that city's brand to be built upon a solid platform of sustained improvement of infrastructure and services.

HOSTING EVENTS

The hosting of events is seen by many cities as an important element of the city brand-building process. In his case on Sydney's city branding (Chapter 27), Geoff Parmenter describes how the city has developed its own innovative program of Sydney-specific annual events and festivals in addition to bidding to host the FIFA World Cup in 2018 or 2022. The hosting of such events is strategically embedded in the city's brand strategy. The hosting of a mega event such as the Olympic Games is much sought after by cities that compete aggressively for the right to host them. Maria Fola discusses the city branding of Athens (Chapter 14) related to that city's hosting of the 2004 Olympic Games. However, Fola expresses reservations about the durability of any benefits that flow from hosting a mega event on the scale of the Olympic Games and suggests that policy makers need to ensure that branding efforts continue well after the event in order to sustain the post-event impact of the city brand strategy.

The significant role of an events-centered approach to city branding is echoed by Gyorgy Szondi in his discussion of the branding of Budapest (Chapter 16). Szondi notes that hosting mega events can act as a starting point for city branding campaigns and that whilst the hosting of some events will appeal only to a limited audience, other events can help unite a whole city. The Spring and Autumn Festivals, the Budapest Fair and the Sziget Festival in August are some of the events that constitute an important element of Budapest's city branding strategy.

PARTNERSHIP WORKING

Although a clumsy phrase, 'partnership working' is a concept that has become well established in the context of urban development. Almost all of the cases in Part II display elements of partnership working in the form of collaborative undertakings between a range of public and private sector organizations united in their desire to establish a powerful city brand. A particularly detailed account of this collaborative approach to city branding is given by Kenneth Wardrop in his case on Edinburgh (Chapter 18). Wardrop explains the evolution of the Destination Edinburgh Marketing Alliance (DEMA) and shows how it is based on the principle of constant ongoing collaboration with key stakeholders. The composition of DEMA's Board of Directors reflects this stakeholder approach. The initial ten Board members are drawn from the following wide range of organizations: the City of Edinburgh Council; Edinburgh Business Assembly; Edinburgh Chamber of Commerce; Edinburgh Convention Bureau Limited; Edinburgh, Lothian and Scottish Borders Screen Industries Office Limited; Edinburgh Tourism Action Group; Essential Edinburgh; Festivals Edinburgh Limited; Edinburgh Science Triangle; and the University of Edinburgh.

A similar partnership, collaborative approach is examined by Hulleman and Govers in their case on The Hague (Chapter 19), a city which they view as a relational network brand. The authors illustrate the interplay that occurs between the Dutch Ministry of Foreign Affairs and the city of The Hague policy makers. The relationship between the Ministry of Foreign Affairs and the city authorities is unusually close in the case of The Hague due to the city's explicit positioning as 'International City of Peace and Justice' and the large number of international organizations hosted by the city.

CREATIVITY, INNOVATION AND BOLDNESS

In his chapter on Barcelona, Belloso identifies creativity, innovation and boldness as a common denominator for the city's branding. Other cities also acknowledge and embrace the potential of creativity, innovation and boldness to contribute to the development of a strong city brand. For example, the role of graphic design in city branding is highlighted by Freeman Lau and Angelica Leung in their case on the Chinese city of Chongqing (Chapter 17). Lau and Leung consider the importance of researching what emblems and motifs are instantly recognizable, as well as the need to become familiar with the city's history and culture so that the eventual visual identity system is grounded in the city's culture, which in Chongqing's case can be traced back at least 3,000 years.

The encouragement of creativity by city policy makers is also touched upon in the case on Hong Kong (Chapter 20) by Grace Loo, Saumya Sindhwani, Cai Jing and Theresa Loo. The authors report how the Hong Kong government began in the early 2000s to champion the development of creative industries such as design, advertising, music, film, digital entertainment, performing arts, broadcasting, antiques and art dealing. In his case on Tokyo's city brand (Chapter 28), Roland Kelts reflects on another manifestation of creativity in the context of city branding, focusing on Tokyo artist Takashi Murakami whose unique combination of artistic skill and business acumen has played a major role in establishing Tokyo's position on the global art scene.

REPOSITIONING THE CITY BRAND

The motivation for cities to engage in city branding frequently stems from a feeling that existing perceptions of the city have become outdated and need to be updated to reflect the contemporary reality of the city. Repositioning the city brand is often seen as necessary and urgent. Perhaps the highest profile example of a city setting out with a clear aim to change negative perceptions can be seen in the case of New York, which is described by Peggy R. Bendel (Chapter 24). Bendel describes how various stakeholders in New York City realized during the early to mid-1970s that something had to be done to remedy the city's decline and how this gave birth to the now legendary 'I Love New York' branding.

Another city whose branding strategy has been driven largely by a desire to reposition the city brand is Wollongong in Australia. In their case on Wollongong (Chapter 29), Greg Kerr, Gary Noble and John Glynn note that during the 1990s Wollongong was often the subject of negative media stories related to serious crime, heavy industry, pollution and floods. The city's image was being further tarnished by famous comedians who routinely ridiculed Wollongong in their nationally televised performances. Kerr, Noble and Glynn present a series of verbatim comments from a range of stakeholders involved in Wollongong's city brand in order to provide a vivid picture of the situation that the city found itself in during the 1990s and the steps that it has subsequently taken to reposition its city brand.

SUMMARY

The 18 cases in Part II demonstrate the range of approaches that cities around the world have adopted in their city branding strategies. For some cities, the key challenge is to reposition the city brand and overcome negative perceptions that may be lingering from a period of the city's past which is different from the city's present reality; the need in such cases is to close what could be a potentially damaging identity-image gap. For other cities, the focus of their city branding may be on other objectives, for example, how to ensure that the benefits of hosting mega events are fully realized. Regardless of the specific objectives that are set, successful city branding strategies appear to be characterized by a collaborative partnership approach involving multiple stakeholders who are united around the need to project a clearly identified and mutually agreed upon city brand positioning. Ranging from Accra to Ahmedabad, from Kuala Lumpur to Wollongong, from Paris to Tokyo, the cases in Part II provide numerous insights into the reality of contemporary city branding practice.

CHAPTER 12

The City Branding of Accra

Anthony Ebow Spio

INTRODUCTION

Accra became the administrative capital of Ghana in 1877 when the British colonial authority transferred the seat of government from Cape Coast. Accra was declared a city on 29 June 1961 by Ghana's first President Dr Kwame Nkrumah. Accra has been one of the fastest growing cities in Africa since the pre-colonial era. Central to the development of Accra was the building of three European forts as trading posts in the 17th century. The first of these was Fort Crevecouer, built by the Dutch in 1650, which was later renamed Fort Ussher. In 1661, the Danes built the second, Christianbourg Castle. The British then followed in 1673 with Fort James. The choice of Accra as a location for castles was attributed to the presence of a rocky shoreline and natural harbor. By the 1850s, the British had taken over the interests of other European nations in Accra and defined the Gold Coast (now Ghana) as a geographical entity. In 1877 the British colonial administration was moved to Christianbourg Castle.

THE GROWING ROLE OF ACCRA AND MODERNIZATION EFFORTS

Accra became a very vibrant city bustling with trading and political liberation struggles in the late 1800s and early 1900s. It became a melting pot of Ghanaian culture and a cradle of the independence struggle in Africa. People from other parts of Ghana and abroad settled and traded with the Europeans while agitating for independence.

The population of Accra has grown exponentially since Ghana's independence in 1957. The population grew from 338,396 in 1960 to 1,658,937 in 2000 and is estimated to reach 4,158,728 in 2009. As the administrative capital of Ghana, Accra is the most endowed city in the country with the most factories, the best hospitals, banks and universities. Consequently, Accra attracts people from all over Ghana. Migration contributes over 35 per cent of the population growth of the city (Accra Metropolitan Assembly, 2007). The rapid growth of Accra's population over the years has led to increasing demands on its infrastructure and services such as health care, quality education, potable drinking water and decent housing.

The government of Ghana has taken initiatives in recent years to modernize Accra and use it as a catalyst for development and the promotion of tourism. For instance, in 2004 the government renamed the Ministry of Tourism and gave it the new name 'Ministry of Tourism and Modernization of the Capital City' (the name has now, however, reverted to its original 'Ministry of Tourism'). The aim of the Ministry of Tourism and Modernization of the Capital City was to derive optimum socioeconomic growth and positive environmental impact for the benefit of deprived communities in particular. The Ministry was tasked to promote Ghana as a competitive and quality destination, and support the West African subregional effort to increase tourist arrivals and revenues. Consequently, the government has intensified its investment in infrastructure in the city and commenced a project to rehabilitate tourist attractions such as the colonial castles, namely Fort Ussher, Fort James and other structures in Old Accra. Improvements in the road network, the rehabilitation of historical sites, the euphoria preceding the Golden Jubilee celebration of Ghana's independence, the growing image of Ghana as a beacon of democracy and good governance in Africa, and the macroeconomic stability of the economy have brought numerous benefits. Accra has since become an attractive destination in the West African subregion for business and conferences as well as an attractive location for the affluent to own property.

Major banks in Nigeria such as UBA, Zenith, Guaranteed Trust and Intercontinental have established subsidiaries in Accra. Barclays Bank also set up an offshore bank to provide a safe haven for investors. Foreign direct investment to Ghana grew as a result from $140 million in 2003 to $160 million in 2007. The net industry earnings of banks in Ghana also grew from $214 million in 2003 to $523 million in 2005. The banking sector has become a key provider of jobs for young professionals, particularly in Accra. Real estate developers have taken advantage of the growing attractiveness of Accra to construct and market luxury homes in well planned suburbs of the city. These properties are targeted at and owned by affluent Ghanaians and foreigners who want great comfort, luxury and first class amenities in a relatively safe environment. The houses, infrastructure and amenities in communities such as Trasaco Valley and Villagio Courts, located in prestigious areas of Accra, are comparable to properties in cities such as New York, Los Angeles and London.

The growing importance of Accra as well as the business prospects emanating from the discovery of oil in Ghana attracted investors to open the first Western style shopping mall in Accra in 2007. The Accra Mall houses renowned South African retailers such as Game and Shoprite as well as franchised shops for famous brands such as Nike, Levi's, Apple and Swatch. The Mall also has state-of-the-art cinemas which show Hollywood films in addition to locally made productions. The mall is targeted largely at the expatriate community, tourists and the growing middle class and affluent Ghanaians.

Another achievement by Accra is the rehabilitation and conversion of certain historic structures such as the colonial forts into museums and tourist sites. The rehabilitated structures and communities of the Old Accra have already started attracting tourists, especially from the Americas, with President Lula of Brazil being the most prominent visitor yet.

A DESTINATION FOR INTERNATIONAL CONFERENCES

Accra's location also makes it a very convenient meeting destination. It is only six hours by air from key cities such as London, Paris, Johannesburg and Cairo and there are direct flights to New York and Washington, which take about 10–11 hours. The city of Accra is increasingly becoming a preferred location for international conferences and events. High profile international conferences and events such as the United Nations Conference on Trade and Development (UNCTAD) XII, the 3rd High Level Forum on Aid Effectiveness, and the 2008 African Cup of Nations were held in Accra in 2008 alone. The city has also hosted august personalities and world leaders such as Presidents George W. Bush and Barack Obama of the United States, United Nations Secretary General Ban Ki-Moon, FIFA President Sepp Blatter, and President of the World Bank Robert Zoellick. Much as the Ghana government's diplomatic efforts may be accountable for bringing these conferences and people to Accra, the democratic credentials of Ghana, the location of the city and its improved infrastructure are also major contributors. The reason for President Obama's visit to Accra in July 2009, for example, can be summed up in the words of his speech delivered to the Ghanaian Parliament: 'And I have come here, to Ghana, for a simple reason: the 21st century will be shaped by what happens not just in Rome or Moscow or Washington, but by what happens in Accra as well. ... And the strength of your democracy can help advance human rights for people everywhere' (Obama, 2009).

CHALLENGES TO ACCRA'S CITY BRANDING

Clearly, the Ghanaian government and Accra Metropolitan Assembly's efforts at modernizing the city over the years have brought some rewards. The successes notwithstanding, there are some factors which are militating against Accra attaining the brand status of cities such as New York, London and Sydney. These factors include the lack of a clear brand identity for Accra, over-stretched and inadequate facilities, limited financial resources, and interference from the central government.

Lack of clear identity and image

Identity is the core concept of a product or even a place which is distinctively expressed. For commercial products and services, identity is expressed through logos, slogans, packaging and product design. For cities it is expressed through infrastructure, architecture, and facilities of the city as well as emotional associations such as the arts, people, politics and goods of the place. The identity is a means by which the brand seeks to build a reputation or create an image in the mind of consumers. Anholt (2007) observed that image includes a range of associations, memories, expectations and other feelings that are bound with the product, service or the company. The image of a place is critical to the way citizens, businesses and indeed tourists respond to the place (Kotler *et al.*, 1993; Kavaratzis, 2004). For instance, the recent massive investment in infrastructure such as shopping malls, hotels and establishment of financial services centers coupled with the hosting of prestigious sporting events seek to promote Dubai as a modern city. The opening of the tallest building in the world with environmentally friendly features in Dubai in December 2009 helps to reinforce its image as a modern and innovative city for business and leisure.

In contrast, Accra does not seem to have a clear identity, although it is home to historic landmarks and the city has seen significant structural development and modernization in recent years. The managers of the city have not sought to define the identity of the city, let alone articulate it to the people who matter. In other words, the work in Accra can be characterized as modernization without branding.

Limited financial resources

There has been some progress made in improving the infrastructure in Accra. However, corresponding rapid growth in population means infrastructural development has not kept pace with population growth. The road network in most parts of the city is still poor and inadequate. There is huge pressure on electricity and water services. There is still a housing deficit as well as waste management challenges in the city. Although city administrators have developed a comprehensive plan to address these challenges, they do not have adequate financial resources. The metropolitan authority relies on the central government to fund most of its projects, because its internally generated income is rather inadequate.

Government interference

The dependence of Accra Metropolitan Assembly on the central government to fund its development projects makes it vulnerable to interference from the government. There have also been instances where the central government has subtly interfered with the city Mayor's efforts at decongesting some parts of the city. The government perceives acts such as relocating squatters and removing hawkers from the streets in the principal trading locations as politically unwise. Consequently, such initiatives are either frowned upon by politicians or at worst the Mayor is asked to stop completely, especially during elections.

'A NEW ACCRA FOR A BETTER GHANA'

After winning a keenly contested election, the National Democratic Congress party was inaugurated in government on 7 January 2009 with a mandate to pursue its promise to Ghanaians, dubbed 'Better Ghana'. A new Mayor was appointed and together with his team has created a development plan covering the period 2010–2013, titled 'A New Accra for a Better Ghana' (Accra Metropolitan Assembly, 2009). The vision of this new plan is to develop Accra into a clean, safe and beautiful city where people and businesses will thrive in a sustainable environment. This vision was translated into seven goals as follows:

- decongest Accra

- sanitation and waste management

- improve the drainage system of Accra

- modernization of the educational and health service delivery system

- enhance and mobilize revenue

- improve roads and transportation

- provide other social facilities such as electricity, water, security, and so on

Accra was declared a Millennium City on 15 January 2010 by the Earth Institute of Columbia University of New York in the presence of Dr Jeffrey Sachs, Director of the Earth Institute and the architect of the United Nations Millennium Development Goals (MDGs). The city signed a memorandum of understanding with the Earth Institute, which will enable Accra to tap into the vast expertise of the institute (Bentil, 2010). The overriding aim of the MDGs is to promote and accelerate the well being of people in developing countries. The new development plan for Accra aligns very well with the MDGs both in terms of overall objectives and also specifics. Accra's association with the Earth Institute will give the city access to development experts and enable it to attract both private and donor funds to transform the city. This will serve as a good foundation for embarking on a credible city branding initiative.

Being declared a Millennium City and aligning itself with the Earth Institute, Accra has publicly declared its preparedness to achieve the MDGs. This could create a unique identity for Accra as the city makes progress in improving its infrastructure and realizing the MDGs. This newly found identity, coupled with Ghana's reputation for good governance and democracy, could lead to a favorable and unique image for Accra.

Grabow (1998) has observed that the communicative competence of a city is a vital requirement for all phases of successful urban marketing. The city of Accra, as well as the wider nation of Ghana, are well aware of this need for communicative competency. The President of the Republic of Ghana has established the Brand Ghana office and appointed a brand and marketing expert in September 2009 to coordinate the development of a compelling national image for Ghana. Two key elements of the Brand Ghana office mandate include ensuring that harmonized Brand Ghana office internal initiatives are integrated with other sub-brands, and developing constructive relationships and networks with partner institutions, external organizations and personalities who directly or indirectly affect Brand Ghana's success. The managers of the city of Accra need to liaise with and tap into the expertise of the Brand Ghana office to ensure that the city's modernization initiative is harnessed into an attractive city brand which also aligns with the national level objectives of Brand Ghana.

SUMMARY

Accra's efforts over the years can be described as modernization without branding. Nevertheless, historical associations with the city such as slave castles and the fight for African liberation from colonial rule, Ghana's growing image as a symbol of good governance and democracy, and improvements in infrastructure serve as a foundation for building a unique city brand image for Accra. As Accra pursues its new vision and MDGs, the city should consider embarking on a formal branding exercise.

Accra and its people stand to derive the following benefits from a city branding initiative: more effective bidding for international events, better investment and tourism promotions, and the transformation of a bad reputation associated with African cities to a much better image and greater profile in the international media. Critical to Accra's branding initiative will be substantial investment in infrastructure, development of a clear identity and image, pursuit of its development goals, accessing of marketing expertise, and obtaining government support. Once these are done, Accra's immense potential for creating 'A New Accra for a Better Ghana' shall be realized.

CHAPTER 13

The City Branding of Ahmedabad

Satish K. Nair

INTRODUCTION

Ahmedabad is the most prominent city of the state of Gujarat, in western India. Gujarat has since time immemorial been renowned for its entrepreneurial spirit. It has made significant contributions to the Indian economy. Gujarat has spearheaded India's march to global superpower status, prompting the state to label itself the 'Growth Engine of India' (Shah and Shukla, 2009). Ahmedabad was the state capital of Gujarat until 1970. Not only is it a bustling industrial and commercial center, it also has a fascinating old quarter of high historical and cultural interest. Mehta and Jamindar (1988) trace the history of Ahmedabad from prehistoric times, with its stature of a capital city nearly uninterrupted from the 15th century to almost the present day. The Vastu-Shilpa Foundation (2002) has chronicled the city's growth over the centuries. Called by various names over the millennia including Ashapalli, Ashaval, Karnavati, Rajnagar, Ahmedabad/Ahmadabad and Amdavad, the city's unique essence resides in its self-reliance and commercial flair.

Mahatma Gandhi chose Ahmedabad to establish his Sabarmati Ashram and spearhead the non-violent 'Satyagraha' movement for the independence of India from the British Raj. The resulting political importance of Ahmedabad, juxtaposed with the pre-British Raj era that has seen the meshing of cultures in the arts, craft, architecture and commerce of the city, has given it a distinct flavor where modernity and heritage go hand in hand (*Ahmedabad Mirror*, 2010). The plethora of textile mills that dotted Ahmedabad's landscape in the latter half of the 19th and early 20th centuries earned it the sobriquet 'Manchester of the East'. Generations of industrialists have patronized institutions – scientific, educational and cultural. Educational, scientific and cultural institutions of international and national stature have been set up in Ahmedabad over the last century through the munificence of its leading business families.

AHMEDABAD'S GROWTH

From a small habitation in prehistoric times, to a small fortress of an invading Muslim Sultan in the 15th century on the banks of the River Sabarmati, the city grew in size steadily between the 17th to early 20th centuries. Post-independence from British rule in 1947, and especially after the formation of Gujarat as a separate state in 1960, Ahmedabad grew in stature owing to its political and commercial significance. The city was governed by the Ahmedabad Municipal Corporation (AMC), with the adjoining areas brought under the control of Ahmedabad Urban Development Authority (AUDA) and certain other areas adjoining the city under the governance of 'Village' Panchayats (local governance bodies).

This arrangement lasted for quite a few decades after independence. However, in recent times, the city limits have expanded, with more and more areas under the AUDA and Village Panchayat controls being brought under AMC limits.

GUJARAT'S MAJOR BRANDING EXERCISE

Vibrant Gujarat: Global Investors' Summit

The Gujarat Government has instituted a branding exercise primarily consisting of an event, the Vibrant Gujarat Summit, aimed at positioning Gujarat as a preferred industrial destination. Targeting foreign direct investment, Indian companies on the throes of rapid growth, and non-resident Indians with business interests in the United States, United Kingdom and other parts of the world, the summit has been an immensely successful initiative for Gujarat and by implication also for its leading city, Ahmedabad.

Instituted in 2003 as a biennial event, the Vibrant Gujarat: Global Investors' Summit has seen phenomenal growth in participation in the four summits that have taken place thus far. A website (www.vibrantgujarat.com) has been developed by the Government of Gujarat specifically for the purpose of promoting the event. The significance of the Vibrant Gujarat Summits has to be noted in the context of the mammoth task of building investor and other stakeholders' confidence in the state. The first summit was envisaged in the wake of two consecutive years of disasters – the massive earthquake that shook many parts of Gujarat in 2001 causing widespread destruction to life and property, and the communal riots in the state in 2002, with its political ramifications in the multi-party democracy that is India.

Over the four summits that have taken place between 2003 and 2009, this biennial event has grown in stature and also in the size of investments that it has drawn to the state. One interesting facet of the Vibrant Gujarat Summit 2009 was the active participation of the city's locals who volunteered to host the non-resident Gujarati summit participants.

Vibrant Gujarat 2011: An exercise in rebranding and repositioning the state

The fifth biennial global investors' summit of January 2011 focused more on branding the state as a business hub where deals are done, rather than just as an investment destination. In a gradual deviation from previous events, the 2011 summit was rebranded as 'Vibrant Gujarat 2011: The Global Business Hub' instead of the tagline 'Global Investors' Summit'. The Chief Minister's Office (CMO) identified the 2011 summit as a opportune time to take the event to the next level, with the main objective not limited to the signing of Memorandums of Understanding (MoUs). During the January 2009 event, nearly 7000 MoUs worth $240 billion were signed, with participation from nearly 45 countries. The 2011 summit sought to leverage on this international participation and was positioned as a networking event along the lines of the World Economic Forum (WEF) in Davos or Global Entrepolis @ Singapore. With MoUs scheduled to become a small part of the event, the focus was on top chief executive officers discussing global issues and an ambitious target of forging at least 100 tie-ups with leading institutions from across the globe for exchange of knowledge (Mehta, 2010).

Marketing Vibrant Gujarat to the world

The seriousness of the Gujarat Government with regard to marketing the state and building the brand 'Vibrant Gujarat' can be gauged from a recent development. The Washington-based global lobbying firm Apco Worldwide has been contracted to market Gujarat across the world as an ideal investment destination (*The Times of India*, 2009). The brief for Apco Worldwide includes strategizing to develop Vibrant Gujarat into a 'super brand' over the next two years, by positioning Gujarat to opinion makers and international thought leaders. The lobbying firm has been tasked with strengthening Brand Gujarat and creating a platform for investors and opinion makers to forge partnerships in emerging sectors and emerging geographies.

The repositioning exercise for Vibrant Gujarat 2011 envisages intangible gains in the long term. The significance of such a move as envisaged along the lines of the World Economic Forum event in Davos is not lost on Ahmedabad, which is on its way to becoming Gujarat's only megapolis by the year 2020. The city of Ahmedabad and the state of Gujarat both stand to gain from the place branding initiatives that have been put in place over the past few years.

RECENT DEVELOPMENTS OF SIGNIFICANCE IN AHMEDABAD

A much-publicized event that has contributed quite significantly to the positive image of the state in general, and the city specifically, is the decision of India's leading business conglomerate, the Tata Group, to relocate its proposed small-car plant from West Bengal in the eastern part of the country to Gujarat. Tata's much awaited Nano (the brand name given to its sub-INR 100,000 car) was to have its plant in Singur in West Bengal. However, a hostile political environment and violent protests against land acquisition for its plant and the ancillary units that were to be developed in the vicinity led to Tata abandoning the project there and looking for more amenable locations. Gujarat won in the face of stiff competition from a few other such industrially advanced states in India (Shah, 2008). The significance of the approach of locals in the two states (West Bengal and Gujarat) was striking in its contrast. Locals on the outskirts of Ahmedabad came out in open support of the Gujarat Government's decision to assist in Tata's small-car project (Parmar, 2008).

Further initiatives that will greatly contribute to Ahmedabad's urban development include the successful launch of its Bus Rapid Transit System (BRTS), the Sabarmati Riverfront Project and the ambitious Gujarat International Finance Tec-City (GIFT). The state government has developed dedicated websites to showcase the three projects: www.ahmedabadbrts. com, www.giftgujarat.in and www.sabarmatiriverfront.com. Within a few months of its launch, the BRTS had already won many international accolades (*The Times of India*, 2010a). Already the denim capital of the country, the GIFT and other projects are set to give Ahmedabad a winning chance over Mumbai, which is currently the commercial capital of the country, in its positioning as a global finance hub (*The Times of India*, 2010b).

An important element of Ahmedabad's identity is its architectural landscape that stretches across the centuries. The city is host to buildings from different eras that coexist in testimony to the Indian phenomenon of adaptive assimilation (Vastu-Shilpa Foundation, 2002). Ahmedabad is home to a plethora of step-wells, temples, palaces, mosques, mausoleums and institutions of national and international fame and the architectural identity reveals an amalgamation of deep-rooted traditional values with the aspirations of changed times. A significant recent development in this respect is the establishment of the 'Ahmedabad Heritage Walk', which is essentially a tourism package intended for both domestic and international tourists, showcasing the unique architecture of the old city. The walk covers the major attraction of Ahmedabad's 'pols' (enclosed residential areas within the city, populated by families of a particular profession, religion, or other group membership) in addition to monuments and temple architecture (Jain, 1988). An important feature of this tourism package is the active participation of the local residents of the pols who have agreed to showcase their unique homes. Without the help of the residents, it would have been difficult for the Ahmedabad Municipal Corporation, the civic body in charge of the event, to offer such a package. The congested interiors of the old quarters of the city would have posed a serious challenge to the civic authorities in conceiving and implementing such an 'experience' tour package. A replica of a pol house in another part of the city – for example, a convention center or museum – would never be able to capture the actual experience. The active participation of the locals in maintaining their surroundings, taking pride in showcasing this historically significant architecture, has made the Ahmedabad Heritage Walk an important revenue generator as well as brand image builder for the civic authorities.

LEVERAGING AHMEDABAD'S UNIQUE FEATURES AND ITS RECENT PACE OF DEVELOPMENT

Ahmedabad has continued with its long history of self-reliance and entrepreneurial spirit and this has had an interesting effect. Ahmedabad is quick to rebound from any calamity, natural or man-made, and the resilience of its citizens is manifest in the zeal and dedication with which people from all parts of society, led by its 'army' of entrepreneurs, assemble into task forces in various localities and take 'ownership' of the relief works. Rather than waiting for the civic authorities or other agencies to take the lead and assisting such agencies, the citizens go about their tasks without fear or favor.

Ahmedabad's population at an estimated 5.5 million today is seen as an immense resource for the city's future growth. The city population may surpass ten million by 2020. Projects like the Gandhinagar–Ahmedabad metro rail and BRTS are poised to become landmark projects for the country (Prashanth, 2009). The civic authorities have spent in excess of INR 20 billion on city development over the last five years and another INR 100 billion has been committed for strategic planning under the

National Urban Renewal Mission (http://jnnurm.nic.in/). Hailing Ahmedabad as the 'Entrepreneurship Capital of India', a senior corporate professional has written that if the past decade belonged to Bangalore and Hyderabad, the next one (2010–2020) belongs to Ahmedabad (Khera, 2009).

SUMMARY

Steeped in its glorious ancient past, prominent pre-independence position, post-independence contribution to the country's industrial growth, and its distinct amalgamation of cultures embodied in the Indo-Saracenic style that evolved with the advent of the Mughals, Ahmedabad is well placed to embrace the challenges of the future. Leveraging on its uniqueness and historical significance as well as the active participation of its citizens, Ahmedabad is well on its way to resurrecting its glorious past. Will it now regain the 'Manchester of the East' tag? An important corollary here would be: In the wake of recent developments, is it worth investing in trying to regain the past glory?

In a decade's time, Ahmedabad will become a world class city, not just another metropolis. With a ring of ports developing near Ahmedabad, backed up by massive Special Investment Regions and Special Economic Zones (SEZs) for engineering goods, gems and jewellery, textile and apparel parks, the city is poised for a giant leap forward. Ahmedabad also draws upon the impact of the 'Vibrant Gujarat' brand that has been established at state level in recent years. Ahmedabad demonstrates itsown vibrancy through celebrating its festivals with gusto, whilst the Gujarat Government has developed theme-based international events such as the International Kite Festival on the banks of the Sabarmati and the 'Nine Nights' of dance specific to Gujarati culture, the 'Navratri', around which another international festival has been promoted. With Ahmedabad poised to be at the center of major infrastructural developments in the coming decade, the vibrancy of fast-paced change is going to be felt the most here. Which prompts the question: Should Ahmedabad shake off its past and position itself as the preferred modern megapolis and finance capital of India?

CHAPTER 14

Athens City Branding and the 2004 Olympic Games

Maria Fola

INTRODUCTION

Winning an Olympic Games bid is largely regarded as a significant victory in the never-ending contest between the world's leading cities for prestige and investment. In recent years the Games has turned into a mega event and serves as a platform for host cities and countries to tell a new story to the world about themselves. This chapter examines the case of Athens and the Olympics of 2004 and looks at the efforts of the Greek capital to capitalize on the opportunity of the Games, not only to improve its infrastructure but also to launch a new image of itself to the global audiences of the Games.

BIDDING FOR THE 2004 OLYMPIC GAMES

On 5 September 1997 in Lausanne, Switzerland, the Greek delegation of the Athens 2004 Bid Committee was enthusiastically applauding the short but meaningful phrase of former International Olympic Committee (IOC) President Juan Antonio Samaranch, 'the city that will have the honour and responsibility to host the games of the XXVIII Olympiad is … Athens!' At the same time, thousands of Greeks joined the applause from Zappeion Megaron, a landmark building at the heart of the Greek capital, engaging in a long party to celebrate the return of the Olympics to their homeland. Greeks had indeed waited long enough. Since the revival of the modern Olympics in their country of birth in 1896, the Games traveled a long journey before their homecoming in 2004. What made this homecoming even more unique was the fact that the Greeks had previously lost the competition to host the Games on their centennial anniversary in 1996, as the

IOC had decided in favor of the city of Altanta, Georgia. However, the motivation and enthusiasm for the winning bid seemed to lie in more than the national Greek pride and Olympic heritage. One of the smallest nations ever challenged to host such an event, the Greek organizers appreciated that the opportunity of the 2004 was a unique one for the country and for the city of Athens to relaunch themselves in the eyes of an estimated 3.9 billion global audience and tell a story not only about their rich history and culture but also one of contemporary accomplishments.

Therefore, the strategy of Athens as the host city of the 2004 Games was to demonstrate that, at the dawn of the 21st century, contemporary perceptions of the city could include – perhaps for the first time – modern characteristics and attributes. It is important to acknowledge that prior to the Olympic Games there had been no comprehensive form of city marketing for Athens with the exception of the activities of the Greek National Tourism Organization (GNTO), which is tasked to promote the whole of Greece as a tourism destination rather than Athens specifically.

BALANCING THE OLD WITH THE NEW

For Athens, as it turned out, the balance has not been an easy one and the path towards showcasing modern achievements has for long been doomed by international media reporting on the progress of Olympic preparations – or rather the lack of it – attributed to typical Greek-related mass perceptions such as lack of organization, lack of professionalism, leaving everything to the last minute, and so on. In a qualitative international survey carried out among opinion leaders in six countries by the Athens 2004 Olympic Games Organizing Committee (ATHOC) in December 2003 (while Olympic preparations were well under way), Greeks were perceived to possess a large degree of self-assuredness, as people who manage to solve problems rather ad hoc thanks to their creativity and ability to improvise. Such skills or attributes, however, are often perceived in juxtaposition to what is required for the economic and political life of a modern state to progress. Respondents thought Greeks seemed to be lacking the qualities of careful planning, reliability and organizational skills, which are perceived as key to the success of a modern state (Fola, 2007).

This was exactly the type of perceptions the organizers tried to fight against. Therefore, they set themselves highly aspirational projects – next to the task of preparing for the Games which itself proved to be extremely demanding – that would bring about the new character of the city of Athens and would create new landmarks and memories, both in the natural environment and in the hearts of all involved. At the same time they reflected upon elements of the Olympic heritage of Athens that would bring a unique character to this event and worked to emphasize the message of the Olympic homecoming both in terms of visuals as well as in terms of main messaging and concepts.

The logo

This approach is clearly demonstrated in the selection of the logo for the Games, which was a wreath made from an olive tree branch. This was a direct reference to the Greek heritage of the Games, as the olive wreath or 'kotinos' was the prize of the Olympic Games from classical antiquity. Also, the olive tree was the sacred tree and symbol of the ancient city-state of Athens and represented the classical Olympic ideal of peace. The wreath of the 2004 logo had the shape of an open circle to illustrate an open invitation to humanity to participate in the Olympic celebration, and was rendered by hand in a free, modern and unrestricted manner, reflecting the human element.

The slogan

When ATHOC launched the first international media campaign in 2001–2002, the slogan, 'There is no place like home' was selected. The slogan was obviously a direct reference to the Olympic heritage of the host city but was perceived by international audiences as somehow arrogant and rather uninviting and was soon replaced by the new slogan, 'In the true spirit of the Games' that signaled the campaign leading up to the Games. During the Games the slogan that prevailed was an open invitation for everyone to join in, expressed in two simple, unpretentious words: 'Welcome home'. At the same time, the slogan that signed the GNTO promotional campaign for Greece was 'Live your myth in Greece'. The campaign featured new land-marks of the Athenian capital such as the Calatrava roof of the Olympic Stadium.

The mascots

The mascots of the 2004 Games were two siblings, Athena and Phevos, and their look related directly to ancient Greece. An ancient bell-shaped terra-cotta doll from the 7th century B.C. served as source of inspiration. Their names were inspired by two Olympian Gods: Athena, goddess of wisdom and patron of the city of Athens, and Phevos, the Olympian god of light and music, also known as Apollo. Athena and Phevos quickly became part of

Greek everyday life and impressed everyone with their presence during the Games.

Traditional landmarks and modern architecture

For more than five years, the city of Athens and the surrounding areas looked like a major construction site. Efforts to relaunch an image of a new city had begun prior to the Games with the opening of the new Athens International Airport in 2001. During the Olympic preparation of the city, of the 16,000 km of road network in the greater Attica Region, 2,800 km were built or upgraded prior to and in view of the Olympic Games. Attiki Odos is perhaps the most important Olympic legacy project, 70 km of modern motorway that forms a ring road around the Attica basin and connects the city to the new airport. Last but not least, the new metro lines 2 and 3 together with refurbishment works in the existing light rail system as well as the Suburban Rail gave the city of Athens the look and feel of a contemporary European capital.

One of the most famous new city landmarks is the largely refurbished Olympic Stadium of Athens with the new glass and steel roof designed by the famous Spanish architect Santiago Calatrava. The new roof was part of extensive renovation works carried out at the Athens Olympic Sports Complex known as OAKA and was fit-for-purpose just in time for the Games, generating massive controversial media coverage for many months.

The balance between the old and the new is perhaps best highlighted in the case of the Marathon route and the city's Marble Stadium (also known as Kalimarmaro). In the 2004 Games, the marathon route followed the original route Pheidipides ran in 490 B.C. to announce the outcome of the battle of Marathon, and finished in the Marble Stadium of Athens, the site of the first modern Olympics in 1896.

The Opening Ceremony

The widely praised Opening Ceremony by avant-garde choreographer Dimitris Papaioannou successfully linked the heritage of the Olympic city to contemporary concepts in a truly unique way. The story began with a 28-second countdown (the number of the Olympiads up to then) paced by the sounds of an amplified heartbeat played by two drummers, one located in the main stadium and another one located in Olympia, the venue of the ancient Olympic Games. The first part of the artistic program, called 'Allegory', introduced some of the main themes of the Cycladic, archaic and classical periods of Greek art, symbolizing the evolution of humanity. At the end of this sequence, a man started slowly balancing himself on a rotating cube while representations of mankind's greatest achievements, juxtaposed with humanistic representations and images of men, women, and children of various ethnicities and ages, were projected onto pieces of broken sculpture. This was designed to symbolize the birth of logical thought, higher learning, and humanity finally making sense of the world in which it lives. The next sequence, called Clepsythra, brought to the eyes of a captivated audience figures from Greek mythology, art, and popular culture in a full stadium parade. It ended with a pregnant woman, representing the future of all humanity and history. Finally, all the characters of the parade began to walk towards the center of the stadium, mixing the past and the present in a single marching beat of the drums.

THE IMPACT OF THE GAMES ON THE IMAGE OF ATHENS

The Olympic Games of Athens 2004 was a successful mega event. The 17 days of the Games attracted worldwide media attention. Athletes, spectators and all parties involved experienced a unique celebration of sports, hosted by a country that managed to showcase a new image to the world. However, as Athens discovered rather too late, the event itself does not automatically do anything for the city's brand. It is a media opportunity, not a branding activity itself and, as Anholt (2007: 110) points out, the most important thing for countries as they prepare for such events is to know precisely what they are going to say and prove about themselves while the global media spotlight is switched on.

It transpired that, after the Games, Athens did not have any further stories to tell that were strategically generated, served a specific media agenda, or aimed to promote consistent strategic objectives. It is now clearly understood that branding efforts before and during the Games should be followed up after the event by governmental efforts to enhance specific characteristics of the city that draw upon its core values and identity as well as to showcase modern attributes. In this respect, as Zhang and Zhao (2009) also highlight in the case of Beijing, international mega events can provide good opportunities to promote certain aspects of the city but will have limited effects unless followed by a longer-term strategy that links the city to its current social and economic environment, and to its own identities and core values; and perhaps most importantly, such events must be embraced by the people of the city themselves.

SUMMARY

In the case of Athens, almost six years after the Games of 2004, it appears that the effect of the Games in respect to building a new brand image for the city has been a truly limited one. What is more, Greece is still focusing on attracting tourists based on traditional sea and sand messaging and very little public or private initiative aims to portray the country's modern achievements, to promote different forms of tourism, or to send out consistent, strategic messaging to the world about who we are, what we are good at, and what different opportunities the city and the country offer to explore.

CHAPTER 15

The City Branding of Barcelona: A Success Story

Juan Carlos Belloso

INTRODUCTION

With just over 1.6 million inhabitants (the entire Greater Metropolitan Area totals 3.2 million), Barcelona is Spain's second largest city in terms of population and the capital city of the region of Catalonia. In spite of not being a capital of state, Barcelona is one of the world's most admired cities with one of the best images at an international level. According to one well known study (Saffron Brand Consultants, 2008), Barcelona is one of the cities with the greatest awareness, image and reputation on a worldwide scale, and the third ranked European city brand together with Berlin and Amsterdam, behind only Paris and London and in front of many European capitals such as Athens, Madrid or Rome. The study mentions cosmopolitanism, creativity, innovation, culture and quality of life as the pillars of this great image.

Another study, conducted by a real estate consultancy (Cushman and Wakefield, 2009) and based on the opinions of top executives from 500 European companies, placed Barcelona in fourth position in the ranking of favorite European cities to do business in, behind only London, Paris and Frankfurt. According to a study carried out by Ernst & Young (2008), Barcelona is emerging as the leading city in the Euro-Mediterranean area, followed by Rome. The International Congress and Convention Association (2008) reports that Barcelona occupies third place in Europe by number of meetings organized in 2008, just behind Paris and Vienna. Finally, in the Anholt-Gfk Roper City Brands Index (2009), one of the most high profile city ranking indexes, Barcelona ranks sixth in terms of brand image, behind Paris, Sydney, London, Rome and New York, and ahead of cities like San Francisco, Los Angeles, Vienna and Madrid. Barcelona is, in addition, one of the most popular tourist cities on a global level, with more than 6.5 million tourists per year, and is also considered to be the best European city in terms of quality of life.

These are only some of the many indicators which reflect the strength and reputation of the Barcelona brand on a worldwide level. What, then, were the key success factors in obtaining this brand positioning for Barcelona?

THE CITY BRANDING OF BARCELONA: A SUCCESS STORY

The case of Barcelona brings together a range of elements that we can consider as ideal for the successful branding of a city and constitutes an excellent example from which to extract interesting learnings and conclusions. These key success factors are:

1. The branding of Barcelona grounded in a profound transformation of the city
2. The vision and leadership of the municipal leaders
3. The involvement and participation of civil society
4. The key role of the 1992 Olympic Games
5. The unique and differentiated identity of the city
6. Creativity, innovation and boldness as a common denominator

1.   The branding of Barcelona grounded in a profound transformation of the city

The first aspect to consider in the success of the branding of Barcelona is the conceptualization of city branding as a process of radical and global transformation of the city, with a long-term vision. A city brand is not built in a day; rather, it is a long-term endeavor that requires years of consistent and persistent actions and projects for the brand to take shape.

The first major transformation project of the city, which occurred from the beginning of the 1980s until 1992, the year when the Barcelona Olympic Games took place, and which was reflected in the first Strategic Metropolitan Plan of Barcelona, included a number of areas critical to the development of the city: new infrastructure – airport, port, entry and exit roads to and from the city, opening the city to the sea, the recovery of neighborhoods, re-urbanization, creation of more universities, modernization of the public health and education systems, plans to create new businesses, new cultural facilities, and so on.

2.   The vision and leadership of the municipal leaders

After 40 years of continued repression by Franco's dictatorship, after which the lack of public investment as well as the degradation of the physical space of the city were clearly evident, Barcelona started a new era full of ambition and hope and with the desire to move on from one of the greyest periods of its history. 1979, the year in which the first democratic elections in Spain took place, marked the beginning of the global redesign of Barcelona, with two main objectives: to improve the quality of life of its citizens and to put the city on the map in terms of global awareness. The redesign needed, on one hand, a new vision and strong leadership, and on the other hand, a significant allocation of resources to make it happen.

The visionary leadership of then-Mayor of Barcelona, Pascual Maragall, and the participation of the civil society itself throughout the whole process, were essential. The achievement of the organization of the Summer Olympic Games in 1992 did the rest, speeding up the process and providing the resources needed to complete the planned redesign.

3.   The involvement and participation of civil society

Civil society has played a key role in Barcelona's development and transformation. Barcelona has had to apply all its creativity and innovation capacity to move forward, looking for continuous challenges and boosts from which to catalyze and sustain its transformation processes, of which the organization of the 1992 Summer Olympic Games constitutes the best example. The city's Strategic Metropolitan Plans, instruments created for pooling and encouraging participation and cooperation of public and social institutions from the city in the definition of its future vision and strategies and in the management of projects of change and transformation of the city, are another example of the importance of civil society in the development of a city brand.

The redesign of Barcelona was accompanied by effective municipal campaigns of support and communication which helped to explain the objectives and transformation initiatives, to align the interests of the various key public and private city stakeholders, and to generate confidence and spread optimism among them to obtain their maximum involvement and commitment to the project.

4.   The key role of the 1992 Olympic Games

The 1992 Barcelona Summer Olympic Games marked a before and after, a turning point in the push for the transformation and international projection of the city. The resources generated and the tremendous energy unleashed by a challenge of such magnitude acted as a catalyst for the process of transformation that the city had planned. The great international shop window that are the Games, allowed Barcelona to show the world the redesigned city as well as the enthusiasm and capacity of the people of Barcelona to develop and manage with creativity and efficiency an event of such characteristics and complexity. The great success of the Barcelona Olympic Games can be found in the ability of the city to make the most out of this event in order to:

1. Stimulate the transformation of the city
2. Involve all the citizens in a collective city project
3. Show the redesigned city and its differential attributes to the world
4. Demonstrate the people of Barcelona's capacity for organizing and managing an event of such magnitude
5. Make the most of the developed infrastructure for the future benefit of its citizens

The Olympic Games helped to completely re-imagine the city and present it on the international scene as a modern capital, creative, innovative, welcoming, daring, cosmopolitan, initiative-taking, with its own style, and as a city with an excellent quality of life, developing a great feeling of self-esteem and pride on the part of its citizens. Only 13 years after the arrival of democracy in Spain, the objectives of transforming and repositioning the city on an international scale had been accomplished and Barcelona had positioned itself amongst the leading cities of the world.

5. The unique and differentiated identity of the city
Another fundamental aspect in the success of the branding of Barcelona is the combination of a series of unique and differentiated elements which are part of its identity. These elements include its history, culture, language, cuisine, location, landscape, and climate. It possesses a distinct identity as a Mediterranean city, an accessible and human city with an enterprising spirit. Furthermore, the welcoming and open character of its inhabitants is another aspect which contributes to the overall uniqueness of the city and its high quality of life.

6. Creativity, innovation, and boldness as a common denominator
Creativity, innovation, avant-gardeness and boldness were the common denominators of the whole process of transforming the city. The urban model, its avant-garde architecture, the taste for design, the way the Olympic Games were conceived, as a project by the city for the city, the Strategic Metropolitan Plans as a model of participation or the model of organization and municipal management of the city, are only some examples.

FROM THE 1992 OLYMPIC GAMES TO THE PRESENT DAY

Barcelona has continued with success to redesign and reinvent the city. This redesigning, combined with the visibility and awareness achieved with the Olympic Games, bore its fruits quickly. Tourists, students and professionals from around the world wanted to visit, to study and to work in the city. Barcelona had become very fashionable.

In the years following 1992, Barcelona continued redesigning the city. New plans in 1994, 1999 and 2003 succeeded the first Strategic Barcelona Metropolitan Plan and continued with the process of redesign and consolidation of the metropolitan area of Barcelona as one of the most important metropolitan areas in the European city network. 'Thematic years' were created – The Gaudi Year, the Design Year, The Books and Reading Year, the Picasso Year, the Year of Science – which structure the whole cultural offer of the city around specific areas of interest. The Universal Forum of Cultures in 2004 was invented, a new platform to mobilize economic energies and to complete the renovation of the city.

In 2000, a new urban order was approved to transform what, for over 100 years, had been the main economic engine of Catalonia and the principal industrial district of the city, by the transformation of factories which had become obsolete and that were shut or with little industrial use, in a new pole of economic activity. The project, named 22@Barcelona, contemplated the transformation of 200 hectares of land into an innovative district offering modern spaces for the strategic concentration of intensive knowledge-based activities. This initiative was also a project of urban regeneration and a new model for the city, providing a response to the challenges posed by the knowledge-based society. It is the most important project in the urban transformation of Barcelona in recent years and one of the most ambitious projects of its kind in Europe.

The Barcelona brand today is one of the best known city brands with an excellent reputation on a worldwide scale. Barcelona continues to be the European city with the best quality of life, one of the favorite cities for businesses and international meetings as well as for foreign investment. Every year an increasing number of tourists, students and professionals want to come and visit, to study and to work in the city. The percentage of immigrants attracted by the quality of life and the opportunities that the city offers continues to grow and the city constantly receives visits from other cities and countries in order to better understand the 'Barcelona Model'.

The municipal authorities are trying to maintain and increase the Barcelona brand value on the international scene, trying to capture the highest possible number of big international sporting events, such as the Davis Cup finals, the Tour de France in 2009, the 2010 European Athletics Championships, and so on. Barcelona also hosts a diverse range of top level events and meetings including medical conventions, the Mobile World Congress, and the Sonar electronic music Festival.

The recent sporting successes of Barcelona F.C., the biggest sports club in the city, or the awareness obtained through the Woody Allen film, *Vicky Cristina Barcelona*, continue to inject more vigor into the city brand. More and more local companies with a strong international presence associate Barcelona with their brand name. New and better infrastructure is being developed, improving direct international connections with the major world cities. The district 22@Barcelona continues the economic transformation of the city into a city which is intensive in knowledge and high value-added activities. Barcelona has been recently designated as headquarters of the Permanent Secretariat of the Union for the Mediterranean. Finally, its current mayor has announced the intention to present the candidacy of Barcelona, together with the Pyrenees, to host the 2022 Winter Olympic Games.

However, the changes that occurred in the city in the last decade, with the phenomenon of immigration and the industrial (economic) transformation of the city as fundamental points of change, together with the profound changes originating at a global level, make it necessary to develop a new impulse for Barcelona so that the city can better adapt itself to the current environment and to make it more competitive, reinforcing its position as a city of reference worldwide.

At the time of the preparation of this case, the city of Barcelona is working on a new Metropolitan Strategic Plan with the objective of defining a new strategic model for the metropolitan area of Barcelona, with an eye on 2020, and intends to bring new creative ideas to improve the competitiveness of the city and to consolidate its positioning in the world. In order to do this, a new vision and a strong and shared leadership is needed and, above all, the participation and involvement of all the city's key public and private stakeholders; and, again, a great dose of ambition, creativity, innovation and boldness.

SUMMARY

Barcelona is today one of the most admired cities in the world, with an excellent image worldwide. The key success factors in its city branding are grounded in a thorough and ongoing process of transformation of the city, the vision and leadership of its municipal leaders, the involvement and participation of its civil society, the important role played by the Olympics in 1992, the uniqueness of Barcelona and the creativity, innovation and boldness that represent a common denominator of the entire process.

CHAPTER 16

Branding Budapest

Gyorgy Szondi

INTRODUCTION

Budapest, the capital of Hungary, is home to two million people which means that every fifth Hungarian lives in the capital. The branding of capital cities is a special genre within city branding, given that capitals symbolically represent the entire country and therefore a strong link exists between the country brand and its capital brand. This is particularly true for Eastern Europe where capitals serve as the first – and often only – calling point for visitors, investors, multinational companies as well as creative talent.

Very little attention has been devoted to branding Budapest in the scholarly literature which is not surprising given the city's limited experience in city branding. Puczko, *et al.* (2007) explored Budapest as a tourist destination brand, while Kavaratzis (2009b) investigated the marketing efforts of Budapest with some valuable lessons learned. The application of marketing to cities is a necessary but not sufficient condition for the development of a comprehensive city brand, however. As marketing professors Sheth and Sisodia (2005) have argued, marketing increasingly suffers from a lack of trust by consumers who are turning away from marketing by consciously avoiding any marketing messages. City marketing has also come under criticism as manipulative and tricky (Hospers, 2009b). An all-embracing, policy-driven city branding with an interdisciplinary approach is yet to emerge in both theory and practice.

CHALLENGES OF BRANDING BUDAPEST

The branding of Budapest faces several challenges. The concept of city branding is open to a wide range of interpretations and how mayors, civil servants, tourism organizations and investment agencies interpret and relate to the concept has a bearing on the activities under their auspices. This 'branding worldview' may be cultural and may vary from city to city or from country to country. There has been much skepticism among Hungarian policy makers towards brands in general and place branding in particular, as they often view branding Budapest either as an unrealistic or not very intellectual endeavor. That is why creating and fostering a city brand culture among stakeholders is paramount. Making the branding concept an intellectual and interdisciplinary process rather than a simple promotional or marketing campaign has presented an ongoing challenge to the Budapest City Identity Office, which has been responsible for the coordination and management of a synchronized city brand since 2006. The Office, which serves as a think tank organization inside the Budapest Municipality, is headed by the appointed City Identity Advisor, who has a background in arts history and architecture and therefore a very broad interpretation of city branding.

The administrative structure of Budapest is a particular issue which hinders a coherent and holistic approach to city branding. Budapest has a two-tier local government system, consisting of the Budapest Capital Municipality headed by the Mayor of Budapest, and the district councils. The city is divided into 23 districts, which have their own local councils, headed by the district mayor. The municipality as well as the district councils have their own Communication and Public Relations departments, which are often responsible for promoting the district. It is clear that without the full involvement and support of these district councils any attempt at strategic and consistent city branding is doomed to failure. Simplifying the administrative system is one of the goals of the newly elected national government in 2010, possibly by reducing the number of districts as well as the power of the district councils.

Another serious challenge to overcome is the politicization of city branding, which can easily fall prey to local district politics or party politics. While the city government's involvement is crucial in coordinating as well as financing branding campaigns, it is not unusual in Eastern Europe that during the implementation favoritism and corruption prevail instead of professionalism.

BRANDING CONCEPTS

Branding Budapest as a concept and process has recently been 'on the agenda' as more and more forums, conferences and discussions are devoted to the topic. In the last decade several city branding initiatives and concepts have been developed by tourism organizations, marketing agencies or various think tanks. Most of these initiatives, however, were promotional campaigns with limited stakeholder focus (for example, aimed at tourists only) and many were never put into practice. During the 1990s, the focus was on the visual dimension. Budapest has had many different logo versions, most of them developed by the Tourism Office. Outdated and recent Budapest logos and slogans co-exist, particularly in the tourism sector. Budapestians do not lack ideas and creativity, as demonstrated by the increasing number of calls for logo and slogan competitions for the city which are, however, further contributing to the confusion. The City Identity Office protested against these initiatives, given that the brand name 'Budapest' is bound by copyrights and cannot be used by anybody and everybody. Language is an often overlooked factor, as the English translation of a creative Hungarian slogan may not cover the original idea ('The City of Senses') or it may be difficult to find the Hungarian equivalent of a catchy English slogan.

The Budapest Tourism Office launched several campaigns to attract more domestic and foreign tourists, relying heavily on advertising whose initiatives were successful in terms of a destination brand but limited as a city brand. A more comprehensive approach to branding Budapest started in 2009 under the auspices of the City Identity Office.

The first step involved the development of a detailed typography guide-book for Budapest that outlines the visual elements of the official logo of Budapest and how it ought to be used by all the institutions that belong to the municipality. Red, yellow and blue are the official colors of Budapest and are represented in the Budapest logo. Up to 2009 there was no coor-dination whatsoever in the visual identity of the different organizations. There are more than 300 organizations run by the municipality, ranging from cultural (schools, libraries, nurseries), economic (investment, budgetary, commer-cial) to social (care homes, hospitals, child protection agencies), city image (tourism agencies, architecture, environmental protection, heritage, utilities, public transport) as well as administration. These five types of organizations construct the pillars of the corporate identity typography and are represented by five different colors in the city brand's visual identity mix.

The second step was the identification of brand values, based on organic and induced values. Organic values include the panorama of Budapest, its waters, lifestyle and architectural heritage. Several organic values center on the River Danube, which has been suggested as the core element of the Budapest brand with its integrative function. Recently, however, induced values, such as creativity, knowledge generation or business friendliness have been gaining importance. Budapest remains a strong economic and business brand. The Budapest Business Region (BBR) plays a key role in promoting and representing Budapest's business interest with the aim of raising awareness of the Hungarian capital as a fast-developing invest-ment area and attracting more investors to the region. For example, the role of innovation as a core value in the Budapest brand is demonstrated in a promotional video by the BBR (http://www.youtube.com/watch?v=e0wko-kaybWA).

In *fDi Magazine*'s European Cities and Regions of the Future 2010/2011 ranking, Budapest achieved the prestigious third position on a list of Central and Eastern European cities, following Bucharest and Warsaw. The cities were ranked based on economic potential, cost effectiveness, human resources, quality of life, infrastructure, business friendliness and FDI promotion strategy. In 2008 Budapest was chosen by the European Union to host the European Institute of Innovation and Technology in acknowledgment of the long tradition of excellence in Hungarian education, research and innovation. The International Congress and Convention Association ranked Budapest as the sixth most attractive international conference destination in 2009, well ahead of any other Eastern European cities.

CITY BRANDS AS COMMUNITIES

Building communities and fostering relationships among these geographical and virtual communities is an emerging dimension of the branding process. The 'I love Budapest' movement started in 2004 with the aim of gathering and uniting enthusiastic and committed individuals who are willing to do something for the city and make Budapest a more exciting, dynamic, successful and likeable place. This movement was the forerunner of the City Identity Office hosted by the municipality and initiated several projects, such as making Budapest graffiti-free and removing illegal posters throughout the capital, particularly prior to local and national elections. The movement has also addressed the problem of homeless people occupying subways and begging, contributing to a negative image of the city. They have organized several urban festivals to 'occupy' and take hold of the city. Another initiative is the 'Let's invent Budapest' movement, which is a platform for exchanging ideas and concepts, discussing views and counterviews about Budapest, the city and how its citizens would like to imagine it. These initiatives are from the bottom-up, rather than an elite driven top-down approach where marketers invent and force an artificial, external brand concept upon the city and its citizens.

These civic, bottom-up initiatives can be vital in branding a city and can help reconceptualize city brands as communities. Based on commercial products, Muniz and O'Guinn (2001) introduced the idea of 'brand community' which can, however, be applied to places as well. This approach to place branding adds a new dimension to the previous conceptualizations of place brands outlined by Hankinson (2004). Social media are a vital platform in creating these geographic and virtual communities, such as the

52,000 fans of Budapest on Facebook (twice as many as Prague or Warsaw) or the 22,000 fans of 'I Love Budapest'. A city brand rooted in the local community will be perceived as being more credible and trustworthy than an official one.

AN EVENTS-CENTERED APPROACH

Hosting large events can play a vital role not only in the regeneration of cities, but also in significantly contributing to city branding. Mega events often kick off branding campaigns, and can help reposition city brands. If the city has already a strong brand (either cultural, tourist or economic), it can attract events to the city which in turn can further reinforce the brand. Budapest has long been committed to organizing annual festivals, which attract a large number of domestic and overseas visitors, including the Spring and Autumn Festivals, the Budapest Fair and the Sziget Festival in August when young people from all over the world converge on Budapest for a week. Budapest has long positioned itself as a 'Festival City', striving to become one of the leading cultural capitals of Europe.

While some events may attract only particular audiences, other events can unite the entire population of a city. One example is hosting the Olympics, which can focus the world's attention on the city as well as the country. Despite the fact that Hungary is the seventh most successful sporting nation in the history of the Summer Olympics, and third in terms of the number of Olympic medals per person, it is the only one of the ten countries leading the Olympic championship table that has never hosted the Summer Olympic Games. This is why a movement started in 2008 to host the 2020 Olympics in Budapest (http://www.budapestiolimpia.hu), contributing to the increased need for a comprehensive city brand uniting various stakeholders.

BUDAPEST CITY BRAND RESEARCH AND MEASUREMENT

Brand audits are useful tools to identify the strengths and weaknesses as well as the overall associations of a city brand among tourists, expatriates, local residents or other stakeholders, as well as to assess the city's image in the local, national and international electronic, print and social media. A city communication audit can reveal the disparities between real and perceived communications about a city; the form, style, effectiveness and credibility of its messages; as well as the communication channels and tactics used to communicate with a wide range of stakeholders.

A comprehensive audit was conducted by the Political Capital Institute in 2008, which concluded that the Budapest brand was too segmented, controversial and inconsistent, and lacking any leadership and ownership. It highlighted the contrast and division between the capital and the rest of country, as Budapest has an over-centralized role in the political, economic and cultural spheres.

On an international scale, ranking cities according to different dimensions and factors has become a competitive and lucrative business in the Western world, as more and more organizations provide city brand image measures which sometimes produce contradictory results. How different stakeholder groups view a particular city provides valuable input into a city branding policy as well as particular campaigns.

According to the 2009 Anholt-GfK Roper City Brands Index, Budapest appeared in 38th position, scoring particularly well on the 'Place' dimension but performing poorly regarding 'Presence'. The Saffron European City Brand Barometer among British citizens ranked 72 European cities based on a comparison of their assets and attractions against the strength of their brands. Budapest achieved 93 per cent of brand utilization, which means that the brand is slightly undervalued as the Budapest brand was worse than its assets would predict. The message from this survey is that Budapest should invest more in branding efforts and not let the brand drift. Gallup has developed a strategic decision making tool, 'Soul of the City', which offers a comprehensive benchmark of urban citizens' attitudes towards and satisfaction with a city's governance, socio-economic, sustainability and cultural spheres. It audits a city's non-material assets such as emotional energies, loyalties, and drivers of engagement that all serve to make up a city's vibrant social fabric and soul, defined as a construct of happiness, commitment and passion. According to the 2008 results, Budapest is a disengaged capital in the views of the local people.

While the locals may feel more pessimistic about Budapest, the city's international standing may be different. Indirectly related to a city brand is the Economist Intelligence Unit's 'Liveability Survey', which quantifies the challenges to an individual's lifestyle in 140 cities worldwide. Each city is assigned a score for over 30 qualitative and quantitative factors across five broad categories: stability, healthcare, culture and environment, education and infrastructure. According to the 2009 survey, Budapest ranked as the most liveable city in Central Europe, followed by Prague, which is often identified as Budapest's major competitor in the region. Only these two cities reached the threshold of 'good quality life' in Eastern Europe.

SUMMARY

The theory and practice of branding cities in Central and Eastern Europe are lagging behind those of the West, which often serve as a benchmark for the rest of the world. Although there have been some city branding initiatives and conceptualizations, they were either short-lived or never implemented. The future will tell how far the City Identity Office of Budapest will get in terms of implementing and coordinating the branding project, particularly as the Office may cease to exist after the local elections in autumn 2010.

As long as branding Budapest is campaign-driven rather than policy-driven, and without a coordinating organization that strategically oversees the process and engages a wide range of stakeholders and interest groups, the city brand remains elusive. An additional challenge is to create synergy between the nation brand and the city brand. The branding of Budapest will not succeed if it is 'invented' and forced upon the city from above with the focus on economic interests only. Social and cultural goals must also be taken into consideration, particularly in the development and maintenance of city brand communities.

CHAPTER 17

Chongqing's City Branding: The Role of Graphic Design

Freeman Lau and Angelica Leung

INTRODUCTION

The contribution of graphic designers to city branding has evolved from relatively isolated projects, such as designing stamps and posters, to much more of a visual communication strategy within city branding. In this chapter, we will explore the role of graphic design in city branding and offer introductions to various projects, many of which may not initially seem to be the work of a visual communicator. Graphic designers can use a multitude of media, ranging from a few centimeters on a stamp to the label of a water bottle, to visually communicate city branding.

A graphic designer communicates information, ideas and concepts through a visual language. The language is made up of images, illustrations, icons, photographs, typography and other graphic elements and moving images. Graphic design is all around us, but is rarely noticed unless done poorly. The design of book covers, posters and brochures, product labels, directional signage, logos and corporate branding all involve graphic design.

Before the days of mass email, letters were sent by post. The stamp can be considered a small advertorial a few centimeters large, and sent to a worldwide audience. The challenge for a designer is how to communicate the theme in such small dimensions. Most cities do not have their own stamps, but in Asia due to historical reasons, the ex-colonies of Macau, Singapore and Hong Kong all have their own philately. The first Macau stamp was issued in 1884. In Hong Kong, the Stamp Advisory Committee, comprising prominent local citizens, professional graphic designers and philatelic experts along with government officials, work with the Postmaster General to consider the postage stamp themes, up to 18 months ahead of issue. For each theme, the post office then commissions several designers to submit designs. The challenge for a graphic designer is then how to interpret the theme and to use their understanding of printing techniques to realize the design on a stamp.

In 1997, a new set of definitive stamps was required after the return of sovereignty of Hong Kong to China. A new design was needed to replace the profile of Queen Elizabeth II which had been featured up to then. Kan Tai-Keung, an established Chinese graphic designer and artist, came up with a design that featured the world famous skyline of Hong Kong and a gradation of color for the different denominations of stamps. He also took references from the traditional Chinese scrolls, which often featured continuous landscapes. Hence, it was possible over the years to create a continuum of 'mini-stories' that would be sent all over the world, to build up a snapshot understanding of the place where the letter originated.

Graphic designers are commissioned to create corporate identities, often including the design of the company or organization's logo. Studies have shown that consumers can often recognize a logo, even when only shown a small part of it.

The use of graphic design in city branding is not limited to signage and maps, but can extend to product packaging. In 2002, for example, Watson's Water commissioned Kan & Lau Design Consultants to do a redesign of their bottle to celebrate their 100 years of history. In Hong Kong, distilled water is often preferred over mineral or spring water. The brand is a market leader in Hong Kong and is often supplied to delegates at international conferences and events, which are important venues to showcase a city to incoming visitors. Riding on the launch of the new bottles, a subsequent limited edition series of 12 labels was created, inviting 12 popular culture local artists and graphic designers to feature their work. This limited edition series was available on the market in 2003. The series created a buzz both locally and amongst visitors, and many bottles were saved as collector's items. As the official drink of the 5th East Asian Games held in Hong Kong in December 2009, the labels of the bottles were once again used as a medium of communication, featuring renderings of icons of the nine participating countries and regions.

A *pro bono* project by Milton Glaser illustrates how great graphic design can be simple, yet deliver a clear and powerful message. He used a rebus, which is a representation of words by pictures of objects or by symbols to develop a very successful campaign in the late 1970s to promote tourism in New York State. The I 'heart' NY (I Love New York) has become an icon and is now widely associated with New York City. During that period, the crime rate in New York City was high and many businesses left the city. The campaign generated a lot of support from the public and was furthermore widely used in tourist souvenirs. In 2003, in response to 9/11, Milton Glaser revised the logo, adding a burn mark on the heart symbol, but the original design still remained most popular and a relaunch in 2008 was undertaken by Empire State Development (ESD), New York's chief economic development agency. In response to the many counterfeit products that proliferated over the years, a set of brand guidelines was also created, which aids the use of the brand's logo in a consistent manner. The guidelines offer 15 'Logo Usage Don'ts' ranging from resizing the various elements, changing the colors and redrawing the heart. The entire brand book is 50 pages long.

Other cities have also commissioned graphic designers to create logos and brand usage guidelines for their locations, often choosing familiar icons as the main inspiration. For example, Venice has worked together with Philippe Starck on the 'winged lion' logo, and in 2009, Rome launched a competition for a new logo, complete with brand book to promote tourism and culture. However, does holding a competition or hiring a well-known designer automatically ensure that the logo will be embraced by the community? How does a designer cater for the many different stakeholders involved in city branding?

In response to these challenges, some graphic designers have now taken up the role of working with the client to identify their core values and then to communicate these values through graphic techniques.

THE GRAPHIC DESIGNER AS RESEARCHER

In the United States, there are less than ten cities with a population of over one million people. According to the Blue Book of Cities in China (Chinese Academy of Social Sciences, 2009), China has 118 megalopolises of more than one million people, and 39 super-metropolises such as Beijing, Shanghai and Shenyang with more than two million residents. City branding is already an important topic to many municipal governments, who are vying to attract tourism and investment and for national resources. But in a large country such as China, what icons are specific to a region or to the country? For example, the dragon motif is used to represent 'Chinese' in general all over the world, and is not owned by a specific region. How is the particular region perceived and represented within China? What city emblems and motifs are instantly recognizable?

CHONGQING: 3,000 YEARS OF HISTORY AND A POPULATION OF 30 MILLION

Chongqing, also known more popularly as Chungking, is a major city in central-western China and served as its wartime capital during the Second

Sino-Japanese War. In 1997, it became a provincial level municipality. The other three provincial level municipalities are Beijing, Shanghai and Tianjin. Located at the confluence of two strategic rivers near the Three Gorges, the municipality is seen as an important economic hub for access to west China, with a strong tradition in heavy industry and agriculture. There is a registered population of over 30 million in an administrative area that spans over 80,000 km^2.

There were many negative stereotypes attached to the municipality over the last 50 years, impeding its growth and the attraction of talent and foreign direct investment. These negative images are present both locally within China and also overseas. To name a few of the general impressions – pollution (the area is a heavy industrial base), poverty, hot-tempered people. Many of the more recent developments in transportation, education, arts and the economy went unnoticed. As a directive of the upper echelons of the local government, action had to be taken to remedy the city's negative image and to show the world what the new Chongqing had become.

The city's new visual system would be used to communicate the new developments of the municipality and to give it a strong identity separate from the adjacent province of Sichuan, which Chongqing was formerly part of until 1997. It would also be used to enhance investor confidence in the organizational structure of the government and to communicate the interest and professionalism of the administration. At the same time, there was a need to communicate the local tourism opportunities and to encourage the flow of human talent from around China, attracting and retaining quality residents and their families, contributing to social cohesion by providing a focal point and renewed interest in the image of the municipality.

The government bureau in charge of the project, the Chongqing Information Office, started with the most popular way to get lots of ideas in a fast and convenient manner, by organizing a competition with a prize and some form of publicity for the winner. From November 2003 to June 2004, the Municipal Government of Chongqing organized the Taiji Cup Competition for the Chongqing Slogan and Visual Identity System – 'New Chongqing, New Image'. However, the resulting entries did not provide a level of professionalism that the administrators had hoped for, which led to the decision to invite bids from professional design consultancies. Through a comprehensive and transparent tendering system, Kan & Lau Design Consultants was selected, with Kan Tai- Keung taking up the role of Chief Designer.

WHAT DOES A CITY MEAN TO YOU?

Designing a city logo is a participative event, involving both the public and private sectors. The absence of such a participative approach risks the designs not being accepted by the public. Before the design process can begin, it is paramount to understand how the city sees itself and how it wants to be perceived externally. When multiple stakeholders are involved, this task can become complex.

In the early brainstorming sessions, workshops were set up with the art and design students of the local universities. They were given the opportunity to interact and become involved in the process of city branding, and they provided invaluable insights through 'core value' brainstorming sessions, as well as the design of posters which featured their interpretation of the city.

Taking the initial flood of ideas and transforming them into visuals was the next step. A panel of local government officials was then invited to vote and give their opinions on almost 50 variations of designs. The key stakeholders in terms of Offices and Bureaus that were involved in the discussions are shown in Table 17.1.

For the initial proposals, the design consultants looked at tourist products, maps of the region and government publications aimed for the local market. One important source was the local weather report that shows iconic pictures of each city as the weather was reported. This was an important and insightful guide to which images the local residents associated with each city from a regional perspective. For example, Chengdu (the capital of neighboring Sichuan province) is well known for Sichuan opera, tea-houses and pandas.

TABLE 17.1   Stakeholders in the design discussions

Stakeholder Organization	Role
Mayor's Office	Final decision maker
Representatives of the People's Congress	To ensure Party interests
Chinese People's Political Consultative Conference Committee (Party representative)	To ensure Party interests
Chongqing Information Office	Project leader and operations
Cultural Bureau	To ensure cultural dimension of the city brand
Chinese Academy of Social Sciences	To provide input as a social policy think tank
City Committee	To represent local interests
Communication Bureau	To advise on communication strategies
City Planning Bureau	To advise on planning issues
External Trade Bureau	To incorporate external audience perceptions
Tourism Administration	To advise on domestic and international tourism
Urban Construction Bureau	To ensure feasibility of construction agenda

The logo featured on the Chengdu Government website is a curled-up panda. Chongqing was identified with the city's more iconic structures, notably the Chongqing People's Assembly Hall, built in the 1950s with a traditional glazed green roof, and also the cityscape at the confluence of two rivers.

LOOK TO THE PAST FOR INSPIRATION

The area where Chongqing is located is also historically important, with early records of the *Ba* ethnic group living in the area documented in *Shang* (c.1600–c.1100 B.C.) and *Zhou* (c.1100–771 B.C.) dynasty artefacts. Later, during the Three Kingdoms period (c.220–280 B.C.), the Kingdom of *Shu* was located in this area. A visit to the local museum and important historical locations was an effective way to find inspiration. In *Ba* culture, the tiger had important significance, and other motifs derived from early writing styles were incorporated into the supporting graphics. Having a variety of images allowed for greater flexibility in the usage of the designs.

THE FINAL DESIGN

Many places use famous architectural sites or other landmarks to represent the city, for example, the Eiffel Tower for Paris or the Opera House for Sydney. However, other inspirations should also be considered, such as use of the abstract or other symbols to represent the city's spirit. Through the

FIGURE 17.1 | Chongqing design

two-year process of refining the design and eliciting feedback, ten discussion sessions, and numerous interviews with top government officials, expatriates and consular representatives, over 80 design concepts were presented. In the media and in online polls, over 80,000 members of the public voted for their favorite designs. The final developed design (see Figure 17.1) reflected the theme of 'double celebration', the literal meaning of Chongqing, and incorporated two persons forming the character *qing* of the city's name. The color was selected to be vibrant and energetic, like the local people, moving hand in hand with the government to build a prosperous future.

SUMMARY

Graphic design should be an integral component of any city's overall brand strategy. The power of graphic design to influence perceptions, emotions, and attitudes represents a key resource for city branding policy makers in their attempts to develop a strong and distinctive brand identity for their city. We have shown how the Chinese city of Chongqing has harnessed the power of graphic design in order to create a rejuvenated city brand that appeals to the full spectrum of city branding audiences, both domestically within China and also internationally. A participative approach between the public and private sectors, allied with the strategic use of high quality graphic design, represents a solid foundation upon which to build a powerful city brand.

CHAPTER 18

Edinburgh: Scotland's Inspiring Capital

Kenneth Wardrop

INTRODUCTION

Edinburgh is Scotland's capital city and for international visitors to Scotland it acts as the gateway to the country. It is the United Kingdom's second city for tourism after London, is the world's leading festival city, the historic city center is a UNESCO World Heritage Site, it is the first UNESCO World City of Literature (having invented the designation), is regularly voted the United Kingdom's favorite city break destination, in 2009 was 28th in the International Congress and Conference Association (ICCA) rankings, generates 13.5 million visitor bed nights per annum, and has a visitor economy worth £2.1 billion per annum that employs 25,000 people.

The destination has a track record of success and punches above its weight, given the size of the city (the city region population is 1.3 million) and its geographic position on the north-western periphery of Europe. The city has, however, recognized that it cannot be complacent in a competitive global marketplace, and has also embraced the thesis that the high brand awareness and currency of our visitor brand can be capitalized on for place marketing focused on attracting inward investment and talent, and utilizing the Edinburgh Inspiring Capital Brand with its cross-selling messaging across visit, invest, live, work and study.

CITY OF EDINBURGH BRAND REPOSITIONING

This destination promotion case study reflects on the City of Edinburgh's brand repositioning since 2005, when it adopted the new 'Edinburgh Inspiring Capital' brand promoting the city as a place to visit, invest, live, work and study, and the recent evolution of the place marketing of the city through the creation on 1 April 2009 of the new city promotion body (and private-public partnership) the Destination Edinburgh Marketing Alliance Ltd (DEMA), described as bringing a third dimension to the brand, taking it from being a passive to a proactive promotional tool for the city.

In late 2002 initial research into the development of an Edinburgh City Region Brand was initiated by the City of Edinburgh Council under the auspices of an inter-agency chief executives group, the Edinburgh Partnership, with a special working group of the Edinburgh Tourism Action Group being tasked to develop the brand strategy for the city. Funding of £800,000 was secured to develop the brand on the strength of this strategy from a special Scottish Government fund for the period 2003–2005. A brand working group oversaw the recruitment of a project manager in February 2004, and the procurement of specialist consultancy support in the shape of the international brand consultants Interbrand appointed in June 2004. The Edinburgh Inspiring Capital Brand was launched in May 2005 with an additional £1 million being secured for the period 2006 to 2008 from the Scottish Government.

Objectives of the initial destination branding project were to develop a brand or family of brands which would represent a cohesive marketing image for the city region. The brand was identified as a tool to develop and enhance Edinburgh's reputation as a successful and dynamic world class city region with the objective of increasing the attractiveness of the city region as a place in which to live, work, visit or do business, and to improve the economic and social prosperity of the city region.

More specifically, the brand reinforced the Edinburgh region's position as:

- a place for companies to locate and to grow their business

- a place which attracts talent to meet the skill needs of key sectors and organizations, for example, key industrial sectors such as financial services, electronics and biotechnology, higher education, research institutes

- a magnet for world class research and education and a region of innovation

- a location with a high quality of life for its inhabitants

- a high quality tourism destination

- a confident and contemporary city region with remarkable history and built heritage

Overall the brand provided a shared clear vision for the city region, ensuring a more joined up and effective approach in promoting the city region which promoted better leverage of resources. The city region brand

FIGURE 18.1 | Edinburgh brand pyramid

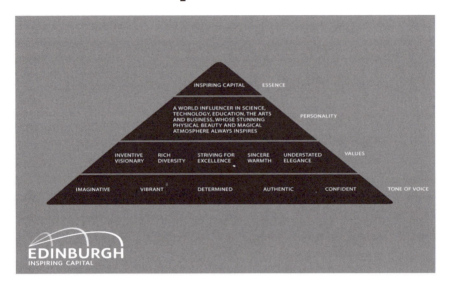

became a key component of the strategy and action plans of both the Local Economic Forum for Edinburgh and the Edinburgh Tourism Action Group (ETAG). The Edinburgh Inspiring Capital brand essence, personality, and values are articulated best through the brand pyramid shown in Figure 18.1.

The graphic representation of the brand is shown in Figure 18.2.

FIGURE 18.2 | Graphic representation of the Edinburgh brand

The brand manager and a small team of staff working with the brand steering group, which was made up of a mix of senior representatives of the business community and public bodies, worked hard from the brand launch in May 2005 to achieve brand ubiquity by encouraging the adoption and utilization of the brand by institutions across the city.

An important component of the brand was the creation of two websites: a business-to-business site (www.edinburghbrand.com) that aims to build the community of brand adopters, and a consumer-facing site (www.edin-burgh-inspiringcapital.com) that aims to be a single official web portal for the city to provide comprehensive and accessible information to consumers and to act as a signpost and conduit to other relevant consumer-facing websites across visit, invest, live, work and study. In 2009–2010 the site was on target to attract 350,000 unique visitors per annum with the aim of doubling this figure in 2010–2011.

COLLABORATION WITH KEY STAKEHOLDERS

The organizational framework for tourism promotion in Scotland changed significantly in 2005 with the creation of a new integrated national tourism body following the amalgamation of the local area tourist boards (including Edinburgh and Lothian Tourist Board) into a new VisitScotland Integrated Network. At this time the decision was taken by the City of Edinburgh Council, working with private business partners and VisitScotland, to create the Edinburgh Convention Bureau Ltd (ECB) as the new city-focused business tourism partnership. The creation of the ECB was based on the premise that given the competitive nature of the business tourism market, the city was best served through a strong city-based convention marketing organization focused on bidding, selling, and aftercare support of convention business, working with the national tourism organization whose focus was on building broader awareness of Scotland as a business tourism destination.

When working with city-based organizations on the extension of the ubiquity of the Edinburgh Inspiring Capital Brand through 2005 and 2006, a clear view developed from businesses that there was a need for the city to raise its competitive profile. This view emerged in light of the competitive global market environment in which Edinburgh was operating in terms of attracting visitors, inward investment, and talent.

This led in May 2007 to the calling together by a group of city partners including the Chamber of Commerce, Convention Bureau and City Council of a summit to discuss the competitive positioning of the city and to establish if there were structural issues in the way city promotion was being tackled. The outcome of this summit was a consensus that the status quo was not an option; the city needed to raise its competitive profile; there was duplication and fragmentation in the way the city was being promoted; and there was a need for a common purpose in approach and strong leadership. A task group was formed to look at the three areas of tourism, talent and trade promotion.

The Communication Group was appointed to advise this task group and produced its final report 'Promoting Edinburgh as a destination' in February 2008. This report made several recommendations:

- a customer-focused approach in identifying the best organizational or structural solution and the need therefore for the preparation of a Destination Promotion Strategy for the city

- capitalizing on the assets of the destination and achieving competitive advantage by cross-selling between tourism, talent and trade (or visit, invest, live, work and study)

- leadership to bring parties involved in city promotion together and speak with one voice thus creating a common purpose and addressing issues associated with replication and duplication of effort and fragmentation

Based on this report, the task group concluded that there was a need for a new structural or organizational approach and took forward the recommendations of the Communication Group's report to proceed with the creation of a

FIGURE 18.3 | **Five objectives for Destination Edinburgh Marketing Alliance**

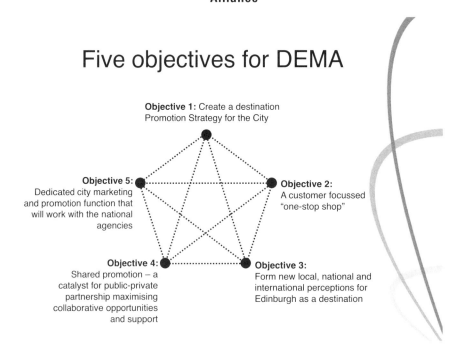

Five objectives for DEMA

Objective 1: Create a destination Promotion Strategy for the City

Objective 5: Dedicated city marketing and promotion function that will work with the national agencies

Objective 2: A customer focussed "one-stop shop"

Objective 4: Shared promotion – a catalyst for public-private partnership maximising collaborative opportunities and support

Objective 3: Form new local, national and international perceptions for Edinburgh as a destination

new Alliance for City Promotion. Five objectives were identified, as shown in Figure 18.3.

Further institutional consolidation of national government organizations in Scotland at the start of 2008, in particular a restructuring of VisitScotland and EventScotland, Scottish Development International (the national inward investment promotion organization), and Scottish Enterprise (the national economic development agency) created an increased centralization that led to the City of Edinburgh Council being the logical organization to take on the championing of the work of the task group.

There was considerable debate amongst the partners involved in this strategic review as to what delivery model or vehicle was most appropriate for this new city promotion body. There was a clear split in view between the national organizations and the city-based organizations. The city-based organizations were keen to create a strong independent leadership body, whereas the national government agencies were in favor of the creation of a formalized alliance rather than a full blown destination marketing organization. City stakeholders were of the view that Edinburgh as an 'attack brand' for Scotland and a capital city was unusual amongst its competitor set of cities in not having an independent dedicated destination marketing body. The national agencies' concerns related to potential duplication and replication of effort, and less efficient and effective utilization of resources.

Ambiguity in relation to the negotiations on the final form and function the new organization would take continued amongst the collaborative partners until the creation of the new organization in April 2009. There was, however, consensus amongst the partners around the benefits of cross-selling between visit, invest, live, work and study. This, coupled with the view that the city needed to present a more contemporary image and to exploit the strong cultural offer in the city, resonated with work being undertaken at the same time by the Scottish Government on the place marketing of Scotland.

DESTINATION EDINBURGH MARKETING ALLIANCE

In May 2008 a new Project Board made up of city-based private and public organizations and national government agencies was established to take forward the creation of the new Destination Edinburgh Marketing Alliance with the target of a soft launch date of 1 April 2009. The author of this case study was seconded in May 2008 to lead the creation of this new promotional body for the city.

Governance arrangements for DEMA have led to the creation of a company limited by guarantee that was fully formed on 15 July 2009. DEMA is a business-led private-public partnership that aims to communicate Edinburgh's status as a world class place to visit, invest, live, work and study – through strong leadership and coordination guided by the city's destination promotion strategy and utilizing the Edinburgh Inspiring Capital Brand. The Board of Directors is a twelve-strong body made up of one representative of the City of Edinburgh Council, the Chief Executive of the company, and ten private business representatives bringing a mix of skills and experience from the key business sectors across the tourism, talent and trade agendas.

For participating organizations or individuals the main criteria for involvement with DEMA is a commitment to, passion for, and involvement in the promotion of Edinburgh as a destination.

DEMA provides:

➤ a unified voice for Edinburgh: leadership, support and collaboration with like-minded people and city-based organizations

➤ consistent and coherent promotional messaging that encourages cross-selling

➤ communication of the city's strengths globally

➤ a unifying destination promotion strategy

➤ coordinating partners' activities to ensure alignment and maximization of resources which amplify Edinburgh's assets through shared marketing campaigns, and to establish who is best placed to message to specific target audiences

➤ Edinburgh Inspiring Capital Brand collateral

➤ customer knowledge: providing robust, focused and current market intelligence

➤ maximization of web-based tools to build customer databases, relationships and communication

➤ media messaging ('open for business', reputation, and perception management) for the city

➤ promotion: working in partnership with businesses and public agencies.

DEMA is looking to build its support in the city and has identified four groups of partners we wish to cultivate:

Supporters;
Participators;

Contributors;
Champions (or Ambassadors).

The organization is also a member-based company and over time the Board of Directors and initial members will be looking to invite additional appropriate members to formally participate in the governance of the Company. The initial 10 members are:

- The City of Edinburgh Council

- Edinburgh Business Assembly

- Edinburgh Chamber of Commerce

- Edinburgh Convention Bureau Limited

- Edinburgh, Lothian and Scottish Borders Screen Industries Office Limited

- Edinburgh Tourism Action Group

- Essential Edinburgh

- Festivals Edinburgh Limited

- Edinburgh Science Triangle

- The University of Edinburgh

VisitScotland and the Edinburgh Hotels Association are at December 2009 currently considering whether to join as member organizations. Further organizations will be invited to join over time. The next steps in 2010–2011 include the proposed merger of DEMA with the ECB and the Edinburgh Film Focus (EFF) film location promotion organization.

DEMA is currently funded through a £1 million contribution in cash and £0.45 million of 'in-kind' support from the City of Edinburgh Council covering eight staff, office accommodation, and associated overheads. DEMA aims to leverage at least equivalent amounts from partner organizations through the alignment of promotional project spend, direct contributions, or sponsorship. The Board of Directors in July 2009 signed off the company's first three-year business plan for the period 2009–2012.

Edinburgh's first Destination Promotion Strategy was published in September 2009. It identifies a consistent and coherent set of cross-selling messages across visit, invest, live, work and study, as well as the key target audiences for the city to take forward the new 'place marketing' agenda. A responsibility for DEMA is to ensure product-market fit translating knowledge of audience, customer intelligence, and market positioning into product innovation and the matching of visitor experience with the values promoted through the city brand.

TRACKING AND MANAGING PERCEPTIONS OF THE EDINBURGH BRAND

As part of the ongoing assessment of the impact and outputs from the Edinburgh Inspiring Capital Brand, we have subscribed to the Anholt City Brand Index. Edinburgh currently ranks 22 out of 50 cities in this index. The most recent report on Edinburgh stated: 'Edinburgh clearly needs to gain more recognition for its contemporary assets and achievements. It seems unlikely that "business as usual" will result in any significant enhancement of Edinburgh's international profile… If Edinburgh is to compete on profile with any of the higher ranking world cities in the list, a step change in the scale and importance of its activities – sporting, cultural, political or economic – will be required' (Anholt City Brand Index Report on Edinburgh 2007).

Areas where the city was underperforming in relation to consumer perceptions were in 'contemporary presence and pulse'. The Anholt City Brand Index Study for Edinburgh also suggested a step change was required in the scale and importance of sporting, cultural, political and economic activities if the city is to realize its full potential. Consequently, amongst DEMA's main objectives is the task of changing customer perceptions (see Figure 18.4) of Edinburgh to match the reality of our city in the 21st century, building on the strengths of our brand awareness as a city of heritage, history, stunning architecture, and traditional culture while overlaying this with messaging about the

FIGURE 18.4 | **Managing perceptions of the Edinburgh brand**

DEMA: CONSISTENT, COHERENT, & CONTEMPORARY MESSAGING

Our proposition needs to communicate Edinburgh's reputation as a beautiful, compact city with a unique heritage and history

And balance this with messages about Edinburgh's role as a dynamic, contemporary and innovative capital city

cosmopolitan, contemporary, innovative, dynamic, and cutting edge cultural character of Scotland's capital city.

The Destination Promotion Strategy also sets out the tactical messages the city needs to broadcast to ensure that perceptions are shifted to present the more contemporary nature of the city and that destination reputation continues to be managed. These tactical messages are shown in Figure 18.5.

FIGURE 18.5 | Edinburgh brand tactical messages

Visit	Invest
• The world's greatest stage for the world's greatest festival • Boutique city – high class, independent, human scale • You'll never have the same experience twice • Real, authentic people and place	• A global financial centre • Knowledge & R&D = innovation capital • 'In good company' (with the world's most successful companies) • Creative, competitive, & connected • A skilled – talented workforce
Live & Work	**Study**
• A dynamic career in one of the most liveable cities in the world • An active city embracing world class heritage, culture and sport • Compact and cosmopolitan • Full of green spaces and with easy reach of countryside • A place to love and raise your family	• World class academic pedigree • Graduate job opportunities in a diverse knowledge economy • Vibrant, friendly student life • Compact and accessible • Culturally diverse

DEMA's reputation management role has been tested in these straitened economic times with major shocks relating to the turmoil in the financial services sector, which remains the city's major economic sector, employing approximately 60,000 people. This is achieved through media relations activities as well as Web 2.0 social media activity utilizing, for example, blogging, Twitter, and Facebook to broadcast positive counter-balancing messages.

DEMA also continues to benchmark the success of the city in reputation and perception management through the monitoring of global city ranking studies and reports as well as monitoring of the activities and delivery models being adopted by a number of competitor cities. The Edinburgh Convention Bureau is also, for example, a member of the BestCities Global Alliance (www.bestcities.net) consortia of the world's leading business tourism destinations.

DEMA's work plan in its first year of operations 2009–2010 is focused on:

- 'brand ubiquity' – increasing support and utilization of 'Edinburgh Inspiring Capital'

- 'knowing our customers' – market intelligence

- maximization of digital platforms for building customer databases, relationships and communication

- PR messaging ('open for business' – reputation and perception management)

- leading destination promotional messaging and cross-selling

- building effective collaboration, facilitation and coordination

A good example of how cross-selling is to be achieved will be through the collaboration between DEMA and Festivals Edinburgh, the body which represents Edinburgh's 12 major festivals. The summer festivals (including the Fringe, International, Tattoo, and International Book Festivals) attract an audience that is also a key target audience for the city's talent attraction messaging. In United Kingdom terms, this audience comes from affluent areas of major metropolitan centers and many are educated young professionals. Many are first-time visitors to the city. Research has shown that those who have visited the city are more disposed to Edinburgh as a place to live, work or study following a visit to the city. DEMA can therefore add value by communicating Edinburgh's compelling live, work and study propositions to this festival audience when they are in town. Convention delegates also represent a strong target audience for similar messaging as Edinburgh's business tourism strengths link closely to its key business sectors and centers of academic excellence.

DEMA's role has been clearly defined now as a leadership role while at the same time acting as a coordinator and facilitator in a consortia approach with city partners. Thought is now being given to a name change for the new body to more clearly reflect the leadership role, with Marketing Edinburgh being the current preferred option. This is likely to be implemented when the merger takes place with the Convention Bureau and Film Location Office in 2011. In order to advance the Destination Promotion Strategy in a consortia approach, DEMA has now entered into engagement agreements with various strategic partners.

SUMMARY

The development of Edinburgh's approach to place marketing, increasingly functioning as an 'attack brand' for Scotland (often with greater brand currency than the country itself), has witnessed a marked shift over the past five years towards a more proactive and high profile approach. Edinburgh continues to offer an excellent case study in relation to emerging trends in place marketing. The strong private-public partnership in the city, the collective vision that is emerging, and the clear message that the city could not afford to become complacent because of the highly competitive global market place in which it operates, has led to the development of a powerful new city promotion leadership body in the Destination Edinburgh Marketing Alliance.

This organization in the role of custodian of the Edinburgh Inspiring Capital Brand is taking forward the thesis that competitive advantage in place marketing can be achieved from the exploitation of cross-selling opportunities across visit, invest, live, work and study (or tourism, talent and trade). Based on the new Destination Promotion Strategy for the city, DEMA is developing a set of new contemporary messages about the destination highlighting its vibrant cultural offer, quality of life, and innovation in the commercialization of the city's intellectual capital and knowledge economy.

DEMA is developing new insights into specific target audiences by committing resources to knowing our customers, such as Generation 'Y' (the 18–35 year old social media generation), seeking to utilize digital platforms and Web 2.0-based promotional (social media) messaging to communicate with these and other target audiences. The primary objective is to maintain in an increasingly dynamic marketplace the city's strong market positioning and high international brand equity, awareness and positive profile, thus ensuring that the city continues to maintain its global competitive positioning as Scotland's Inspiring Capital.

CHAPTER 19

The Hague, International City of Peace and Justice: A Relational Network Brand

Bengt-Arne B. F. Hulleman[1] and Robert Govers

INTRODUCTION

In 1993 Mr Boutros Boutros Ghali, at the time Secretary-General of the United Nations, stated that 'The Hague is the legal capital of the world'. The question is whether this free publicity and strategic advice has been built upon in the meantime. This chapter reports on a study that was conducted in order to identify which actions need to be taken in order to exploit the unique identity of the city of The Hague in order to build a global place brand. This has been done by specifically focusing on bringing together the concepts of public diplomacy, place branding, hospitality and networks in a relational network brand (Hankinson, 2004).

In 2005, The Hague started focusing on its role as a city that is host to many international organizations. Building on Mr Boutros Boutros Ghali's quote, the choice of the brand The Hague, International City of Peace and Justice, was made. Being host to many international organizations brings both economic opportunities and challenges, not only for the city but also for the country as a whole. However, it also creates responsibilities and requires specific measures to be taken so as to ensure 'customer satisfaction' or fulfilling value-matched experiences among employees and stakeholders of these international organizations, as they are

---

[1] This chapter is based on research work that was conducted as part of a successfully completed Master of Science in Hospitality Management at Erasmus University/Hotelschool The Hague and as such cannot, in any case, be considered to reflect the views of the International Criminal Court, The Hague. Robert Govers was supervisor of the research reported upon in this chapter.

instrumental in building the brand. The Hague already has a long history in hosting international players dealing with peace and justice, dating back to 1899 when the first Peace Conference was held. However, the city would have never been able to become this important a hub in hosting the international organizations without the support of the national government. In 1988, the Dutch government recognized the importance and advantages of hosting international organizations within its national borders and started a campaign to attract such organizations to be domiciled in The Netherlands (Dutch Ministry of Foreign Affairs, 2008). The economic added value of the presence of international organizations in The Hague is substantial. A recent study (Gemeente Den Haag, 2008) showed that the total economic effect in The Netherlands as a whole is close to €2 billion, consisting of both direct economic effects and of indirect effects such as expatriate spending. The effect in the Haaglanden region (Greater The Hague) is €1.6 billion, that is, 3.9 per cent of the gross regional product.

As host to international organizations, the Netherlands and especially the city of The Hague are constantly involved in public diplomacy, place branding, hospitality management and networking. The Hague therefore offers many opportunities to study the aforementioned issues and it will consequently serve as a case study in this chapter. Important hosts to international organizations in The Netherlands and as such involved in branding The Hague are two dominant actors: the Dutch Ministry of Foreign Affairs, with an emphasis on (public) diplomacy and the city of The Hague, which is trying to align its recently launched place branding policy with the concept of hospitality, being a good host to international organizations. Although there are more actors involved, including ones from the private sector, this chapter focuses on public sector initiatives. The question to be addressed is whether a network model of public diplomacy, place branding and hospitality actors leads to a strengthened brand for The Hague, International City of Peace and Justice.

CONCEPTUALIZATION

In general, one could argue that public diplomacy focuses more on international relations whereas place branding focuses more on the commercial side (Anholt, 2006b). In comparing public diplomacy and place branding, Melissen (2005) suggests that place branding involves a much greater and better coordinated effort than public diplomacy and that place branding and public diplomacy are very closely related, which explains why in recent years many Ministries of Foreign Affairs have shown a growing interest in place branding. Place branding tries to bring many things together including policy, people, sports, culture, products, tourism, trade and investment and the recruitment of talent (Anholt, 2006b). This also includes managing the level of hospitality in a place, which may indeed be one of the most important aspects in place branding, linking place identity, product offering and perception together through consumption experience (Govers and Go, 2009). Melissen (2005) argues that public diplomacy and place branding complement each other. Both focus on the image of the country as perceived by foreigners, but largely depend on the identity of the local community. Both need a long-term approach to be successful, instead of a reactive approach.

Public diplomacy and place branding focus mainly on the perceptions that people have of a place. It is the concept of hospitality that determines whether or not the image created by both concepts can be justified. But how can all these concepts be brought together? Building on network theory, Hankinson (2004) has developed the concept of relational network brands. In designing this model, Hankinson builds on his earlier work in which he argues that issues associated with organizational structure and managerial control need to be taken into account when designing a destination brand (Hankinson, 2001). In Hankinson's model, the place brand is used as the central theme with four categories of brand relationships, thus designing a small network. Hankinson states that these relationships are dynamic, they strengthen and evolve over time, and stakeholder partnerships may also change as the brand develops and repositions. He further contends that the success of cities such as Manchester, Sydney and Barcelona in building successful brands was based upon their ability to develop strong relationships between stakeholders who would benefit from that success. The main focus of this approach lies in viewing the city brand as a relationship or network, where the roles of different stakeholders in building a successful brand are recognized. Another good example is Davos, where the organization of the annual World Economic Forum has resulted in most world leaders visiting this little town and even feeling honored if they are invited to give voice to their views at that annual event. A common felt goal by the locals, long-term persistence and the will to cooperate has ensured that everyone now knows Davos (Berács, 2005).

To study the applicability of the relational network model, we adopted a case study analysis approach as it is appropriate for a thorough analysis of a single phenomenon – the application of a relational network brand – within the specific setting of one city and two lead organizations. To investigate how the research concepts are applied at the Dutch Ministry of Foreign Affairs and the city of The Hague, in-depth interviews were conducted with eight senior officials involved in place branding, public diplomacy or international hospitality within their organizations. To broaden the research, additional interviews were held with people dealing with these issues outside these two organizations. So as to facilitate triangulation of data, additional documents and websites were studied, including those of the Dutch Ministry of Foreign Affairs and the city of The Hague, as well as other organizations, describing aspects of relevance to the case study.

THE HAGUE AS A RELATIONAL NETWORK BRAND

Public diplomacy aims to influence the image that a foreign audience has about a country or city. Therefore this concept is very well suited for a relational network brand such as The Hague, International City of Peace and Justice. It would move the city forward if it is successful at building a positive international image, so as to ensure that when international organizations seek domiciliation, automatically The Hague/The Netherlands is approached. The same applies to international high-level meetings such as the 2009 conference on the future of Afghanistan, which was held in The Hague.

Place branding identifies the core brand, preferably based on a unique identity of place and competitive advantage. It tries to align the image, identity and experience and serves as the link between the concepts of public diplomacy and hospitality. The image of the brand can be influenced by the use of public diplomacy. The identity of the brand depends largely on the strength of the chosen brand and sense of belonging of all stakeholders involved in this brand. Place branding is successful when the residents of the place feel they 'are' the brand and live the brand with a strong feeling of pride. The place experience should confirm the image portrayed about the place, linking supply and demand, host and guest, interacting in the multiple forms in which hospitality exists. The Hague is slowly but surely putting more emphasis on place branding in order to be able to compete both with neighboring cities as well as cities worldwide. The concept of place branding is a key factor in the relational network brand.

Hospitality is crucial in fulfilling visitor experiences. Hospitality needs to confirm or even surpass the expectations formed by public diplomacy and place branding. In the case of The Hague, the brand International City of Peace and Justice can only be confirmed if the users of this brand feel that the level of hospitality meets their expectations. Hospitality focuses more on the demand side of the issue, trying to please the guests/visitors. To be able to fulfill the promises made by public diplomacy and place branding actors, hospitality actors need to be involved in the relational network brand; without these actors the value of the brand would diminish as promises are not delivered. Again it would help move the city forward if The Hague became known worldwide for its hospitality towards expatriates. This would be a good indicator that the brand experience dimension of the brand 'International City of Peace and Justice' is strong.

Bringing all the above stakeholders together in networks offers many synergy effects. Other cities around the world have benefited from such a network approach. The research conducted in this specific case of The Hague has shown that such an approach, certainly at local governmental level, has not yet been pursued. The government actors, however, acknowledge that a more coordinated approach should yield benefits for all parties involved in The Hague International City of Peace and Justice brand. At national government level, such a network approach is partly used in the cross-ministry steering committee 'Stuurgroep Nederland Gastland' (Steering Committee Host Country Netherlands). Nevertheless, this network only consists of actors that represent the supply side and does not involve the actors on the demand side.

In successful tourism destinations it has been established that the formation of a hub organization within the network has delivered considerable advantages. In the case of The Hague, 'The Hague International Spirit' (www. thisunites.nl/) is a good example of such a hub organization trying to bring demand and supply together involving as many parties as possible. However, contrary to international practice where such organizations are generally government controlled or sponsored, in The Hague this is largely a private initiative. The role played by the national and local government in The Netherlands/The Hague could thus be improved, further focusing on their role as a creator and facilitator of the networks dealing with 'The Hague, International City of Peace and Justice'. This facilitating role should suit the government, as it is increasingly accepted that one single government actor is no longer able to control all the channels of communication and interaction, thus forcing such actors into cooperation. Networks and a proactive approach have become essential for building a place brand. Furthermore, there seems to be a lack of coordination between the Foreign Ministry and the city of The Hague regarding how to communicate the concept of hosting international organizations. The Ministry of Foreign Affairs puts emphasis on foreign audiences whereas the City of The Hague targets its own citizens. To be able to bring a strong message across to both foreign and domestic audiences, the messages need to be aligned.

Development of a long-term vision to align the identity and experience within the City of The Hague is not yet apparent. The search for the competitive advantage of place has been done, but the alignment of image, identity and experience is still incomplete. In terms of the coordination of stakeholders and messages, no action has been taken yet. The contact between the Ministry of Foreign Affairs and the City of The Hague could be intensified as most of the international organizations in the Netherlands are domiciled in The Hague, thus making these two organizations the most important stakeholders on the supply side.

A 3-CONCEPT PERSPECTIVE ON THE HAGUE'S CITY BRAND

Based on the results described above, it can be concluded that not only for The Hague but also for other cities dealing with place branding, the three concepts researched – place branding, public diplomacy, and hospitality – fit very well into a network. The concepts partly overlap but also strongly complement each other. Place branding is the umbrella concept; public diplomacy strengthens the image and perception of the place brand; hospitality takes care of the place brand experience; and the network brings all the actors together and aligns them. This alignment offers possibilities for synergy effects resulting in a stronger brand.

It is irrefutable that The Hague has a rich history in the fields of Peace and Justice. This history, however, seems relatively little known to The Hague's local residents and to the Dutch general public. Being the International City of Peace and Justice could be a very strong competitive advantage for the city based on the presence of international organizations. Focusing its place branding on this competitive advantage will result in both economic and political advantages for the city of The Hague and its residents. Many stakeholders are involved in this brand and the branding process, but it has not yet resulted in a real commonly felt identity on which all actions are focused. Therefore, at this moment, the branding can still cause many conflicts of interest among stakeholders involved.

Up to now, The Hague has followed a more reactive approach to public diplomacy, place branding and hospitality management and has given limited attention to the concept of networking. Important advantages can, however, be obtained when taking a more holistic, long-term approach. This encompasses bringing together all actors involved in the concepts mentioned, with The Hague's city officials taking on a leading role within the networks. Furthermore, it also requires coordination with the national government departments in consideration of their respective roles at the national level in the process of attracting and hosting international organizations.

The introduction of a hub organization that deals with the branding of 'The Hague International City of Peace and Justice' as an intermediary within the network is advisable. This hub organization should act independently and have the power to make decisions that are in the interest of strengthening the brand. This ensures a long-term commitment to building a sustainable brand and makes sure that political changes in the future, and different political agendas in the present constellation, are overcome.

SUMMARY

This chapter has examined how the city of The Hague can strengthen its recently launched branding as the International City of Peace and Justice by asking whether a network model of public diplomacy, place branding and hospitality actors leads to a strengthened brand of the city of The Hague by attracting and benefiting from the image effects of international organizations. To answer this question, several interviews were conducted with the main government stakeholders involved in this brand: the Dutch Ministry of Foreign Affairs and the city of The Hague itself, in addition to a content analysis of policy documents and websites. The results show that both government actors face several challenges. The city of The Hague is recommended to take on a more holistic approach to branding the city as International City of Peace and Justice and to be more proactive in facilitating the different networks that have recently started to develop. The installation of a hub organization could solve the challenges of sudden changes in the political landscape and agendas and make sure that the desired long-term approach can be guaranteed through long-term and intense cooperation. It is concluded that public diplomacy, place branding and hospitality actors can easily be brought together into a network because they partly overlap, but also, and more importantly, they complement each other, which will lead to synergy effects and therefore a strengthening of the brand of The Hague, International City of Peace and Justice.

ACKNOWLEDGEMENTS

The authors would like to thank the Dutch Ministry of Foreign Affairs and the city of The Hague for providing access to the data required to perform this study. We are particularly indebted to Mr Zaagman, Ambassador for International Organizations at the Ministry of Foreign Affairs and Mr Dijkstra, Deputy Head of the International Desk at the city of The Hague, for their support.

CHAPTER 20

Brand Hong Kong

Grace Loo, Saumya Sindhwani, Cai Jing and Theresa Loo

INTRODUCTION

A city brand is a complex entity. It has to encompass all the different facets of a city and face multiple stakeholders with a coherent image. Often, the different facets of the city brand may not be well coordinated, or the city image may leverage excessively on its tourism image. Brand Hong Kong, however, is a case of successful city branding in terms of its well-balanced character. The brand captures the spirit of the city's people and its core competences, from attracting foreign direct investment to tourism and culture. The different pillars under the overall city brand positioning are compatible and mutually supportive when taken together. Hong Kong's branding strategy builds on what the city has and provides a blueprint to identify areas in which it should engage in further development. The successful branding exercise is one of the reasons why Hong Kong ranks among the top five global cities behind New York, London, Paris, and Tokyo in the 2008 Global Cities Index (*Foreign Policy*, 2009).

MANAGEMENT OF BRAND HONG KONG

The Hong Kong government began exploring branding in 1996 out of fear that the return of sovereignty to China in 1997 would affect the city's status as a trading, financial and logistics center. In the years immediately following the handover, the government began to take action in using city branding to differentiate Hong Kong from its competitors. The government's vision was for Hong Kong to become a world class city on par with New York and London. In 2000, a report was released (Commission on Strategic Development, 2000) on the city's long-term development over the next 30 years. Its vision for the city is to achieve both economic prosperity and a high quality of life.

The Brand Hong Kong initiative is coordinated by the government's Information Services Department, which works with different bodies to ensure the projection of a consistent branding message (Advisory Council on the Environment, 2008). Brand Hong Kong was launched in 2001 before an international audience at the FORTUNE Global Forum. It positioned the city as 'Asia's World City', a place 'where opportunity, creativity and entrepreneurship converge'. This positioning reflects the fact that Hong Kong is strategically located to be a dynamic physical and cultural hub in Asia. It has a network of people with an impressive record of success that can make things happen. Brand Hong Kong presents the city as offering unlimited potential and unsurpassed opportunities. Having the quality of East meets West, Hong Kong has a contemporary outlook and business culture, yet is rich in culture and tradition. The city is also open to innovation and vision. All these facets converged together under a city brand that has the following core values: progressive, free, stable, opportunity and high quality. A dragon logo was designed to capture the positioning and core values of the city for the world to see. It incorporates the letters H and K and the Chinese characters for Hong Kong. The dual expression of the dragon image symbolizes a combination of modernity and antiquity, and the meeting of East and West. It also suggests Hong Kong's passion for the daring and innovative, incorporating a can-do spirit which brings visionary ideas to life.

The Brand Hong Kong communications plan unifies a wide range of activities, publicity events, advertising and promotion. The brand values and attributes are reinforced in a number of ways, particularly through co-branding and association with particular events and programs both within Hong Kong and abroad. A wide range of activities have been organized in diverse areas covering culture, sport, fashion, finance and so on, in order to appeal to a broad spectrum of different audiences. Some of the key dimensions of Brand Hong Kong are discussed in the following sections.

TOURISM

Hong Kong wants to become the ultimate travel destination in Asia. Yet it does not have much in terms of natural tourism resources, especially when compared to other cities in China. Therefore, it develops its initiatives towards entertainment and leisure.

Tourism plays an important role in the Hong Kong economy, comprising 3.4 per cent of its GDP in 2008 (Hong Kong Information Services Department, 2009). The Hong Kong Tourism Board launches new marketing campaigns each year to showcase the diverse range of attractions and activities available in Hong Kong, including shopping, dining, and cultural heritage.

It runs mega-events and promotes cultural festivals to attract tourists. It also leverages the city's geographical position as the gateway to China by engaging in joint promotions with tourism bureaus in the Pearl River Delta to promote multi-destination tourism. Furthermore, the Hong Kong government devotes significant resources to the development of a wide range of world class tourism projects. Examples include Hong Kong Disneyland, Hong Kong Wetland Park, and Ngong Ping 360 (see Table 20.1).

TABLE 20.1   Initiatives by the Hong Kong Tourist Association

Date	Initiative
2003	Hong Kong – Live it, Love it
2003–2004	Seeing is Believing
2005–2006	Hong Kong Disneyland, Ngong Ping 360, Hong Kong Wetland Park
2006	Discover Hong Kong Year
2007	Hong Kong Shopping Festival, Hong Kong Salsa Festival
2008	Olympic Games Equestrian Events
2009	East Asian Games, Hong Kong Food and Wine Year

The initiatives shown in Table 20.1 demonstrate the multidimensional nature of Brand Hong Kong and its attempts to promote itself as a vibrant city brand.

The government also takes a proactive approach in diversifying the territory's tourism industry. Hong Kong is now a popular place for meetings, conventions and exhibitions in Asia, with more than 300 events taking place each year (Hong Kong Information Services Department, 2008). Hong Kong has become associated with a wide range of events such as the Fortune Global Forum, Forbes Global CEO Conference, World Newspaper Congress, Hong Kong International Rugby Sevens, and the Hong Kong International Cricket Sixes. The territory is also a popular medical tourism destination, especially with mainland Chinese, offering low-cost services with high quality. In 2008, the government began to explore marketing its traditional Chinese medicine capabilities to overseas visitors.

CULTURE AND CREATIVITY

In the early 2000s the government began championing the development of creative industries such as design, advertising, music, film, digital entertainment, performing arts, broadcasting, antiques and art dealing (Hong Kong

General Chamber of Commerce, 2003). It provided funding for design-related activities; created the Hong Kong Design Center, which organized the Business of Design Week, a major international design, branding and innovation conference in Asia. It also established Create HK, an agency dedicated to driving Hong Kong's creative economy. In 2005, the development of cultural and creative industries was included as part of the program to sustain Hong Kong's world city status. The Hong Kong government banks on what it already has existing in the city and then consciously builds up what else is necessary to make the city a cultural and creative stronghold. Hong Kong already has the third largest art auction market in the world (Seno, 2009). Though its film industry has declined since its heydays in the late 1980s and early 1990s, it has nonetheless continued to maintain a presence in international cinema. Separately, its animation industry is also making progress. The comic character turned movie star McDull, a pink piglet that is not very smart but always tries hard, has spawned high success domestically and amongst the Chinese diaspora all over the world.

INVESTMENT

As a place of investment, Hong Kong is attractive to both mainland Chinese and overseas investors. According to the 2010 Index of Economic Freedom (Heritage Foundation, 2010), Hong Kong has been ranked the freest economy for 16 consecutive years. It also ranked second in the Ernst & Young Globalization Index 2009 (Ernst & Young, 2009). A stable government, good law and order, open access to information, solid banking and financial systems, low tax rates and excellent geographical location, plus a highly skilled and motivated labor force, are all incentives for foreign investors. In terms of attracting foreign direct investment, the Hong Kong Trade Development Council, with its wide network of offices all over the world, enhances business relationships with current and potential investors.

PEOPLE

The people of Hong Kong have abilities that exemplify the essence of Hong Kong as 'Asia's World City'. They have a high level of education, good language skills and are well-versed in doing business in the international arena. These skill sets are combined with a 'can-do' spirit (Gilmore, 2002) and an ability to think on their feet and be flexible in getting things done. Individuals who contribute to the Brand Hong Kong equity include Li Ka Shing (entrepreneur), Jackie Chan (movie star) and John Woo (movie director).

They prominently exemplify the essence of Brand Hong Kong on the world stage.

PRODUCTS AND SERVICES

While still famous for its high quality production of garments, timepieces, toys, electronics and light industrial products, most production activity has now moved north into China. Hong Kong's economy now places more emphasis upon services and focuses on information technology, multimedia technologies, telecommunication services, trading and transportation, and so on. Hong Kong has also shifted towards higher end services such as investment banking, asset management and finance. Corporate brands such as HSBC and Cathay Pacific, which are internationally famous, act as endorsements for Brand Hong Kong.

SUMMARY

Maintaining a city brand is an ongoing exercise. To this end, the Hong Kong government has been relentless in its efforts to ensure that Brand Hong Kong is kept up to date. In 2006, a Brand Hong Kong Group was formed to ensure that the brand is sustained both locally and overseas. Two years later, the government launched an initiative to review the shared vision of the community for the future of Hong Kong and what Brand Hong Kong should stand for in 2020. In this exercise, public response showed that cultural heritage and the environment had taken on an increasingly important role in the public's mind (Wong, 2008). It will be interesting to see how Brand Hong Kong incorporates these concerns of the Hong Kong people into its image in the future.

CHAPTER 21

Kuala Lumpur: Searching for the Right Brand

Ghazali Musa and T. C. Melewar

INTRODUCTION

City branding is a relatively new concept which has been adopted by cities in their efforts to differentiate themselves from other cities, to instill civic pride in their residents and to help the decision making of visitors and businesses. This chapter begins with a consideration of the definition of city branding. This is followed by an examination of the various developments and activities carried out in Kuala Lumpur, which represent attributes that carry city brand values. These values direct the authors to the construction of a possible distinct brand for Kuala Lumpur, a city which is yet to define its own unique brand. The chapter concludes with a proposed promotional brand tagline for Kuala Lumpur which encompasses all the identified values and an icon that can represent the city brand.

DEFINING CITY BRANDING

The conceptualization of the city as a brand (Kavaratzis and Ashworth, 2007) builds upon Aaker's (1996: 68) definition of a brand as a 'multi-dimensional construct, consisting of functional, emotional, relational and strategic elements that collectively generate a unique set of associations in the public mind'. The concept of city branding is largely derived from the corporate branding literature (see for example, Balmer and Greyser, 2003), whereby the whole organization is branded, and multiple stakeholders are addressed. In the context of cities, stakeholders view the city brand as a single entity with values which represent the city's attributes bound together by a vision which gives them meaning, impetus and direction (Kavaratzis and Ashworth, 2006). The branding of a city demands the identification and communication of believable and realistic city attributes. The attributes need to be built into the city through planning and design interventions, infrastructure development and organizational structure (Kavaratzis, 2004). These attributes must then be communicated through promotional activities. Trueman, Klemm and Giroud (2004) propose that the communication of the city should have a distinctive appeal and be valid, believable, and simple. The following section details the attributes which are being created in Kuala Lumpur in an effort to differentiate it from other cities in the region.

PLACE BRANDING EFFORTS OF KUALA LUMPUR

According to Ashworth (2009), place branding is the idea of discovering or creating some uniqueness which differentiates one place from others in order to gain a competitive brand value. Ashworth goes on to elaborate that such uniqueness is normally created through three efforts: personality association, flagship building (signature urban design and signature district) and hallmark events. Personality association takes place when cities associate themselves with specific individuals (normally an artistic personality), in the hope that the unique qualities of the individual are transferred to the place. Kuala Lumpur lacks such association with artistic personalities. However, celebrity branding could be promoted by Kuala Lumpur, especially among citizens who have an international presence, such as Datuk Michelle Yeo (a famous actress), Jimmy Choo (a celebrity shoe maker) and Tun Dr Mahathir Mohamed (a famous politician). Two excellent sports personalities are Datuk Nicol Ann David and Datuk Lee Chong Wei, who are the current world number one female squash player and male badminton player respectively. Another prominent name is Dato' Tony Fernandes who has led AirAsia to become hailed as the best low cost airline in the world (Hooi, 2009). All these names could be used to endorse Kuala Lumpur as a city which is active and vibrant with talents.

Flagship buildings are the visual qualities of buildings and urban design that could be used in order to stimulate wider cultural and economic development of the city (Ashworth, 2009). This could include an individual flagship building, signature urban design and signature districts. Such physical developments can make important statements about a city brand. The example of a flagship building in Kuala Lumpur is the Petronas Twin Towers, which represents a deliberate government-sponsored statement to position Malaysia on the world map (Sya, 2005). The towers are not only glorious in height but also majestic in their beauty and unique architectural design. The building has been recognized as among the top 20 of the world's best city icons (Boer, 2009).

Another physical manifestation of signature city developments in Malaysia can be seen in the planned city of Putrajaya to the south of Kuala Lumpur, which is the new federal administrative capital of Malaysia, with investment capital of US$16 billion. The city design of Putrajaya is unique with its blend of Islamic and modern architecture. The street lights and the several bridges were built beyond their utilitarian purposes. Also known as 'City in a Garden', 60 per cent of its land area is covered with greenery, open spaces and parks, and a 600 hectare man-made lake. Putrajaya sits within the Multimedia Super Corridor (MSC) and has been developed as an intelligent city with multimedia technologies to facilitate communication among Government offices, the business community and residents. There is a plan to develop the city and its neighbor Cyberjaya as carbon-neutral cities (*New Straits Times*, 2010). All buildings in Putrajaya and Cyberjaya need to be certified by the Green Building Index (*New Straits Times*, 2010). This development gives Kuala Lumpur the image of a modern and innovative city.

Kuala Lumpur also has distinctive districts that represent important attributes of the overall city brand. Examples of such districts in Kuala Lumpur are Bangsar, Bukit Bintang and China Town. Bangsar is both an entertainment and residential area for affluent city dwellers. There is a huge expatriate community who live in the area, attracted by its low rise, low density, greenery and high quality living. Bangsar is often equated to Holland Village in Singapore. Bukit Bintang is perhaps the most popular destination for both domestic and international tourists. The area is a stone's throw from the Central Business District and the iconic Petronas Twin Towers. It contains many luxurious five star hotels, as well as trendy shopping centers such as the Pavilion and the Starhill Gallery. The third unique district is China Town. The area is famous for its night market and bargain shopping. All three districts contribute to the images of diversity, vibrancy and tolerance in Kuala Lumpur.

In terms of hallmark events, Kuala Lumpur has leveraged the city brand-building potential of such events by hosting the Commonwealth Games in 1998 (Musa, 2000: 146). This was the first time the Commonwealth Games host city had been situated in Asia. The Games were attended by 70 countries which sent a total of 5,250 athletes and officials. The government spent US$5 billion (RM21 billion) to complete Games-related mega projects including Kuala Lumpur International Airport, roads, stadia and other facilities such as the International Broadcasting Centre. The Formula One motor racing which is held yearly in Kuala Lumpur creates huge awareness of the city around the world. Other than hosting sporting events which portray images of the city as vibrant and active, the city also hosted the World Halal Forum in 2009. Kuala Lumpur has affirmed its Islamic credentials through economic activities such as Islamic Banking and halal food production.

CREATION OF THE CITY OF KNOWLEDGE THROUGH DEVELOPMENT AND IMPROVEMENT OF INFRASTRUCTURE AND SERVICES

Edvinsson (2006) has stated that a knowledge city is purposely designed for encouraging and nourishing intellectual capital. The creative class appreciate talent, technology and tolerance, and is attracted by the labor markets, a diversity of cultural scenes and vibrant lifestyle amenities. Kuala Lumpur was described by Edvinsson (2006: 8) as one of the most impressive and interesting examples of a knowledge city. The MSC was initiated in 1996 by then Prime Minister, Dr Mahathir Mohamed, in line with the Vision 2020 which aimed at achieving a developed nation status by 2020. MSC was intended to attract the import of foreign knowledge migration and investment. The corridor, which covers an area of 750 square kilometers from Kuala Lumpur International Airport to Kuala Lumpur City Centre, functions as a modern free port area with impressive information and communication technologies (ICT) infrastructure for foreign partnerships (www.msc.com.my). New establishments into this area receive a special attractive MSC status which offers free flow of knowledge migration, few currency restrictions, and tax-free status for the first ten years. A total of 22,000 jobs have been created and more than 1000 international companies are now located within the MSC (Edvinsson, 2006).

A short distance from Putrajaya is another vibrant city, launched in 1999, called Cyberjaya. Its development adds further to the country's status as a knowledge-based economy. Cyberjaya promotes itself as a regional and global ICT hub (www.cyberjaya-msc.com/cyberjaya-town.asp). When completed, Cyberjaya's population is expected to be 210,000 with business developments providing for up to 120,000 employees and 30,000 students. Cyberjaya is home to many multinational companies such as Shell, EDS, Ericsson, BMW, HSBC and DHL. It is also the chosen location for some of the nation's top schools and institutions such as Limkokwing University College of Creative Technology, Multimedia University, and Cyberjaya University College of Medical Sciences. Many private colleges have sprung up with a great number of them twinning with prestigious universities overseas. International students in Kuala Lumpur numbered 70,259 in 2008 (Education Malaysia, 2009) and are expected to reach 100,000 by 2010 (Robertson,

2008). The development of Kuala Lumpur as a city of knowledge carries images of a modern, innovative and progressive city.

The city's progress is also reflected in the improvement of services and infrastructure in Kuala Lumpur. Transportation facilities and services are an example. In 2009, government committed to spend the sum of RM35 billion to improve traffic congestion in the city over the period 2009 to 2014 (*The Star Online*, 2008). The Light Rail Transport system in Kuala Lumpur will be extended to benefit 2.6 million residents upon its completion. There are plans to increase the green spaces for residents, to reduce traffic congestion and to increase pedestrian walkways (Kuala Lumpur City Hall, 2008). Already the country's manufacturing products have shown a remarkable commitment to quality, design and innovation (Sya, 2005). The technology used for the development of the SMART tunnel and monorail are evidence in Kuala Lumpur of innovation in design and quality.

BRANDING THE CITY FOR TOURISM DEVELOPMENT AND INTERNAL AUDIENCES

Kuala Lumpur as a city benefits from tourism development at the national level. Over 50 per cent of international tourists who come to Malaysia visit Kuala Lumpur. The country has promoted itself using the tagline 'Malaysia Truly Asia' for a decade with notable success (Sya, 2005). Malaysia is proud of its large multi-ethnic populations of Malay, Chinese, Indian and indigenous people, who live in harmony to practice and celebrate their religious beliefs and festivals. Malaysia attracted 22 million tourists in 2008, which is substantially more than its stronger tourist image neighbors of Singapore (10 million) and Thailand (14 million) (Zanina, 2010). Even though Kuala Lumpur has been identified as the cheapest city in the world (Finfacts, 2008), its attractions, services and infrastructure are comparable to those of cities in the developed world (Sya, 2005). Thus the city has a strong image of value for money (Finfacts, 2008) and as the world's best travel bargain (Sesser, 2006).

In searching for the brand for Malaysia, the Prime Minister, Dato Seri Najib Tun Razak in one of his speeches stated that diversity is how Malaysia could define its identity, together with a moderate outlook and progressive practice of Islam and in the post-September 11 period, Malaysia has gained a justifiable reputation as a progressive, modern and moderate Muslim country (Sya, 2005). The country is spared from terrorism. Kuala Lumpur is the main representative of Malaysian diversity and moderate Islamic practices, and these could easily be adopted as attributes for the Kuala Lumpur brand. The city continues to attract the highest growth of tourists from the

Middle East (Ariffin and Hasim, 2009). The strict Islamic codes in their home countries may have drawn the tourists from that region, in search for a more relaxed and tolerant Islamic culture. At the same time these tourists may avoid the possible prejudices of the west.

In addition to the promotion to attract tourists, the government also launched its most recent campaign of 1Malaysia. The campaign is intended to strengthen the unity of different races in the country and strongly emphasizes the government's seriousness in the matter (*Daily Express, East Malaysia*, 2009). This demonstrates the tolerance and diversity of the country and of Kuala Lumpur, as well as acknowledges the importance of engaging as full a range of possible of stakeholders in the branding of the city and country.

WHAT IS THE BRAND OF KUALA LUMPUR?

Many efforts have been carried out to create images, attributes and values of Kuala Lumpur which could be communicated to stakeholders. The question remaining to be answered is how such attributes and values can be fitted by any city into a single brand which is consistent and unique (Chalip and Costa, 2005). From the description of attributes for Kuala Lumpur as discussed earlier, the city possesses values of being active, vibrant, modern, innovative, progressive, diverse, tolerant, and offering value for money. These attributes show that Kuala Lumpur has its brand values in place. All the values listed could be shortened to five without sacrificing any major values, as follows: modern, vibrant, progressive, value for money and tolerant.

Attaching these values to a single brand is the next task. There is a current campaign for the country to be described as 'Malaysia Boleh' or 'Malaysia Can Do It', mainly to promote an ambitious spirit in the people (AllMalaysia, 2010). However, this spirit could also be extended to other stakeholders such as visitors and businesses. Therefore we propose that for consistency of promotional message, the spirit of 'Malaysia Boleh' should also be adopted by the city as 'Kuala Lumpur Boleh', or 'Kuala Lumpur Can Do It'. All the brand values that have been discussed could fit in easily to this brand and could be communicated to all residents, visitors and businesses.

For the purpose of easy recall the city brand requires an icon. A consultation study carried out by Kuala Lumpur City Council in 2008, which surveyed quantitatively and qualitatively all the main tourism stakeholders (travel agents, hotel managers, tourist guides, academicians, domestic tourists and international tourists), stated that the Twin Towers should be the icon of

Kuala Lumpur (DBKL, 2008). According to Sya (2005), the Twin Towers are a symbol of Malaysia's vibrancy, progress and potential and the impressive structure boosts national confidence and redefines the country's identity, reputation and image as an independent, ambitious and forward-looking country. The government should recognize this fact and feature the Twin Towers on postage stamps and other official paraphernalia, and the private sector should use them in their design, packaging and promotional material as a symbol of Malaysian progress and quality.

SUMMARY

In summary, the Kuala Lumpur Brand could be represented by the tagline of 'Kuala Lumpur Can Do It', which supports similar branding efforts by Malaysia at the national level and which carries the values of the city as modern, vibrant, progressive, value for money and tolerant. The Petronas Twin Towers is the best icon for Kuala Lumpur as they carry the elements of vibrancy, progress and potential. With the brand and icon in place, Kuala Lumpur could start its international branding communication with a close partnership between the private and public sectors, in order to ensure that the brand is successfully impressed on the mind of residents, visitors and businesses as unique and distinctive compared with other cities in the region.

CHAPTER 22

Branding Lisbon – Defining the Scope of the City Brand

João Ricardo Freire

INTRODUCTION

It can be argued that place branding is now a well-established concept. The last few years have witnessed a flow of new research and publications in the area. The year 2002 can be seen as a pivotal one for the field. In that year, Nigel Morgan, Annette Pritchard and Roger Pride (2002) edited a book titled *Destination Branding: Creating the Unique Destination Proposition*. This book, a collection of articles within the place branding field, was the first of its kind. That same year, the *Journal of Brand Management* published a special issue dedicated exclusively to place branding. In 2004, following the success of that special issue and the increasing interest in the area, the publishers launched a new journal named *Place Branding* – now renamed *Place Branding and Public Diplomacy* – with articles focused on the branding of places. Four years later, Keith Dinnie (2008) published *Nation Branding – Concepts, Issues, Practice*, the first academic book written exclusively on the topic of nation branding. Since then there has been a considerable number of new book publications in the area of place branding.

Thus the issue of branding places is well established and is now part of the agenda in most cities, regions and countries. In fact, most places are now sensitive to the issue of branding and are actively trying to apply the concept to their places. Places are now expected to invest and develop strategies to increase the attractiveness of their brands. Although branding techniques can and should be applied to places, it is also true that their application sometimes diverges from the application of such techniques to product and service brands. In fact, the branding exercise applied to places is often more complex than the branding exercise applied to products and services (Freire, 2005). One of the challenges, for example, associated with place branding is ownership. Product or service brands normally belong to an organization, which manages the brands in a specific manner in order to fulfil certain objectives. Furthermore those branded products, services or concepts are protected by legal mechanisms that give exclusive ownership to the organizations.

In contrast, a place is composed of a number of different and independent organizations, which indicates that it is not clear who actually owns the brand. There are the local, regional and national agencies that have concrete planning objectives. There are also a number of privately owned organizations that pursue their own objectives. Adding to this complexity it cannot be forgotten that the people living in each particular place have the freedom to act as they wish (Freire, 2009). This is in contrast to organizations where managers have direct control over their employees, recruiting only the ones that share the same values as the brand. Places, obviously, will have to deal with a multitude of stakeholders who will have different goals, values, attitudes and beliefs.

Another problem with managing places as brands is linked to the definition of the brand. While a product or a service brand's offer is clear and well defined, the place brand's offer is sometimes not clear and often difficult to define. What area does the place brand cover? What is the geographical scope of the brand? These are important and occasionally overlooked questions. In fact, the brand created to represent a particular area might have broader meaning for the target consumers than the one anticipated by the organization that manages the brand. Consumers' image and definition of the place brand might be different than initially planned. It is in this sense one can argue that branding places is highly complex and achieving a predetermined positioning will be more difficult than if one is dealing with a product or service brand.

The Portugal Tourism Board recently felt these difficulties in managing places as brands when they reorganized Portugal's tourism regions. Mainland Portugal is now divided into 11 tourism regions: Porto e Norte de Portugal, Douro, Centro de Portugal, Serra da Estrela, Leiria-Fátima, Lisboa e Vale do Tejo, Oeste, Alentejo, Alentejo Litoral, Alqueva and the Algarve. These regions were created to be managed as brands and each has a dedicated regional organization responsible for managing its image.

Prior to the creation of the 11 tourism regions or place brands supported and recognized by the Portuguese Tourism Board, a number of individual organizations took responsibility for managing the image for many more, smaller place brands. However, there was a lack of rationale for the scope and geographical coverage for each of these smaller brands and therefore some of the organizations were underfunded and inefficient. For these reasons the Portugal Tourism Board believed in the need to integrate and merge some of the regions which created, in effect, new tourism regions or place brands. These new place brands would obtain economies of scale and would provide better geographical coverage for the entire tourism system of Portugal. The objective was to have fewer tourism regions but for each region to have better resources in order to improve efficiency.

The 11 organizations in charge of the 11 different tourism regions had at their disposal several marketing variables that could be used to manage their regions in order to reach a set of proposed objectives. The goal of each regional organization was the management of these marketing variables with the intention of influencing the behavior of a selected target group. Infrastructure, attractions, landscape, quality of life and people are a few examples of the marketing variables available to the place brand managers. It was then important for the managers within each organization to understand the role each variable had on their region's brand image formation. It was felt that each manager could only successfully work with the variables if they knew the relevant impact of the variables on brand image formation.

In this context the Portugal Tourism Board initiated a research project to identify and understand the variables that Portuguese tourists used to form the image of the 11 tourism regions. This study was especially relevant because some of the tourism regions, such as Lisboa e Vale do Tejo (Lisbon and the Tagus Valley), were new regional creations with new naming. Other place brands, such as Alentejo or the Algarve were existing regions and therefore consumers could already easily identify their meaning. From the research it became clear that the integration and creation of new place brands solved some of the efficiency problems. However, the integration also created a new set of problems as some of the newly created place brands did not have a clear meaning or significance for the market.

BRAND LISBOA E VALE DO TEJO

The region Lisboa e Vale do Tejo, for example, demonstrates the problems and difficulties of managing places as brands. The new brand Lisboa e Vale do Tejo covers an extensive area and incorporates the city of Lisbon, which itself constitutes just a small part of the new tourism region. During the research conducted by the Portuguese Tourism Board, when the Portuguese consumers were asked for their image of Lisboa e Vale do Tejo the majority had nothing to say about the region; for consumers, the brand Lisboa e Vale do Tejo had little meaning.

One of the problems with the brand Lisboa e Vale do Tejo is its apparent lack of focus. The brand unites the city of Lisbon, which is urban and cosmopolitan, with the area of Vale do Tejo, which includes rural areas, natural parks and picturesque cities like Santarém. Combining so many different offers defined by distinct variables under the same brand name created a complex and incongruous brand image. In fact, the majority of the research participants could not even clearly define the brand's boundaries. Due to the lack of focus and meaning of the brand Lisboa e Vale do Tejo, another problem emerged. When the participants were asked, or forced, to define their image of Lisboa e Vale do Tejo there was a general trend for the participants to focus on variables that characterized the urban area of Lisbon. Nightlife, restaurants, museums, art galleries and shopping centers were some of the relevant variables used to define the brand. These variables are strongly associated with the urban area of Lisbon yet have little meaning for the more rural area of Vale do Tejo.

Consequently, it can be concluded that using the same brand name to represent the city of Lisbon plus the extensive and diverse area of Vale do Tejo can be considered a risky solution. Lisbon overpowers the rest of the region and consequently the brand name benefits the urban area of Lisbon but jeopardizes the rest of the area. The area of Vale do Tejo tends to be ignored by the market. Hence, the brand name Lisboa e Vale do Tejo to represent this new tourism region might not be the optimal solution. Possible solutions in overcoming this problem might be the creation of two different brands: Brand Lisboa and Brand Vale do Tejo, or creating a new name to represent the area of Vale do Tejo.

BRAND LISBOA VERSUS CITY OF LISBON

Branding Lisboa, however, faces its own challenges and difficulties. Lisbon is a city defined by clear boundaries. The city is managed by a mayor and city hall. Nonetheless, one may ask if the brand Lisboa covers only the area of the city of Lisbon. If the answer is yes and if the brand Lisboa covers exactly the same area defined by boundaries of the city of Lisbon, then the owner and manager of the brand Lisboa should be the responsibility of Lisbon's mayoral office. If the answer is no and if the brand Lisboa does not coincide with the defined boundaries of the city, then the ownership and the management of the brand Lisboa should not be the exclusive responsibility of Lisbon's mayoral office. In this case, the management of brand Lisboa should be shared with the other cities that compose the brand. The issue then becomes: What is the brand Lisboa? How can the brand Lisboa be defined? Which geographical area does the brand Lisboa cover?

For Portuguese consumers, the brand Lisboa appears to cover an area larger than the city of Lisbon. When consumers were asked to define their image of the brand Lisboa, they repeatedly used variables, such as, art galleries, restaurants, nightlife, shopping, beaches and sea. These last two variables, beaches and sea, that consumers used to define the brand indicate that, in fact, brand Lisboa is composed not only of the city of Lisbon but also of some of the cities surrounding Lisbon. This is a reasonable conclusion since the city of Lisbon does not have any beaches while cities bordering Lisbon, such as Oeiras or Cascais, have beaches. In fact, when consumers were directly asked if neighboring cities like Cascais, Oeiras and Sintra belonged to Lisboa the great majority considered that yes, those cities were part of the brand Lisboa.

Therefore, for the Portuguese, the brand Lisboa is composed not only of the city of Lisbon but also of some of the neighboring cities. In fact, it was the variables from the other cities that made the brand Lisboa so attractive when compared to other destinations. The beaches and casino of Cascais and the gardens and palaces of Sintra, for example, were important variables in characterizing the brand Lisboa. Hence, in order to maximize the attraction of the brand Lisboa, its definition should include other cities such as Cascais, Oeiras and Sintra. These cities, however, might resist the idea of being included in the brand Lisboa. These cities might argue that they are sacrificing their own brands to the city of Lisbon's gain. Although these arguments might be valid, the reality is that there is a symbiotic relationship between the city of Lisbon and its neighboring cities. Therefore, on the one hand there are advantages for these neighboring cities to be included in the brand Lisboa as these cities benefit from the power of attraction of the city of Lisbon. On the other hand, the brand Lisboa is leveraged and becomes more valuable if it includes not only variables of the city of Lisbon but also variables from the neighboring cities.

SUMMARY

To conclude, although the city of Lisbon is a well-defined concept, the definition of brand Lisboa is open for debate. The definition of the brand Lisboa, in fact, should be broader than the city of Lisbon and should include some of its neighboring cities. Therefore, the city of Lisbon and the surrounding cities, each with their individual objectives and functions, should be seen as belonging to a common structure. The conceptualization of this structure is an exercise in brand architecture, which in this context seeks the optimization of each of the brands' variables in order to benefit the whole. It is then important to consider the scope of the brand and which kind of brand architecture maximizes the efficiency of the brand Lisboa and all the other brands that are part of it. The essential point to guarantee the success of brand Lisboa is to make sure that there is the creation of a common platform where all relevant stakeholders from the different cities can communicate and share their vision. It is their role not only to develop a vision of what the brand is and what the brand wants to achieve, but also to consider the best method of how to achieve that goal.

From the recent experience of the Portugal Tourism Board and the difficulties encountered with branding the region of Lisboa and Vale do Tejo, it can be concluded that the definition of the scope of the brand is an extremely relevant aspect for place brand management. This aspect must be taken into account when building or developing a brand identity for a city or a region. How broad the place brand should be is a matter that must be strategically analyzed and well thought out. Nevertheless, this important issue in place brand building is sometimes overlooked.

CHAPTER 23

Montevideo City Branding

Pablo Hartmann

INTRODUCTION

Montevideo is the capital and principal city of the Oriental Republic of Uruguay. It is also the administrative seat of Mercosur and of ALADI, the Latin American Integration Association. The city of Montevideo is situated in the south of Uruguay, on the coast of the River Plate with a bay that is a natural port which, since its foundation by the Spanish at the beginning of the 18th century, became the route that linked Buenos Aires and Rio de Janeiro with the European ports. Due to its strategic position, Montevideo was occupied by the English for a year in 1807. In 1930 Montevideo hosted the first FIFA World Cup, which was won by the Uruguayan team. At present, Montevideo is one of Mercosur's main points of cargo movement and one of the main ports of the Southern Cone.

The population of Montevideo is 1.3 million. The city's most distinctive characteristic is open urbanism with many green areas and parks and numerous historical, cultural and geographic attractions. The streets are lined with 150,000 trees. A recent survey carried out by Mercer Human Resource Consulting (2008) showed Montevideo to be the city in South America with the highest quality of living and also one of the safest cities in the world.

THE IMPORTANCE OF TOURISM FOR URUGUAY AND FOR THE CITY OF MONTEVIDEO

The arrival of tourists to South America is strongly influenced by intra-regional tourism. In fact, visitors from the region represent almost 80 per cent of tourists in South America.

With approximately two million tourists per year, Uruguay is the fourth top tourist destination in South America with a market share of around 10 per cent, behind Brazil, Argentina and Chile. In 2008, tourism in Uruguay generated an income representing six per cent of GDP. Tourism generates more than 125,000 direct jobs. The principal markets which generate tourism to Uruguay are Argentina, Brazil, North America and Europe. Many of the visitors from the northern hemisphere are Uruguayan nationals, who represent 14 per cent of arrivals and are the third market in importance following tourists from Argentina (50 per cent) and Brazil (16 per cent). Visitors to Uruguay are very loyal and generally return more than once. The majority of tourists (93 per cent) have visited Uruguay before and three out of four tourists have made more than four visits. The main reasons for visiting Uruguay are rest and recreation (65.5 per cent), to visit family and friends (21.3 per cent), business tourism (5.4 per cent) and tourism in transit to other destinations (4 per cent).

In 2008, the city of Montevideo received 688,331 visitors, of which 87 per cent were from the region, mainly from Argentina (67 per cent). Tourists visited Montevideo for the following reasons: rest and recreation (47 per cent), visiting friends and family (37 per cent) and business (12 per cent). Although in terms of visitors Montevideo is Uruguay's main tourist destination with 35 per cent of visitors to the country, in terms of income it is second to Punta del Este, a tourist resort to the east of Montevideo.

In recent years, Uruguay appears to have understood the importance of tourism as a factor to make the economy more dynamic and has started to compete more aggressively to lure tourism from less traditional markets. The Ministry of Tourism has led and promoted the coordination of dialogue between the different stakeholders in the tourism sector. To this end, the Ministry of Tourism set up the National Council of Tourism (CONATUR) with representatives from the public, private and third sectors, as well as the community, and designed the National Sustainable Tourism Plan.

The tourism strategy for Montevideo was taken over by the Montevideo Tourism Cluster, integrated by the public sector through the Ministry of Tourism, the Municipality of Montevideo and the Presidency of the Republic, and the private sector. The Montevideo Tourism Cluster has developed a 'Competitiveness Reinforcement Plan' (Muntal, 2009) with the following working premise:

- Cooperation: aligned with the efforts carried out in the country for promoting and supporting tourism in Uruguay.
- Participating focus: the inclusion of local actors has been constant at all stages of the development of the project.

– Orientation of results: the strategic recommendations aim to attain specific results in a certain temporal horizon.
– Sustainable focus: the development of tourism in Montevideo must meet sustainable development criteria.

The 'Competitiveness Reinforcement Plan' of tourism in Montevideo included a detailed inventory of resources, the city's tourist attractions and the tourism support system. At the diagnostic stage a SWOT analysis of Montevideo as a tourist destination was carried out with the following results. The strengths of the city lay in its geographic location; high number of tourist arrivals, high level of accommodation occupancy and average length of stay; high levels of security in the city; good cultural, leisure and recreation options; the city's tourist infrastructure; the hospitality of the population; its status as the capital of the country and of Mercosur; open urbanism and riverside coast; diverse attractions such as parks, restaurants, commercial facilities, and so on. The city's weaknesses include the weak tourist image of the city; insufficient integration of available resources; the poor history of cooperation between the public and private sectors; poor knowledge of the market; limited regional and international connectivity; an insufficiently trained tourist sector; low daily expenditure per tourist.

Opportunities for Montevideo as a tourist destination include increasing demand for safe tourist destinations in times of crisis; operations by low cost airlines and greater regional connections; the increase of special interest tourism as a reason for travel; and, the greater integration and political weight of Mercosur within the region. Threats faced by Montevideo include the appearance of new tourist destinations; the world economic crisis; health and international security issues; competition from the established destinations of Argentina and Brazil; and, low recognition of tourism as an important contributor to the country's economic development.

Once the analysis stage of the plan was finished, the 'Competitiveness Reinforcement Plan' defined the vision, objectives and action plan for Montevideo as a tourist destination. The definition of the tourist image and the promotion and commercialization of Montevideo were identified as major strategic priorities.

THE MONTEVIDEO TOURIST BRAND: 'DISCOVER MONTEVIDEO'

As stated above, one of the main weaknesses identified regarding Montevideo as a tourist destination lies in the city's poor tourist image. It is vitally important to create a brand for Montevideo as a tourist destination. The Montevideo Tourism Cluster has decided to maintain and build on the brand 'Discover

Montevideo' as defined in 2007 by the Municipality of Montevideo. On taking office in 2005, the city's municipal government made changes to the visual identity of Montevideo. A new logo and a new tagline were rapidly activated, mainly on the city's street signs. The new brand, 'Montevideo for All', transmitted a new vision of the municipal government, based on inclusion. On the basis of this new brand, the Municipality developed a coherent and complex brand architecture with the sub-brand 'Discover Montevideo' as the city's tourist brand.

The Montevideo Tourism Cluster chose to maintain the brand 'Discover Montevideo', conceived in a different context, rather than creating a new tourist brand for the city. The Cluster is designing a new marketing plan for Montevideo as a tourist destination under the brand 'Discover Montevideo'. To this end a call for tenders has been put out to consultancy firms. The objectives of this marketing plan include aspects such as the tourist image of the destination, national and international promotion, plan of action (following the guidelines of the strategic plan), institutional marketing, and proposals for the city's street signs.

SUMMARY

The city of Montevideo has understood the impact of tourism on its economy. Together with representatives from central government, the private sector and the third sector, the city authorities have created the Montevideo Tourism Cluster, the body responsible for the 'Competitiveness Reinforcement Plan' in Montevideo. This strategic plan has been carried out through a process of participation which has stimulated dialogue between the public and private sectors, the community and the third sector, thus ensuring a broad basis for consensus.

The tourist brand 'Discover Montevideo' has emerged, however, from a process that is different to the 'Competitiveness Reinforcement Plan'. In its definition a restricted brand concept appears to have been preferred. Under this narrow perspective of a brand, the name, the visual identity or the tagline get more attention than the set of associations that should provide functional, emotional and self-expression benefits to the target markets and thereby impact positively on their attitudes and behaviors. The marketing plan must give content to the 'Discover Montevideo' brand and promote it aggressively in the most attractive target markets.

CHAPTER 24

Branding New York City – The Saga of 'I Love New York'

Peggy R. Bendel

INTRODUCTION

Can a city or its Convention and Visitors Bureau (CVB) ever bypass the formal process of conducting a branding exercise to determine their brand? If the answer is 'Yes', 'Maybe', or 'Sometimes', what are the conditions that allow – and even encourage – that? And is this a trick question?

NEW YORK'S MULTIFARIOUS IDENTITY

'The Big Apple', 'World Financial Capital', 'The City So Nice, They Named It Twice', and even 'The City of Light', as electricity took over the city – and the world: with more than 100 nicknames in its history as a world class city, New York boasts an identity so multifarious that perhaps no single phrase can capture its essence as a destination for travelers, let alone for residents, business, real estate investors and politicians from around the world. The essential conditions for building a brand for such a city include:

- a prepared industry
- an unmistakable wake-up call (some people might say crisis…)
- credible research
- adequate funding
- the right people, in the right place, at the right time!

In New York City's case, all of these elements came together in the early and mid-1970s. After the high of hosting the 1965 World's Fair, there was a dramatic drop-off in the number of visitors to New York, particularly among the most lucrative segment, business travelers.

Not coincidentally, during that same time period, many companies were moving their headquarters from New York – that world financial capital! – to nearby Connecticut, where many CEOs had their homes. With no income tax at the time, Connecticut was seen as an upscale and desirable place to reside, and an easy commute to New York, should that be necessary. Simultaneously, the economy of the State and the City was worsening (with the exception of the media/advertising/public relations industries, which were thriving), exacerbated by the almost-forgotten oil crisis of the mid-1970s, with long lines at the pumps, and a general feeling of 'What's happening to America – and to the Empire State?', whose very motto ('Excelsior') projected a sense of power and even entitlement, at odds with the prevailing economic realities.

THE 'BIG APPLE' AND 'I LOVE NEW YORK' CAMPAIGNS

In the early 1970s, the Association for a Better New York (ABNY) grasped the seriousness of the situation and launched the 'Big Apple' campaign, designed to highlight the City's many assets, directed at residents, businesses and visitors, resulting in the proliferation of 'Big Apple' pins, stickers, posters and more, and enlisting the aid of those media and marketing partners, who had not given much thought to the fact that their success might be linked to their location.

That campaign prepared the fallow ground for an even more high profile initiative: 'I Love New York'.

Summarized by one of the most memorable headlines ever written, New York City's fiscal crisis had reached epic proportions, with default on the City's debt a possibility. Seeking help from Washington, then-Mayor Abraham Beame woke on the morning of 30 October 1975 to the *New York Daily News* blaring on its front page: 'Ford to City: Drop Dead!' Then-President of the United States Gerald Ford had indeed turned down the City's appeal for help – though not in quite those dramatic words.

A wake-up call indeed – and a crisis, too: New York was on its own to solve its problems. The State was in little better shape. Losing manufacturing jobs for decades, the State was facing its own financial issues: tax revenues had fallen, jobless rates had grown, and no palatable solution seemed in sight.

Newly-appointed Commissioner of the New York State Department of Commerce (DOC) John Dyson recognized that tourism presented the best job creation opportunity of the moment: after all, travelers can make a decision to visit a destination today, and be there tomorrow, spending their travel budget on theater tickets, shopping, museum admissions, accommodations and meals – and in the case of upstate New York, camp grounds, theme parks, historic sites, wineries and more.

Recruiting top marketer William S. Doyle on loan from Chase Manhattan Bank (as it was then known) to handle economic development and tourism marketing, Dyson charged him with structuring a marketing campaign that would boost visitor numbers, while improving the image of New York as a location for business, meetings and conventions as well. With funding coming from a skeptical State Legislature, Doyle knew his pitch would need to be backed by world-class research.

Spending the entire marketing budget of DOC's Travel Bureau (then the lowest among the 50 states, at $US.08 per capita), Doyle turned to Consumer Behavior, Inc. to produce the required research. The resulting data showed that New York State had two primary products:

- New York City, whose primary draws were Broadways theater, shopping, dining and museums, appealing primarily to couples and singles from around the region, the country and internationally

- outdoor recreation, throughout non-urban New York State: mountains, lakes, spectacular and varied scenery and outdoor recreation opportunities drew families from around the State and surrounding New England, New Jersey and Pennsylvania

Taking these findings to the Legislature, Doyle succeeded in convincing them to appropriate $US 4.3 million for the initial campaign, to run in the summer and fall of 1977. The next step: finding the right agency to create the compelling messages that would move travelers to choose New York, State and City. In a competition against several top New York agencies, Wells, Rich, Greene's creative credentials won them the assignment. Brainstorming sessions ensued, but who first said 'I Love New York' remains a mystery!

Renowned graphic artist and designer Milton Glaser, then design director of *New York* magazine, signed on to create the graphic identity, and Steve Karmen, known for such catchy commercial tunes as 'Double your pleasure, double your fun' for Doublemint chewing gum, composed the 'I Love New York' theme music. The first television commercials, one for New York City and one highlighting the State's outdoor recreation, are classics and play well even today.

Missing from those commercials, which ran in summer 1977 and spring 1978, was one element – and the one that is now, 33 years later, most recognizable around the world, and in many non-New York incarnations: the distinctive 'I Love New York' logo. Glaser had produced several logo options, and everyone had signed off on the apparent finalist, the words 'I love New York' within a lozenge outline and using a heart for the 'o' in 'love'. But he was not satisfied, and continued to experiment: he sketched the now-famous 'I (heart symbol) NY', and knew that was it. The logo was trademarked, but the decision was made to freely distribute the logo speci-fications (American Typewriter as the typeface, and Pantone Warm Red for the generously-rounded heart) to all tourism-related entities in the State, in order to increase awareness well beyond the reach of the DOC's budget.

Collateral items such as T-shirts, pins, and bumper stickers were pro-duced; the New York State (NYS) Thruway Authority began printing the logo on toll tickets; Steve Karmen's theme music was released commer-cially and climbed to the top of the disco charts. Separate travelers' guides to New York City and New York State were produced as inserts to *New York* magazine, maximizing distribution at minimal cost. Within the year, fall foliage and winter sports campaigns followed, and in the spring of 1978 the legendary 'Broadway' advertisement was launched. The original 'Broad-way' commercial featured the stars and casts of top-drawing Broadway plays and musicals, and it was this remarkable talent pool – all working for scale, with the support of the League of New York Theaters and Producers – who first sang 'I love New York':

- Yul Brynner, then appearing in a revival of *The King and I*

- Hume Cronyn and Jessica Tandy, partnered in *The Gin Game*

- Angela Lansbury, star of *Sweeney Todd*

- The casts of *A Chorus Line*, *Annie*, *Grease*, and *The Wiz*

- Frank Langella, who concluded the spot by sweeping his *Dracula* cape and intoning 'I Love New York: especially in the evening!'

For the New York Convention & Visitors Bureau, the response was over-whelming: more than 17,000 requests for the Broadway Show Tours brochure mentioned in the commercial in just the first two weeks after it aired – and an average of 1,500 requests a day for information, double their past record. And the following year, in response to this increased volume and the cam-paign's demonstrable impact on both ticket sales and hotel occupancy, Mayor Koch authorized a tripling of the City's contribution to the CVB's budget, to $2 million. Soon, there was also mayoral support for the long-delayed pro-posal to erect a convention center on the city's West side, partially redressing the disadvantage New York City had long faced in comparison with such cities as Chicago which had vastly greater convention and exposition space at their disposal to draw the lucrative spend of convention attendees and exhibitors.

In subsequent years, funding for cooperative advertising, collateral and other marketing activities was predicated on use of the now-iconic logo, further amplifying its visibility. Every adaptation – or imitation! – of the logo harkened back to the original, already firmly imprinted in the minds of travelers by the consistent marketing, which soon included international advertising and promotions in cooperation with major airlines in Europe, South America and Asia, though the core markets remain North America and the Northeast United States in particular.

Fast forward a few decades to today, and ask travelers to New York City, 'What is the city's brand identity?' Possibly carrying a shopping bag or coffee cup, wearing a T-shirt or baseball cap, or about to buy a shot glass or piggy bank, each emblazoned with the logo, they will not be at a loss for an answer.

SUMMARY

Perhaps this *was* a trick question posed at the beginning of this case study. After all, no city can count on the good fortune that was New York's when the State took on the development of what has turned out to be one of the most memorable campaigns in destination marketing history – and one of the longest lasting, predated only by 'Virginia Is for Lovers'. And a classic branding process *was* followed, but by the State, not the City itself.

As I write this, we are approaching the 32nd anniversary of the campaign's launch in 1978, a remarkable record of persistence through changes of political parties in the State Capital in Albany, as well as the legendary fickleness of marketing clients, always eager for something new, which they can claim as their own. None of us – not visionary Milton Glaser, charismatic Mary Wells Lawrence, catalyst John Dyson or marketing architect Bill Doyle – and certainly not those of us who were fortunate enough to be on the DOC staff when 'I Love New York' was aborning, in effect earning a marketing MBA on the job as I did – could have predicted its enduring appeal. The stars, and market forces, were aligned. The preconditions noted above were in place, and most of all, those right people in that right place at just the right time. The result: 'I Love New York' continues to proudly blaze from airport gift shop counters, television screens, T-shirts, posters – and the hearts and minds of all who *do* love New York, around the globe.

CHAPTER 25

Paris as a Brand

Jean-Noël Kapferer

INTRODUCTION

In an interview in *The Economist* (2008), John Ross, the economic consultant to the London Mayor, reacted to the old rivalry between Paris and London by stating: 'We do not consider ourselves competing with Paris anymore. We have won that battle. Now we measure our strength against New York.'

This quite direct assertion reminds us that cities do compete against each other for scarce resources and for fame. This competition is assessed by the regular publication of hit parades comparing the main capital cities of the world on a number of objective indicators that act as measures of the city's strength. In fact, *The Economist* added that London was ahead of Paris on 'most of the big economic indicators'. By pointing out selected economic indicators, it is clear that London had chosen the economic field as its battlefield. One cannot compete on all fronts. Choosing where to fight with the highest chances of winning is the essence of strategy.

CITIES ARE IN DIRECT COMPETITION

Now, interestingly, after having learned in 2008 that Paris had lost against London for the hosting of the 2012 Olympic Games, Bertrand Delanoë, Paris Mayor, emitted a diagnosis according to which he had a better objective 'product' (the proposal itself) but the Paris 'brand image' was not as sexy as that of London.

Our point is not to say who is right or wrong, or to question the relevance of the economic indicators put forth, or to propose alternative indicators where Paris would lead, but to notice that these two quotes from non-marketers can be easily reframed in the context of brands. Ross talked about tangible, material proofs of performance, Delanoë about the intangibles. In fact a brand is made of both aspects: a tangible and an intangible part, both being of course tied together intimately into a value proposition.

Among the economic indicators selected to show who wins, one finds the number of square meters of offices, of headquarters of multinational companies, of congresses and conferences, or the presence of corporations from the most dynamic sectors such as internet and telecommunications. Such indicators do measure the fact that the city is indeed attractive to business and multinational companies. Other indicators measure well-being and thus signal the desire to compete on an experiential field, that of quality of air, number of parks and playgrounds, quality of infrastructure, as well as number of kindergartens, primary schools, doctors, the costs of healthcare, social security, and so on. Finally, one could also compete in terms of the city's cultural life. Then the indicators of success would be the number of theaters and cinemas, the intensity of nightlife, artistic dynamism, the number of exhibitions, ballet, the number of tourists from abroad, the number of foreign students living there, and so on.

Of course the competitors are not the same in each field. Now Paris competes against Berlin or Amsterdam for international companies' world congresses or conventions. It is quite complicated to go from Roissy Airport to Paris itself, because of traffic jams and the absence of a direct tube link. As a consequence, most managers now prefer the ease and convenience of a city like Berlin, which in addition to security has a lot to offer in terms of culture and nightlife, or Amsterdam, which is so close to Schiphol airport.

BUILDING BLOCKS OF THE CITY BRAND: FLAGSHIP PRODUCTS, SALIENT COMMUNICATIONS, AND PEOPLE

Cities can really be conceived as brands with all their constituent parts as follows: they have a name which embodies latent or explicit universes and values; they have a symbol, often rooted in the past; they have a historical proverbial sentence (for Paris it is 'Fluctuat nec mergitur', which literally means 'it floats but never sinks'); they sometimes add a slogan (like 'I love New York'); they are perceived with strengths and weaknesses, on material but also intangible dimensions.

City brand image is built by everything we learn about the city. This includes the city's prototypical products, its salient communication (whether it is managed or not), and finally by the people we meet. Flagship products (Florek and Conejo, 2007) are those which build the positive dimensions of the city image abroad. For London, these 'products' would include the Stock Exchange, the City, the London School of Economics, the Tate Museum, and the original mix of cultures exemplified by Buckingham Palace and Carnaby Street. For Paris, the key salient products include The Eiffel Tower, Beaubourg Modern Art Museum, The Louvre, haute couture and all temples of luxury designer brands on the Faubourg Saint Honoré.

As for communication, one can think of the constant flow of pop music coming from Great Britain, hence attached to its capital city, to the BBC, to the Times or The Economist, but also to salient people such as the dynamic Tony Blair who renewed the image of what a Labour politician looks like, all the respect that flows to the figure of the Queen, interesting maverick entre-preneurs such as Richard Branson, City bankers in classic suits as well as the young financial traders with their bonuses. For Paris, beyond the archetypal images of the River Seine and its many bridges so loved by romantic couples, one finds the mythical haute couture catwalks, the magnificent beauty of the city, and its multitude of fine restaurants. However, the people of Paris do not have a reputation for being particularly welcoming. No pre-eminent figure strongly represents France or Paris on the international scene, except perhaps the present President. The Paris football team itself is not a champion and does little or nothing to boost the city's recognition.

CITY IMAGE AND COUNTRY IMAGE: WHAT ARE THE LINKS?

Some of the dimensions of a city brand are also those of its country brand. The capital city could be said to act as the flagship product of its own coun-try. But there is a difference between the country brand and the city brand. The country brand and the city brand can follow different trajectories. One talks about the 'country-of-origin' effect, in which 'Made in Germany' conjures up images of Mercedes-Benz, BMW, Audis, and VW as well as engineering equipment, the concept of order and rational ideals of quality. On the other hand, 'Made in Great Britain' has now become quite empty. Certainly, Aquascutum trench coats do leverage this origin as well as Jaguar cars or MINIs, but what else? There is very little else, as the United Kingdom has turned its back on industry and entered the tertiary world and the dematerialization of economies. On the other hand, when one thinks of France as a country, top of mind evocations are those of Chateaux de la Loire, of vineyards, of quality of life in Dordogne, but also of the remark-able TGV fast train system that ties all major cities together at 300 km/h, energy independence thanks to 50 nuclear power plants, three automobile major brands, and a rare social security system which guarantees health treatment for all.

Regardless of the country brand's image and performance, the city brand has its own momentum. The city brand cannot just be held as a summary or apex of the country brand's assets. London is not the United Kingdom. As for Paris, historically it has been the place where all the revolutions started: 1789, 1848, 1968. When the country was still, Paris was in revolt. As such, it has been the place of a permanent unrest based on Parisians' desire to change the world's status quo. Let us notice in passing that this is typically an intangible facet, whereas the country's industrial resources are generally found in the provinces.

CAN CITIES BE MANAGED AS BRANDS?

Cities can be analyzed with the concepts of branding. However, one should remember that brands are managed; they are not just another name for 'current image'. In fact, brand management (Kapferer, 2008) starts by a statement on what you intend to stand for. But can one really decide what a city wishes to stand for?

Naturally all city mayors should have a long-term vision. Seoul in South Korea, for instance, used to be one of the poorest cities of that part of Asia. After 1980 it was decided to transform the country into the next Japan, with Seoul to be transformed into one of the most dynamic, modern and sophisticated cities in the world. Thirty years on, the city has been fully rebuilt and is renewed and revitalized. Long-term plans such as those adopted by Seoul and South Korea are the essence of what governing should mean.

To make Paris a more attractive city, there is a need to build a fast train line between the center of the city and the airports, reducing the transport time to 15 minutes maximum. But just this will take ten years to achieve, as such a line cuts across very heavily inhabited suburbs. Branding exercises, on the other hand, are often short term, at least in their managerial cycle. An illustration of this came in 2008 when Paris lost the competition to host the 2012 Olympic Games. The Paris Mayor, Bertrand Delanoë, decided to launch a bid around the project 'Brand Paris' (in French, 'Marque Paris'). Advertising, brand identity, and design agencies were asked to compete for the first time on the project. The 'Marque Paris' wording was itself a revolution, beyond just the fashionable use of marketing terms.

A brand is a vision with values, inspiring both internally (city residents in the context of a city brand) and outside, followed by an alignment of major projects to transform this vision into reality. Brand communication helps by revealing the common direction and meaning of all these actions. A brand is a source of understanding and of loyalty. When branding is taken seriously, it involves the full range of stakeholders and tries to make them think strategically, revealing who are the competitors, and what are the city strengths and weaknesses – both real and imaginary. The result is a brand platform with a clear positioning and value proposition.

The problem is that there is a contradiction between politics and management. A brand platform is an explicit statement that engages: it is meant to become public. Politics, however, has become the art of adaptation. It is easier from a political standpoint not to have explicit or binding commitments.

BRAND OR SLOGAN?

In the case of Paris, what the Mayor wanted in fact was a good slogan. This is why the process which was engaged in 2008 to build the brand stopped some months after. For many mayors, branding means merely 'find me a good logo and slogan'. This is not to diminish the role of a good slogan: everybody knows how much it can catalyze both internal and external stakeholders.

All mayors dream of achieving the impact and success of New York's slogan. Interestingly, the New York slogan and logo were created for the New York City tourist office. The same is true for Seoul: their slogan was a demand of the tourist office. The success of the New York slogan is demonstrated by the fact that most people do not attribute it to a methodical managerial process undertaken to invent a slogan. It is not associated with either marketing or advertising. 'I Love New York' is less a commercial success than a citizen success: New Yorkers have appropriated this sentence as theirs. They see no marketing goal or strategy behind this. One of the main strengths of the New York slogan is that it expresses a relationship rather than a difference or consumer benefit aimed at communicating superiority. The city of Amsterdam's slogan 'I amsterdam' operates in a similar manner.

What, then, are the consequences of these insights? Good slogans for a city have to come from inside. They should reveal the true identity of the brand, unlike products which try to convince of their difference vis-à-vis a set of competitors. Cities are first and foremost made for their inhabitants. Cities have a history. The slogan should express a sense of belonging, pride, and symbolic proximity.

SUMMARY

The brand metaphor has its limits when one speaks of cities. Commercial brands such as Coke are artefacts: they invent a universe and stage it in advertising, events, sponsorships, on the internet, and so on. They even have a network of fans on Facebook. Coke is about friendship, dynamism, the joy of doing things together. This imaginary universe is made to be consumed as much as the cola itself. On the other hand, a city is a human reality, local, and quite permanent in the short term. A city is also anchored into a history, a culture, an ecosystem. This gives the city a reality, a force which has resisted time. It should be adapted to present economic conditions, but nevertheless it constitutes the city's DNA.

What are the main consequences of this? First, one cannot make a city brand without the city. Just as for a service brand, one cannot artificially separate the inside and the outside. Second, it should be understood that what is at stake is less to 'manage the city brand', which is a technical assignment, but rather to 'manage the city by the brand', with the brand acting as a lever of collective consciousness and commitment to accelerate social change.

CHAPTER 26

Seoul City Branding: The Case of Seoul's International Brand Communication

You Kyung Kim and Peter Eung-Pyo Kim

INTRODUCTION

Korea's national soft power competitiveness in areas such as culture, tourism, and citizens lags behind its hard power, particularly in terms of the country's impressive economic performance. These soft power sectors including culture, tourism and citizens require cities to play a substantial role. Therefore, Korean cities need to focus their efforts on nurturing soft power. Seoul, the heartland of Korea, has served an important role as a key strategic brand name that represents the country. Seoul has played a pivotal role in enhancing the value and assets of Korea's national brand, while being an example for local cities in their efforts to increase their self-sustainability. The city has conducted branding campaigns at various locations in cooperation with the government, local communities and other cities. In this section, we will explore the strategic process and best practices for managing city brands, which Seoul as the capital of Korea has implemented under strong leadership.

THE MARKETING HISTORY OF SEOUL METROPOLITAN GOVERNMENT

Korea's local autonomy system, which was introduced in 1995, has encouraged local governments to differentiate themselves through individual destination marketing strategies. Seoul Metropolitan Government (SMG) established the City Marketing Taskforce to integrate city marketing affairs directed by various divisions and it has endeavored to create an image for the city as the world's hub. SMG took advantage of the 2002 Korea-Japan World Cup as a turning point to offer the citizens an opportunity to unite and to highlight the positive image of the city. At that time, it was necessary to build Seoul's own unique image beyond simply being the capital of Korea. The City Marketing Taskforce was renamed the Global Marketing Division in 2002.

PRE-2006: INITIAL PROMOTIONAL ACTIVITIES

Since the 2002 Korea-Japan World Cup, the organization in charge of Seoul marketing has launched various activities, such as publishing monthly journals for citizens, creating a promotional song about Seoul, and creating a 'Hi-Seoul' city brand, at the domestic level while focusing only on occasion-based promotion at the international level. International level promotions included setting up light box advertising at major overseas airports such as Tokyo, Beijing, and Hong Kong, providing support for international press tours in Korea, developing promotional programs for Cheonggye Stream, and so on.

2006: THE FIRST YEAR OF INTEGRATED MARKETING COMMUNICATION

Starting from 2006, SMG became actively involved in promoting the city's brand overseas. This was in response to the emerging need to create Seoul's own brand by centralizing overseas marketing practices, which had been sporadically conducted on an ad hoc basis until 2005, in a more strategic manner. In this context, SMG began to push forward with improved overseas marketing strategies aimed at building Seoul's image as a welcoming and environmentally responsible city.

In 2006, the marketing objective of SMG was to create Seoul's image as a first class global city. The slogans 'Refresh your Soul in Seoul' and 'Be @ Seoul' highlighted Seoul's image as a city that is rich in culture and advanced science technology. At the time, Seoul was recognized as the capital of Korea but there was no clear image related to the city, which indicated the urgent need to create a unique and original image of Seoul. Focus group interviews with experts in overseas countries and with foreign correspondents in Korea indicated that Seoul was perceived as a city which has more strengths in the economic sector and information technology than other cities and where diverse cultures coexist with 600-year-old history. Therefore, SMG decided to magnify the image of a high-end, cultural city as already perceived by foreign audiences.

For strategic implementation of the marketing strategies, SMG assigned about US$ 2.5 million in budget and conducted overseas marketing communication centering on Asia in 2006. The marketing budget execution details are as follows. Asia had the highest proportion with 53 per cent, followed by Europe with 34 per cent and other regions including the USA with 12 per cent. In terms of marketing media, outdoor media took up 73 per cent while TV broadcasts, which were utilized for the first time, accounted for 15 per cent and print media for 12 per cent. Regarding advertisements carried out in 2006, the impact survey conducted in the Beijing area shows that about 26 per cent of all the respondents answered that they had seen the advertising, among which 70 per cent said they have a positive impression of the advertisement about Seoul. Some answered that the advertising well described the favorable image of the city, which focused on harmony between the past and present, while others said that it was hard to concentrate on the advertising because it showed too many aspects of Seoul.

What is noteworthy in the marketing execution of 2006 was that SMG for the first time in its branding campaigns adopted strategies based on the principles of segmentation, targeting, and positioning. Within Asia, Singapore and Hong Kong have long been active in conducting brand campaigns, but Seoul only began to do so in 2006. In addition, various media including television and print as well as outdoor advertising were comprehensively employed, which makes 2006 the launch year for an integrated marketing communication approach to the city branding of Seoul.

2007: THE TRANSFORMATION OF SEOUL'S OVERSEAS MARKETING

In 2007, overseas marketing for SMG went through a vast transformation as Mr Oh Se-hoon took office as the new Mayor. Under the leadership of the new Mayor, Seoul set a goal to establish the image of a 'clean and attractive city' and enhance its competitiveness in tourism through city marketing. In addition, the city adopted 'Soul of Asia' as its new brand slogan, with the intention of communicating that 'Seoul is the center of Asia'. Based on the brand identity established under this slogan, SMG has formulated marketing communication strategies with the ultimate goal of attracting more tourists.

In 2007, as a result of environmental analysis, it was found that Seoul had little familiarity and uniqueness compared to its neighboring cities and countries. Analysis based on their similarity in geographical proximity and tourism activity showed that China, Japan, Singapore, and Hong Kong were the major competitors to Seoul. Therefore, Seoul needed to be differentiated from Chinese and Japanese cities. Compared to Chinese and Japanese cities, Seoul has the advantage that it is young in its overall image. Accordingly, in terms of market segmentation the conclusion was reached that Asia was a primary target market considering perception and behavioral involvement towards Seoul. In addition, Japan and China were segmented as focus markets for potential growth in tourist visits to Seoul, while Southeast Asian markets including Singapore and Hong Kong were also categorized as growth markets. The key target groups selected were based on the share of travelers to Korea and type of travelers by country. It emerged that Chinese tourists usually desired to experience Seoul's trendy culture such as fashion, Japanese tourists intended to have an in-depth cultural experience such as visiting every corner of Seoul, and Southeast Asian tourists were attracted to Seoul due to Korean Wave stars in popular culture.

SMG set the marketing positioning to be 'Emotional Modernity' in order to create a sensitive and modern image of Seoul in the minds of its target markets. SMG produced two television commercial films and three print commercials in order to appeal to the needs of each target market. Television was mainly utilized as a communication tool to efficiently spread the city's brand image, and differentiated communication media were also adopted according to the characteristics of each geographic region and consumer target segment. In terms of media execution, television including CNN accounted for the biggest share (43 per cent), followed by outdoor advertising (14.4 per cent), internet (9.5 per cent) and print (7.8 per cent). This blend of media channels was aimed at optimizing media contact to each target group. In the marketing execution during 2007 Seoul tried to diversify its marketing media by utilizing the internet, a preferred communication medium for Southeast Asian tourists. Media-based marketing centered on Asia with 35 per cent of media spend allocated to Southeast Asia, 27 per cent to China, and 20 per cent to Europe in a bid to achieve a regional balance. The achievement of 2007 was meaningful because diverse vehicles were utilized in the target markets in order to support Seoul's brand positioning of emotional modernity. However, no consumer surveys were conducted on Seoul's advertising and the adopted media were not exposed enough to consumers in each target region, resulting in difficulties in accurately assessing the effectiveness of the advertisements used in attempts to enhance the city's image.

2008: HISTORIC INCREASE IN SEOUL'S MARKETING BUDGET

2008 can be regarded as a historic year for Seoul's overseas marketing communication. SMG took innovative actions to increase the overseas marketing budget from 5.3 billion won (about 5.3 million dollars) in 2007 to 40.1 billion won (about 40 million dollars). Out of the new budget, 35.3 billion won (35 million dollars) was used for overseas marketing communication. The reason behind the budget increase was because SMG recognized that the tourism industry is a high value-added industry which earns foreign currencies and creates jobs, thereby greatly contributing to boosting the economy. SMG tried to actively attract tourists by selecting the tourism industry as a core project for economic revitalization. SMG thought that, if

the number of tourists visiting Seoul increased, it would boost the overall economy by attracting investment as well as facilitating the tourism
industry. In this context, SMG undertook several projects to transform the
city's physical assets, including the Han River Renaissance Project and the
City Recreation Project that aimed to develop the Han River, South Gate,
Myungdong Area, and Insadong streets.

   In addition to a physical transformation, there was a need to establish the
brand identity of Seoul. Since 2003, Seoul's neighboring cities in Asia such
as Singapore and Hong Kong had continuously engaged in city branding by
investing more than 50 million dollars annually in building their city identity. As a result, Singapore saw the number of tourists increase by 35 per
cent in 2004, compared to 2003. Up until 2007, SMG had conducted its
branding activities in overseas countries with the budget of one million to
five million dollars and promoted marketing communication through diverse
marketing tools, but the scale of the budget remained at a relatively meagre
level compared to that of its competitor cities. In response to this situation, backed by the Mayor and related officials, SMG expanded the budget
for overseas marketing communication in 2008 to 40 million dollars, an
unprecedented increase. In order to establish the overseas marketing communication strategies, SMG took a strategic approach to establishing the direction
of Seoul's city branding by analyzing the current status of Seoul's brand as
well as the policies of competitor cities. SMG developed a communication
execution plan, slogan, related media campaign, and so on. The marketing
communication positioning was set as 'My Soul Story', which was derived
from the idea that the traveler's purpose is changing from sightseeing into
experiencing the destination. As for the brand positioning for each nation,
SMG adopted 'Stylish Story' for China, 'Humanistic Story' for Japan, 'Fan-
tastic Story' for Southeast Asian countries, and 'Inspirational Story' for the
United States and Europe.

   When acquiring tourism information, tourists appear to be most influenced
by word of mouth by other people. Therefore, SMG adopted a strategy of
producing commercial advertising in which local people tell their experiences about Seoul. The commercials were divided into two categories: one
with ordinary people from the target countries recommending trips to Seoul,
and the other with local celebrities recounting their experiences of Seoul.
Four promotional commercials were custom-produced to meet the characteristics of each of the four regional target zones, namely, China, Japan, Southeast Asia, and the United States/Europe. In the commercials using celebrities,
movie director Kaige Chen (China), novelist Murakami Ryu (Japan), photo-
grapher Anuchai (Southeast Asia), and famous pianist George Winston (United
States/Europe) talked about their experiences of Seoul. A further distinctive

initiative in 2008 was that SMG became a destination partner to Manchester United Football Club. This provided an opportunity to promote Seoul to 190 million people in Asia and 330 million people worldwide, exposing Seoul to 200 countries through more than 20 football games.

As a result of the city's international brand communication, Seoul was named by tourists from China, Japan and Thailand as a city that people want to visit the most within a year. Before the advertising, Seoul was the fifth wish-to-visit city in China, fourth in Japan, and first in Thailand. In addition, since Seoul began to sponsor Manchester United, the awareness level of Seoul increased from 14 per cent in October 2004 to 38 per cent in May 2009 among fans of the football team. In 2008, the number of foreign tourists to Korea reached 6.9 million, an increase of 7 per cent from the previous year. SMG marketing practices, therefore, appear to have brought a positive impact across various sectors.

2009: NEW GLOBAL POSITIONING FOR SEOUL'S CITY BRAND

In 2009, the objective of SMG's overseas marketing was to maximize the effect of Seoul's brand image through the creation of new campaign slogans and to enhance the functions of integrated marketing strategies by utilizing various promotional opportunities and media. The target markets are the same as those of 2008, but the global positionings have changed to 'Trendy City', '24 Hour-Lively City', and 'Digitalization City', based on the newly adopted slogan, 'Infinitely yours, Seoul'. The new slogan 'Infinitely yours, Seoul' implies that Seoul is a city with cultural diversity in which you can enjoy yourself safely and conveniently around the clock and a place with limitless cultural experiences available. Along with the global campaign slogan, local sub-slogans were developed for each target region, thereby carrying out both globalization and localization simultaneously. For example, 'Infinite Pleasure' was adopted as the sub-slogan for China considering the fact that many Chinese tourists enjoy different kinds of Seoul experiences. Under the umbrella campaign slogan 'Infinitely yours, Seoul', the marketing positionings were differentiated for each market.

Different brand campaign advertising was also created separately for each of the four regions: China, Japan, Southeast Asia, and the United States/Europe. The advertising adopted the same format in which local people made their testimonies about Seoul, but their stories were rendered in different ways. The most distinctive feature of the advertising produced in 2008 were the cameo appearances of Korean singers who were popular in China, Japan, and Southeast Asia. For example, TVXQ, Super Junior, and Girls Generation appeared briefly in the promotional films for about two to three seconds, increasing viewers' interest. In addition, behind-the-scene stories from producing the commercials were made into separate shows which were distributed through SMG's YouTube page as part of the viral marketing campaign. The advertising and the behind-the-scene episodes attracted two million views online, an unprecedented figure in the history of the Korean government's overseas campaigns. The viral marketing gained success as the commercials spread among the fans of Korean Wave stars. Particularly, the online comments about how they want to visit Seoul added to the uploaded films indicate that the viral marketing practices have contributed greatly to building a positive image of Seoul.

In 2009, SMG conducted the 'Seoul Infinite Dream Series' along with the 'Infinitely yours, Seoul' campaign. The series of promotions were pursued both online and offline, utilizing sports, Korean dramas and Korean music, with the objective of making Seoul a talked about subject by foreign audiences. The first promotion was 'Seoul Infinite Match', which offered an opportunity to selected people to participate in a mini football game with Manchester United and to receive training from the professional players while the team was on its Asia tour. More than one million people viewed this advertising worldwide and about 5,000 people applied for the promotional event. Among them only five were selected and given the opportunity to play in a mini game with Manchester United. The Dream Match received a lot of media attention from other countries and it became global news through media such as Eurosport and Gillette World Sports.

The second promotion was 'Seoul Infinite Dream Story', which was carried out in cooperation with Yahoo. This gave selected applicants an opportunity to attend fan meetings with Korean celebrities such as famous singers at the Drama Awards held in Seoul. In order to receive applicants, the event page on Yahoo was open to receive stories of people on why they would like to meet the Korean star. Only one couple was selected and invited to Seoul to meet the Korean star. It generated a record of 120 million hits and tens of thousands of applicants.

The third promotion was 'Seoul Infinite Dream Concert', which offered an opportunity to meet Korean stars who appeared in the Seoul advertising. This promotion was carried out on SMG's YouTube page, where an online contest was held to choose two winners. More than 400,000 people visited the page and about 2000 people applied for the contest. The selected applicants for the Dream Match, the Dream Story, and the Dream Concert were filmed when they visited Seoul enjoying city tours and happily meeting Korean stars. When the films were uploaded on YouTube, there were positive responses from many viewers.

The fourth promotion of the Dream Series was 'Seoul Infinite Dream Jump', the Big Air World Cup held by the International Ski Federation at Gwanghwamun Square, the heartland of Seoul, from 11–13 December. For this sports event, SMG set up a 34-meter high slope in the middle of the city. During the Big Air World Cup, more than 300,000 people visited Seoul and the game was aired on ESPN Star Sports, FOX Sports, and Eurosport. The 'Seoul Infinite Dream Series' pursued online and offline promotions simultaneously, and it employed convergence marketing, which is rarely seen in city brand marketing. In particular, it can be considered as evolutionary in marketing practices in that it focused on building a brand image of Seoul by holding actual promotional events beyond the existing methods of online advertisement.

In 2009, SMG conducted diverse activities such as product placement in addition to advertising and promotional events for the overseas marketing of Seoul. In particular, 'Hip Korea', a documentary about Korean culture with a focus on Korean singer Rain and actor Lee Byung Hun, was produced by the Discovery Channel and has induced positive perceptions of Seoul. 'Hip Korea' was divided into two parts with the subtitles 'Seoul Vibes' (Rain) and 'Seoul Savvy' (Lee Byung Hun), in a bid to give the impression that Seoul is infinite. This documentary received highly favorable responses when it was aired on Discovery Channel Asia and NHK, and it was selected as a winner for Best Cross-Platform Content at the Asian TV Awards in 2009.

SUMMARY

City branding is a difficult task. The images associated with a city are intangible and abstract. Therefore, it is necessary to specify and visualize the resources that the city has in order to provide a memorable impression of the experience. SMG's branding strategies began with the idea that a city should be a place where experience and consumption coexist in harmony, instead of simply being a historic location. In other words, a city should not be complacent about its already established roles of providing historic and cultural resources, but should also move forward to revitalize the city economy by increasing the value of what tourists experience based on a balanced tourism infrastructure for shopping and other activities. Only when these conditions are satisfied, can the city be an attractive place which is pleasant to live in, and it will then deserve a reputation as a consumer city. To this end, SMG has established the clear identity of the city brand and made its utmost efforts in adopting innovative methods beyond the traditional practices in order to communicate the brand identity in an effective and efficient manner. Recently, small and mid-sized local cities have been taking bold steps to increase their self-sustainability through cooperation and partnership with other cities. The evaluation of SMG's success stories in city branding has fuelled the joint marketing efforts by local cities in a bid to explore the possibility of city alliances. We are confident that Seoul will continue to perform brand management projects while innovatively enhancing its city identity as a global brand, and ultimately will build a powerful identity and image of its own, comparable to that of Paris, New York, and Singapore.

CHAPTER 27

The City Branding of Sydney

Geoff Parmenter

INTRODUCTION

Despite being consistently acknowledged as one of the best cities in the world, Sydney has been losing ground competitively in recent times to other cities, in Australia and overseas. Prompted by a series of reports written by Sydney businessman John O'Neill, in mid-2008 a broad group of Sydney stakeholders joined in a major city-wide collaboration to unite, align and inspire the city to market itself far more strongly. The initiative has delivered the first ever research validated brand model for Sydney, and has catalyzed and provided the framework to harness a number of large scale initiatives now being implemented across the city. These include tens of billions of dollars worth of infrastructure developments, an innovative, distinctive program of Sydney-specific annual events and festivals, dedicated campaigns and programs from Tourism and State Development, and a leading role in Australia's bid to host the FIFA World Cup in 2018 or 2022.

SYDNEY IN 2008

Sydney is Australia's only global city. The gateway to Australia, it hosts more than half of all Australia's international visitors every year. It is home to Australia's financial services sector, creative industries, performing arts and media, and almost half of the top 500 corporations in the country. It is blessed with a breathtakingly beautiful harbor, and its iconic Opera House, Harbour Bridge and beaches. Sydney has been rated consistently by the annual Anholt City Brands Index amongst the top three cities in the world. Indeed, in March 2008 it was named the number one city brand in the world for the second year running. As one American colleague put it to me recently, 'When God made Sydney, he had a very good day!'

But despite this, in mid-2008 a broad group of Sydney stakeholders put aside their traditional Sydney self-interest and joined in a major city-wide collaboration to unite, align and inspire the city to market itself far more strongly. Why?

The answer is simple. A series of studies and reports have substantiated a local perception that despite its strong assets and successes, Sydney has been losing ground in recent times to other cities, in Australia and overseas, across a range of measures – whether they be tourism, business events or other broader indicators of economic health. Indeed, there has been a recognition that Sydney's strong natural assets and successes have in fact contributed to a certain complacency which left the city vulnerable to the aggressive positioning pursued by a number of enlightened, highly motivated and very capable competitors. There was a belated acknowledgement that having a beautiful harbor and hosting the 'best Games ever' would not automatically translate into enduring prosperity. And so in August 2008, Sydney – the then 'number one city brand in the world' – embarked upon an initiative to deliberately define, articulate and present that city brand for the very first time.

BRANDING SYDNEY

Sydney can be a particularly fragmented city. By Australian standards, it is a big city. The massive waterways that define and divide it create enclaves and villages with distinct and discrete cultures and characters. Its size, geography and status as Australia's only global city can work against the natural development of a community consciousness or a sense of civic duty at a whole-of-city level. The glaring exception to this is the manner in which Sydney in all its parts can rise superbly to the occasion when hosting a singular global event. In the 2000 Olympics, the 2003 Rugby World Cup and World Youth Day in 2008, it has successfully hosted three of the world's five 'mega events' in less than the last ten years. But in the absence of such a uniting 'project', motivating all of the city's primary stakeholders not just to participate in, but to invest jointly in a multi-million dollar initiative to provide the platform to put Sydney back on the front foot, was a considerable, and quite unprecedented achievement.

The inspiration was a prominent Sydney Business Leader, John O'Neill AO, the author of three reports commissioned by the State Government in 2007, which were critical of Sydney's recent complacency. He managed to achieve three vitally important outcomes as Chairman of the Brand Sydney Steering Committee in 2008 and 2009.

Firstly, he designed a governance structure for the research and development phase of the project, which ensured that no single party would 'own' the initiative, and in doing so he created an environment where *all* the participants could claim ownership. The result was a multi-million dollar project jointly funded by some 13 participating stakeholders, from Federal, State and Local Government, and the private sector.[1]

Secondly, he emphasized the critical importance of robust and rigorous research. With guidance from international experts Terrence Burns[2] of Atlanta-based consultancy Helios, and the former Marketing Director of the Sydney 2000 Olympic Games, John Moore, extensive data was gathered and new research commissioned to ensure that the eventual brand model created from this platform would stand up to the intense scrutiny that captains of industry and other prospective partners would give it. Without such research, all branding – and particularly city branding – becomes 'just someone else's opinion'.

Finally, O'Neill advocated an appropriately structured entity to propagate the outcomes of the research and development phase of the project. Once again, the need was recognized for a vehicle that would not be perceived to be 'owned' by any particular stakeholder, and importantly, not by Government. The result was the creation of a company, The Greater Sydney Partnership Pty Ltd, established by private sector representative organization, the Sydney Chamber of Commerce, the Committee for Sydney and the Tourism and Transport Forum, with Directors positions for State and Local Government appointees, and an independent Chair. Seed funding was procured from both the State Government and the Council of the City of Sydney. The Company was formally launched on 30 April 2010.

CREATING A BRAND MODEL FOR SYDNEY

Reams of research already commissioned by the project participants was shared, instantly creating a massive data pool to be collated, analyzed, retained or discarded. Already a number of consistent themes began to emerge. These were supported, amplified and tightened up through six months of custom designed research activity conducted across Australia, and internationally, in

[1]The City of Sydney, the NSW Department of State and Regional Development, Tourism Australia, the Sydney Chamber of Commerce, the Greater Sydney Universities, the Committee for Sydney, Events NSW, the NSW Department of Arts, Sport and Recreation, Business Events Sydney, the Sydney Harbour Foreshore Authority, Parramatta Council, Tourism NSW and the Tourism and Transport Forum.
[2]Burns was responsible for the first ever Global Brand Assessment of the Olympic Brand for the IOC, across 15 countries, in 1996–2000.

Sydney's key geographical target markets and industry sectors. Moore alone conducted more than 100 one-on-one interviews with hand-picked business and opinion leaders around the world.

Some of the results were predictably confronting. Sydney is complacent – 'like a model with fading lipstick' according to one. We had been fragmented, lacked a consistent strategy and have challenges with infrastructure.

But along with being one of the world's most loved cities, blessed with world famous natural beauty, Sydney is recognized globally for its extraordinary vibrancy and an enviable way of life. A unique combination of a 'first world business centre set in a resort'. In Sydney, we work hard, but health and well-being empower us. 'Sydney lives large!'

And the research also supported a notion of Sydney's special creativity. Our uninhibited outlook and free-thinking approach is seen as emanating from the way the city embraces its diversity. Sydney does not *tolerate* different perspectives; Sydney *celebrates* them.

Sydney, over two hundred plus years, has forged a world renowned, highly successful city by considering the way in which things are done in other places, and not being afraid to borrow from the best, while trying it our own way if we believe there is a better option. Nowhere is this better illustrated than in our approach to the Sydney Olympics. We looked carefully at the way it was done in Atlanta and Nagano, borrowed some of their approach, but in many areas, we innovated – very creatively, and very effectively. Many of these innovations have become and remain the 'baseline' for Olympic delivery today.

From an essence of *Vibrant Magnetism*, a brand model was constructed, providing four key drivers or positioning options for stakeholders and partners. These are:

1. 'Can do' attitude – 'Work hard, Live Large'
2. Uninhibited outlook
3. Progressiveness
4. Natural attraction

The research, and this articulation of Sydney's differentiating attributes and desired positioning, underpinned a strong piece of creative development work that was managed by Sydney creative agency Moon. The work has provided a distinctive new look and feel, and a powerful toolkit for marketers and communicators seeking to partner with and leverage Sydney's unique international image and reputation.

SYDNEY IN 2010

Sydney in 2010 is a city on the threshold of an exciting new phase of its young life. Its physical appearance, personality and behavior will be evolved substantially in the next decade.

Miles Young, Global CEO of The Ogilvy Group, talks of 'Big Boxes' and 'Cultural Incubators' as keys to repositioning a city's image and reputation.[3] In terms of 'Big Boxes' or major infrastructure projects, physically, several massive developments will begin in Sydney in 2010. Barangaroo, currently a vacant concrete 22 hectare site, will be transformed to create the last piece of Sydney's spectacular waterfront Central Business District, at a cost of $6 billion. The completion of its world leading green commercial, residential, and public entertainment and park space will for the first time unlock the entire harborside precinct from The Rocks to Darling Harbour. A brand new 5+-star hotel will join the nearby $0.5 billion Star City hotel development as the latest Sydney icons. The 'Central Park' project is taking place on six hectares near Broadway in the heart of Sydney, where a new $2 billion precinct is being created featuring commercial, residential and retail space. The site will be the largest urban development in Australia to introduce on-site tri-generation (known as 'green transformers') for power, heating and cooling. Substantial facelifts are also set for Campbell's Cove near Circular Quay, Rozelle Bay near Anzac Bridge, and the harborfront Museum of Contemporary Art. Together, these developments will present a highly visible physical upgrade for the city, and provide a tangible platform for refreshing and repositioning Sydney's image and reputation.

Complementing these large scale prominent infrastructure projects has been a major push to create Young's 'cultural incubators' in the form of a distinctive, relevant program of Sydney-specific annual events and festivals. A large scale light festival, *Vivid Sydney*, was launched in 2009, for example, and the second edition will open in May 2010. Dubbed Sydney's annual 'Festival of Light, Music and Ideas', it has been custom-built to showcase Sydney's special creativity – our uninhibited outlook and free-thinking approach. It features the spectacular illumination of the Sydney Opera House sails, and international curators Brian Eno (in 2009), and Lou Reed and Laurie Anderson (2010). Two hundred and thirty thousand people attended the inaugural event.

---

[3]Miles Young presentation to Metropolis Conference, Sydney, October 22, 2008.

Each October Sydney's enviable way of life will be highlighted through another specifically developed Festival, 'Crave Sydney' – an international lifestyle showcase, featuring extraordinary food experiences in extraordinary Sydney locations. The inaugural event in 2009 featured a picnic breakfast on a freshly turfed Sydney Harbour Bridge, and a series of themed activities and entertainment on the Harbour Islands, together with the more traditional elements of an international food festival such as international chef master classes, and special events and offers across the city's restaurants.

There is strong recognition of the unique capacity of events to present a highly authentic image for a city – to locals, visitors and media audiences alike – accurately and cost effectively. A structured annual program of events is providing a rallying point for relevant parties across Sydney, and fostering a unity of purpose that has been somewhat absent for a number of years. The ultimate galvanizing force could be Australia's bid to host the FIFA World Cup in 2018 or 2022. One of the few remaining mega events not recently hosted in Sydney, the FIFA World Cup would provide a significant shot in the arm for Sydney, headquarters of football in Australia, and likely host for the final and other major matches, should the bid be successful. FIFA will make their decision in December 2010.

Tourism too has been quick to capitalize on the opportunity presented by the newly defined Sydney brand. A tourism campaign for the city was launched in April 2010, the first in living memory. It introduces the notion of 'Sydnicity' – a catch-all descriptor for Sydney's indefinable *vibrant magnetism* – and will be backed by some $22 million of NSW Government support over the period ahead.

The timing of this work fits neatly with a project embarked upon in parallel by the Australian Government, and designed to define a new brand for Australia. The Federal Government is aiming to release this work at the World Expo in Shanghai in May, where the new Sydney brand and imagery will also have a strong presence in the Australian pavilion. The emerging synergies between the Australian and Sydney brand work are of course unsurprising, but their formalization and validation will enable them to be leveraged in a much more structured and deliberate way.

So 2010 sees the confluence of a number of powerful and exciting initiatives in Sydney. And the newly launched Greater Sydney Partnership is set to play a vital role in harnessing that momentum. One of its first steps will be to convene the 'Sydney Marketing Partnership', a cooperative of many of the more than 70 organizations already identified who are currently marketing Sydney directly and explicitly, or leveraging Sydney's image or reputation to drive added value to their own businesses. Just by providing shared visibility of these marketing and communications activities, the first practical steps will be taken in uniting, aligning and inspiring Sydney, and in doing so unlocking hundreds of millions of dollars worth of communications activity. These are the first steps for Sydney towards taking what New York Mayor Michael Bloomberg called 'direct, co-ordinated custody of our image'.

SUMMARY

Of course the necessary change will not happen overnight. But the ingredients for action are all present. The research and development is done and it is rigorous and robust. It is broadly and jointly owned by all the city's key players. It has been capably articulated, packaged and presented. And the large scale catalysts for collaborative activity are present. The stage is set. Now the hard work has to begin.

CHAPTER 28

Superflat Tokyo: City of Secret Superlatives

Roland Kelts

INTRODUCTION

On his first visit to Tokyo, American novelist Paul Auster remarked to his Japanese translator that the city managed to combine the density of Manhattan with the sprawl of Los Angeles – and still thrive. American poet Gary Snyder, while refusing to live in Tokyo again, has claimed that it is the world's most successful megalopolis – home to millions, yet resolutely functional, clean, safe and efficient. Tokyo is reportedly the brightest city in the world seen from NASA satellites in space, and is now home to the largest number of 3-starred restaurants in the epicurean Michelin Guide from Paris. Tokyo's public transit system is the envy of every city in the world, as are its relatively low crime rates, stable incomes and public services. Still, while it is easy to find people who are astonished by or simply respect Tokyo, it is hard to find people who claim to love it.

Quick quiz: How many songs can you name about the glories of New York, Paris or London? Now try Tokyo.

Tokyo is massive, and Auster was likely awestruck, as many of us are upon first encountering Japan's capital city, lone national center of finance, government, publishing, media and mass entertainment. Imagine New York, Washington, D.C. and Los Angeles sharing the same regional real estate, with a bit of South Beach decadence around the edges and 35 million people, the world's largest metropolitan population, vying for its services and attention. Now imagine trying to make that city livable, even pleasurable.

I have now lived in Tokyo for several years, after visiting numerous times as a youth with my Japanese mother. Yet I will never forget the

40th floor view of the city I took in as a young adult from my room in the Keio Plaza Hotel in Shinjuku. Jet-lagged and bleary, solo in Tokyo for the first time, I watched the lights course deep into the distance and wondered: Does this town ever end?

Thickets of skyscrapers rise haphazardly across the megalopolis, which oozes out from the city's official center, the Imperial Palace, to Chiba in the East, Saitama in the North, and Yokohama due West. South of the city is the natural inlet of Tokyo Bay, but it, too, hosts an armada of skyscrapers and entertainment complexes in a mini-metropolis built on landfill called Odaiba, originally a platform for a fortress of defensive cannons to ward off enterprising colonizers in the 19th century. Japan was officially opened to global trade by the arrival of American Commodore Matthew Perry and his so-called 'black ships', a naval fleet of four vessels that landed at a rocky outpost in Izu, a peninsula south of Tokyo, in 1853. After Japan's nightmarish attempts at Imperial dominance of Asia in World War II, its cannons were transformed, not into ploughshares, but to pachinko (gambling) parlors and entertainment centers. Tokyo is ample evidence of a capitalist emporium gone mad, a postwar playhouse for your every distraction.

Natives of former capitals Kyoto (794 to 1868) and Nara (710–794) still speak of Tokyo as a callow upstart, over-Westernized and insufficiently schooled in the ways of proper cultural etiquette. I have experienced this firsthand, having lived in Osaka for a year. My friends there happily host me in their homes when I visit, but unless they are on business, most refuse to trek north so I can return their favors. 'Tokyo is an artificial city', one of them told me by way of explanation and apology. 'There's nothing real or Japanese about it.'

True: Tokyo is not Japan, any more than New York can stand as substitute for America, or London for England. Many Japanese outside of Tokyo are either deeply skeptical or dismissive of the megalopolis making decisions on their behalf, just as Americans love to decry the actions of New Yorkers or Washingtonians, and rural Britons gleefully trash Londoners. But owing to its mostly mono-ethnic population (roughly two per cent of residents today are foreign-born) and financial and media pillars, Tokyo to me remains deeply *Japanese*. The casual visitor eyeing one or more Starbucks or McDonald's outlets on nearby corners may not immediately grasp this paradox: Tokyo is both Japan's most global city, and a global cipher, resistant to transparency even as it struggles to retain relevance amid its fast-rising neighbors in Asia. Tokyo is a city brand that stubbornly defies comprehension, which may be part of its appeal.

WELCOME TO TOKYO – HYBRID CITY

In the early 2000s, I researched and wrote an article about the Japanese government's then nascent tourism slogan: '*Yokoso*, Japan!' or 'Welcome to Japan!' A Foreign Ministry official told me that their strategy was to make the Japanese word 'yokoso' ('welcome') as popular as the Hawaiian term, 'aloha'. In 2010, no such luck. The banners greet you at the airport, and a few signs are still tethered to streetlamps, but no one in Japan or elsewhere is gleefully high-fiving, fist-bumping or shimmying to shrieks of 'Yokoso!'

The same official's softly expressed concerns may underscore part of the reason why. Tokyo, he noted, has no visual icons it can claim as its own. While the Eiffel Tower *ipso facto* stands for Paris, Big Ben for London, and the Empire State Building evokes New York all on its lonesome, what do you see in your mind's eye when you think Tokyo? The most obvious marker is the Tokyo Tower, a gaudy orange (if slightly taller) mimic of the grand Eiffel in Paris. Tokyo's most emblematic skyscrapers are similarly plagiarized. The Nippon Telegraph and Telephone (NTT) building in Shinjuku is a grim, dark and windowless echo of the Empire State Building. Odaiba, the artificial island in Tokyo Bay, greets incoming ships with its diminutive replica of … the Statue of Liberty, courtesy, again, of France.

Tokyo's brand is about mimicry and hybridization, borrowing influences and recreating them in the context of local culture. That is an image that requires new branding strategies for comprehension and appreciation.

TOKYO'S BRAND IMPRESARIO

I first saw Tokyo artist Takashi Murakami's art in the form of his sculpture called *Hiropon*: a wide-eyed girl-woman with massive breasts swinging a stream of lactating milk like a jump-rope around her skipping body. The torso and legs were lean and athletic, the breasts comically huge. The milk looked nearly lethal – more a bondage device of rippled eaves than a stream of life-enhancing liquid. Hiropon's sparkly oversized eyes above a pert and tiny nose at first struck me as too self-consciously borrowed from anime cliché. But upon closer inspection, I realized why they were making me increasingly uneasy: blank white orbs of reflected light sat just off-center, adding a hint of Orphan Annie inscrutability to the colorful swathes surrounding them. Viewed from other angles, their vapidity could look menacing. She was cute, even sexy by way of hyperbolic parody. But she was also, quite possibly, deranged. I was new to Tokyo then, but discovering Hiropon in an otherwise unremarkable western suburb made perfect sense.

Tokyo had already become for me a city in which stumbling upon the tantalizing amid the mundane had itself become commonplace.

A few days later, I learned that 'hiropon' referred to meth-amphetamines – in particular, the uppers consumed by Japanese laborers building a new Tokyo during Japan's postwar reconstruction. The word was also a street name for heroin. At the time, I was drafting a short story I had been commissioned to write (Kelts, 1999). It was taking shape at least partly as an exploration of two of my frequent obsessions, delusional longing and delusional nostalgia, and I could not resist borrowing Takashi Murakami's sculpture for its title: 'Hiropon my Heroine'.

Murakami has since become well-known internationally as a bridge between Japan's contemporary pop culture imagery, largely via manga, anime and toys, and its contemporary art and fashion scenes – largely via ample commercial success in the former and rampant commercialism in the latter. He has also become something of an impresario, presenting contemporary Japanese artists to the global art market via Tokyo and New York, and offering provocative theories in order to both explain and brand them for consumption. The Takashi Murakami who has been the subject of major shows in Los Angeles, New York and Europe is a seasoned businessman, unabashedly so. Newspapers gleefully call him 'the artist as CEO', and complaints arose from the usual suspects in 2003 when he accepted Luis Vuitton designer Marc Jacobs's invitation to brand the company's famous brown handbags with the smiling colorful flower icons of earlier Murakami paintings.

Murakami has also almost single-handedly opened Tokyo to the buyers, critics and fans of the global art circuit. With his own aesthetic whims as guidance, he selects and helps to cultivate the careers of Japanese artists such as Chiho Aoshima and Mr., both of whom now work in the newly constructed artists' studio space in Queens. Through his Geisai Art Fairs in Japan, Murakami hopes to open the Tokyo art world to the ambitions and achievements of the city's native artists. 'In the West, you [already] have your galleries and exhibitions', says one of his New York staffers. 'But in Japan it's much less rigidly defined. Takashi's fairs are to stimulate buying and selling, and to get young artists exposed. He's trying to establish an art market for less established figures.'

So who is the real Takashi Murakami, emblem of Tokyo? A skilfull huckster, spinning shallow art and consumerism into a capitalist enterprise and shoving it back at the West at inflated cost? A middle-aged postmodern hipster with a native knack for blending high and low in the name of the now that rivals Madison Avenue's brightest? Or a bit of both – plus a genuinely serious trained craftsman who is able to convey today's Japan in all of its cartoonish identities, and show the West what it wants to see in today's Japan? Those of us who have lived and worked in Tokyo may see less reason to begin asking these questions or even raising debate, for Murakami is very much of and about the city in which he still spends most of his time. His most oft-cited boilerplate theories – 'superflat' as a culturally specific aesthetic style and 'little boy' as a culturally specific historical pathology – are better personified in the city of Tokyo than anywhere else in the world.

Superflat is hardly new, but it is handy – a single word to summon images of sleek computer monitors and flat panel television screens while suggesting a historical lineage (pun intended) of respectability and mystique. Japanese artists' relative emphasis on the manipulation of the line, or the outline of shapes and forms, for effect over the shading techniques (classic *chiaroscuro*) of depth perception and perspective pursued by Western artists is an example of superflat that can be traced back to the *emakimono* picture scrolls of the 12th century. The Japanese have always seen and conveyed the world in this way, according to Murakami, and now, with our addictions to streaming Internet videos, computer games, cell phone and LCD screens, so do the rest of us.

When I was forced to describe the contrasting views of New York and Tokyo from above (my airplane porthole window) in my book *Japanamerica* (Kelts, 2007), I used the following metaphors. New York, with its rising stone skyscrapers and falling avenue valleys in grid-like order, its shapely rivers and natural contours and stolid burnished lights, appeared to me as a jewel below, elegant and sturdy, clearly defined as it reached up toward you, beckoning calmly. Tokyo, by contrast, with endlessly circuitous patterns seeming to follow their own Byzantine logic, an uncertain relationship with the sea (an artificial island in the middle of the bay?), and red lights and neons blinking neurotically and sleeplessly, looked more like a computer chip, a tangled mass of somehow interlocking devices that never revealed a start or a finish, pulsing on with perpetual data.

From above, New York is all about rising and falling, foreground and back, the space between the Empire State Building's mighty spire and the broad dark magnificence of 5th Avenue at its side. Gazing down over Tokyo, I can rarely identify a single street, building or neighborhood. Instead there is the seemingly endless, and very flat, expanse of the urban.

As above, so below. Stroll down Broadway from upper Manhattan. Unless you are a native, and thus too frenzied and focused to pause, you will be taking time out to view the balconies and turrets, the forceful thrust of buildings like the Flatiron, or the cavernous gaps of courtyards behind iron gates. The contrast of light and shadow lures you in.

In Tokyo, the casual visitor is awash in light. Buildings assert themselves, to be sure, surrounded by narrow alleyways that are barely visible in the glow. But it is hard to notice them amid the action on the street – flashing signs inviting you to all-night *izakayas* (food and drink bars), karaoke bars, hostess clubs, fast-food counters and noodle shops. They envelop every train station, so where you are matters less than the fact that you are there. Wherever you alight in the city of Tokyo, this is what you expect – and this is what you get. Superflat.

Is it any wonder that Murakami greets us with the proliferating mushroom clouds of the only nation struck by nuclear bombs, that he sends us flowers of power with quizzically broad smiles, that his drugged up, dazed and giddily mindless Hiropon has vast breasts, mammoth milk – and an unnervingly aggressive desire to please?

Superflat is a clever word for an artistic approach that may well have been historically amenable to Japanese tastes. And Murakami may be at least partly right in suggesting that an accidental convergence is taking place in the 21st century, making manga, anime, fashion, high-and-low and East-and-West more blissfully confused and connected than before. To paraphrase English pop band the Vapors, maybe we are, in this manner, 'turning Japanese'.

Murakami's 'little boy' theory – that his nation has for 60 years learned to become servile to Western interests, and developed the appropriate resentments and related irreverence – is a psycho-historic aesthetic of wounded pride and disfigured ambition. To pursue, but not embrace, his positing of America, and the West, as big brother, I still think it is helpful to look directly at Tokyo.

I have a personal stake in this vantage. While my mother was born in Tokyo, she was raised in northern Japan, first in the village of Esashi, later in the small city of Morioka. If you visit either Esashi or Morioka today, you will find little of the combined deference, worship and disenchantment with the West that colors Murakami's vision. Despite harsher economic conditions than those in Tokyo, local citizens in those communities act with sincere beneficence – and also sincere difference. They do not expect non-Japanese to behave like the Japanese do, hence they seem more provincial to the international traveler. At the same time, they do not harbor the vindictiveness or self-loathing inherent to Murakami's best work. They were neither buried in Western icons nor brutalized by American soldiers. No wonder.

Where else in the world would a capital city boast as its landmarks crude copies of other cities' landmarks, and leading artists whose grasp of capitalistic reproduction exceeds that of their primary sources? Tokyo's city brand is rooted in its postwar history – a hybridized, post-industrial megalo-polis of the 21st century, an urban center that questions the value of originality through its native acquisitions, its astute borrowings of what symbolizes other cities, even as it reinvents itself out of necessity. In short, Tokyo's brand is a mashup, a remix, a postwar matrix of temples to spirituality (Buddhism and Shinto, the national faiths) and capitalism (skyscrapers and statues appro-priated from Western models). As such, Tokyo has emerged as a distinctly con-temporary city brand, sprung from obscurity via Western films like 2004's 'Lost in Translation' and native anime masterworks like 'Akira'. Tokyo is a real town full of real people, mega-millions of them. But after decades on the world's stage, it remains as much of a cipher as Hello Kitty – tantalizing and expressionless, massive but hidden, an empty vessel you can fill with your wildest dreams. Oh, what a town.

CHAPTER 29

The City Branding of Wollongong

Greg Kerr, Gary Noble and John Glynn

INTRODUCTION

The city of Wollongong's brand image strategy, 'Wollongong: City of Innovation' was implemented in 1999 and is still in use in 2010. The objective of this chapter is firstly to show how the leaders in the city of Wollongong came to realize that the image of their city had become a barrier to the city's improvement and growth. Secondly, supported by an analysis of recent interviews with some involved in the brand strategy, an explanation is provided of the process which was undertaken to gain support for, and implement, what was to become known as the city image campaign. Advice has also been obtained from some stakeholders as to what could have been done better and what more could have been done. Finally, some concluding comments are provided.

The next section provides some background information on the city of Wollongong. Familiarity with some of its characteristics aids an understanding of the argument for the city's brand image strategy.

THE CITY OF WOLLONGONG

Wollongong is located on the east coast of Australia in the State of New South Wales (NSW), approximately 100 kilometers south of that state's capital, Sydney. Wollongong is the third largest city in NSW, with a population of 201,438 in 2009 (Wollongong City Council, 2010a). Throughout the 1900s, the city's industrial base was dominated by a steelworks located south of the city center at Port Kembla. In addition to the direct export of coal, the local mines were integrated with steel production. Together with a busy port, road and rail freight were important to these industries and further contributed to the working class character of the city. By the 1980s the steelworks was being rationalized, having been subjected to downturns in demand, increased competition and opportunities to reduce costs by the introduction of labor-saving technology. The Port Kembla Steelworks had reduced its workforce from 22,000 to less than 7,000 by the early 1990s (Watson, 1991; Garrett-Jones *et al.*, 2007). For similar reasons, the local coal mines were also succumbing to economic pressures and were introducing more sophisticated mining equipment which required less labor.

Although in 2010 both the steelworks and coal mines are benefiting from their production efficiencies and unprecedented demand from China and India, the experience of the late 1980s and 1990s had provided an incentive for the city's leaders to look to seek ways to diversify the city's industrial base. In 1991, the unemployment rate in the Illawarra Region (Wollongong containing approximately two-thirds of this region's population) was 13.6 per cent and the region was above the state average in all age categories, particularly persons under 25 years (Buchan Consulting, 2003). The experience of Wollongong at this time was similar to many industrial cities throughout the world (for example, see Kotler *et al.*, 1993; Dickinson, 2006).

THE NEED FOR THE IMAGE CAMPAIGN

In addition to the realities of the economic downturn of the early 1990s, Wollongong was often the subject of negative media stories. The Wollongong Image Strategy (Valerio *et al.*, 1999) reported that there had been a wide range of negative articles relating to serious crime, heavy industry, pollution and floods. Industrial unrest was also identified as a deterrent for potential investors. It was common for a number of well-known Australian comedians to ridicule Wollongong in their nationally televised performances.

Despite some broadening of its industry base in the early 1990s, particularly with the growth of the local university and other service-based industries such as information technology (Buchan Consulting, 2003), a number of the city's leaders were deeply concerned about the image of the city and realized that there was reluctance on the part of external investors to even consider Wollongong as a place to invest. One of the then community leaders reflected:

'Those people that we needed to bring as investors into the new economy still had the perception that you wouldn't go there because it's a steel town.'

Another person interviewed explained:

'Well Wollongong had a very bad image. And a lot of it was historic; you know, all the families that used to go down the South Coast and had to wind their way down [the] Highway, through Wollongong, past the smoke stacks, sulphur; and they came down on school excursions in the 1960s and 1970s and so on and visited Port Kembla which was a filthy joint in those days. I think there was just a general view that there was nothing good in Wollongong at all. There were [TV] shows that lampooned Wollongong; so there was this great history of Wollongong as being the laughing stock of NSW and [in reality] its nothing like the image that was portrayed.'

It was realized that there was no attempt being made to control and manage messages about Wollongong, with the comment being made, 'it pretty much had a life of its own'. The 'Wollongong problem', as with many other places which have become involved in place branding, gave rise to what Ecorys Research and Consulting (2008: 7) refer to as a 'sense of urgency' which did eventuate in a 'true commitment of public and private partners to the marketing process'. The impact of a negative image had been identified by some of the city's leaders. On reviewing the process, a number of important phases have been identified by the authors. These are addressed in the following sections.

THE RESOURCING PHASE

One of the main instigators of the brand strategy for Wollongong was the then Chair of the Tourist Board who, as was claimed by one stakeholder, was keen to promote the city for tourism purposes but was concerned about 'the negative impact of our industrial image'. One stakeholder advised that despite the Chair's foresight and enthusiasm 'he really couldn't do anything about it, because he didn't have the money or the power'. The Chair had, however, become a champion of place branding and commenced what Morgan, Pritchard and Pride (2004: 8) refer to as the 'political act of place branding'. To gain resources, political support was required and one stakeholder suggested that the Chair of the Tourism Board, 'through effective lobbying, and use of newspapers, garnered support from [the General Manager] and [the Lord Mayor]'. The proposal for a brand image strategy in Wollongong not only gained high level support, but also a number of the city leaders took on a specific role. One stakeholder explained:

'[The Lord Mayor] had to take up the political salesmanship of it, and that was both to other councillors and the community. [The Chair of the Tourism Board] obviously had to convince the industry that we had to go through some planning steps rather than just sticking some money into a media campaign … and [The General Manager of the council] was as always a quintessential public servant's role, how [to] actually make this happen from an administrative perspective … So there were the distinct roles I suppose.'

The Council allocated $2.5 million over five years to the city image campaign. Not only did the proposed city image campaign have broad political, bureaucratic and industry support, it had financial resources to proceed.

THE CONCEPTING PHASE

In addition to providing substantial funding, the council formed a high-powered Marketing and Promotions Committee, with the executive being the Lord Mayor, the General Manager of the City Council and the Chair of Tourism Wollongong. Committee members included councillors and business representatives. The committee ensured that it recruited people who had the desired capabilities to contribute to the project as explained in the consultant's report (Valerio *et al.*, 1999: iii):

'Driven by a desire to do more than simply produce an advertising campaign, Council engaged the assistance of advisors with experience in strategic destination marketing planning. This assistance was in the form of a small purpose-formed consortium led by Peter Valerio (Tourism Solutions and Marketing Places) in conjunction with Bill Baker (Destination Development Group) and Graeme Gulloch (from Wollongong firm Imagescape Pty. Ltd.). Frank Small and Associates was appointed to undertake primary research into Wollongong's image …'

The consultant's report provided details of the methodology used to undertake the research, which included the adoption of a framework based on internal assets and community values as well as existing and desired demand. An analysis of planning and tourism documents, as well as a review of other place marketing documents from places including Britain, Calgary, Glasgow, Las Vegas and Hawaii was undertaken. Academic literature on place image was also reviewed, such as Echtner and Ritchie (2003).

The consultants recommended that the vision for Wollongong is 'to be known for innovation, creativity and excellence' and that 'Wollongong: City of Innovation' be the primary tagline. They reminded their clients that despite the negative image of the 1980s and 1990s, innovation is a credible proposition for Wollongong (Wollongong City Council, 2010b), citing many examples ranging from the early days of its history (aviation pioneer

Lawrence Hargrave) through to the 1990s (The Intelligent Polymer Research Institute at the University of Wollongong and BHP's innovations in steel production). The consultants argued that the City of Innovation strategy not only included what was already there, but was 'an inclusive approach that can be presented as aspirational for all residents and organisations' (Valerio *et al.*, 1999: 76). Further, they identified innovation as 'the single most important attribute of successful organisations in the next century' (1999: 76).

THE IMPLEMENTATION PHASE

The Council declared the city a 'city of innovation' in June 1999 and the consultants' report provided recommendations regarding the implementation of the strategy, which included extensive advertising and public relations campaigns. The logo consequently developed by the city council is still in use in 2010. Despite detailed recommendations by the consultants regarding the implementation of the image strategy, there were some obstacles encountered, particularly as some elements of the community were not supportive. In an organizational context, the work of Hatch and Schultz (1997) and de Chernatony (1999) might aid the understanding of the brand-culture gap encountered. A community leader involved in the image campaign reflected:

'I don't know that we necessarily have a level of self-belief as a community … I don't know that we have that sort of pride; we can be self-deprecating at times; we can you know, put ourselves down.'

Despite some negativity, those leading the image campaign were able to garner support (see Vallaster and de Chernatony, 2006 regarding the importance of leadership in organizational brand implementation). An individual who was at the time a senior manager of the local newspaper commented:

'And I remember that they came to see me, we had a meeting with [the general manager of council] and [brand manager] … where they were clearly seeking the [local newspaper's] support, … council was spending a lot of money on this, half a million dollars a year and they didn't want I suppose, to have the local media criticising them at every turn.'

REFLECTIONS OF STAKEHOLDERS

There is evidence to suggest that the brand image campaign was successful. When asked to reflect on the process of the image campaign, the issues of a realistic timeframe and commitment were identified.

With regard to the timeframe, one stakeholder commented that stakeholders needed to understand that the brand image strategy was a medium to long-term project:

'The advice would be that it's a long term thing. That it can't be done in 12 months. That you have to set a strategy and follow it through … I would say a minimum of three years. To allow the message to get out and for the message to be consistent, so it needs to be funded and committed to for three to five years. That would be my strongest recommendation, that it can't possibly be a quick fix and that five years is a probably a good time. Even three years might be a bit short.'

Largely because of the required timeframe, the matter of commitment was also identified by stakeholders as being important. While the brand tagline, City of Innovation, is still being used in 2010, most of the instigators have moved on to other positions or retired from the workforce. The need for continuity of commitment was identified:

'The people with the high energy passion aren't as involved now as they were … so we are looking for a renewal … in terms of people with the passion who carry it forward … the nucleus of those that were driving the … strategy … are now out doing other things. Where is the next generation of passion? … we can talk how it is all in a practical sense, and we can map things out, but if you don't have the community spirit and community pride, and you don't have individuals to drive the passion, how do you get these things to happen.'

While it could be argued that the worst has passed with regard to Wollongong's economic and consequent social problems of the 1980s and 1990s, one stakeholder suggested that there is a need to continue with place marketing and not 'down tools'. One key stakeholder reflected:

'There is a lack of a follow-up organisation – if it just stops dead and nothing else happens you have wasted your … money. If it led to something, which in Wollongong it did … that's where we are now … that's the biggest problem.'

Interestingly, in 2008 Wollongong City Council made national and international headlines. Even the English tabloids reported on the sexual exploits of a town planner and property developers and alleged payments from developers to councilors and staff, eventually resulting in the dismissal of the elected council and the appointment of administrators. Some community leaders are now advocating for another city image campaign to counter the alleged damage that has been done to the city's image.

SUCCESS OF WOLLONGONG'S CAMPAIGN

There is evidence to suggest that the city image campaign had been successful. A benchmark study of Wollongong's image was conducted in 1999 by the Illawarra Regional Information Service (IRIS) and by way of comparisons to findings of their 2004 study, the external perceptions of Wollongong had shown significant improvement over that period. For example, it was found that the proportion of people who believed that Wollongong offers beautiful, unspoiled natural attractions had increased from 49 per cent in the benchmark measure to 73 per cent. Equally importantly, it was found that the image of Wollongong as being 'industrially orientated' had weakened over the period since the benchmark survey (IRIS Research, 2004).

The success of the image campaign was not only the result of the public relations and advertising strategies. The functional benefits (see Hankinson and Cowking, 1995; Hankinson, 2005) of the Wollongong brand had changed. For instance, Wollongong Image Strategy (Valerio *et al.*, 1999) reported on the ongoing efforts of the Port Kembla Steelworks to blend and soften the image of the plant by planting 500,000 trees on the site and painting the structures. The city council has improved the city's beach reserves and constructed cycleways. Capital investment has delivered new industrial and residential developments.

SUMMARY

It is a significant challenge for a place brand to have relevance across a number of its sectors, unless of course the brand is specifically designed for one sector. While there is evidence supporting the success of Wollongong's image campaign, tourism operators had difficulty in leveraging the 'City of Innovation' tagline to attract leisure tourists. Other cities have attempted to adopt taglines that have relevance to a number of their sectors, for example 'Accelerate Cape Town' (www.acceleratecapetown.com/) and 'Thrive in Armidale' (www.armidaletourism.com.au/). Attempts are now being made by some community leaders in Wollongong to implement an 'Advantage Wollongong' campaign, which expresses the city's strategic advantages regarding its location, innovation, trade, growth and lifestyle. This was endorsed by the City Council and supported by the local Business Chamber but has yet to be supported or funded to the same extent as the initial city image campaign.

The case of Wollongong shows how a negative image can be a barrier to growth and change. An examination of the case provides some useful lessons. These include the importance of having high level political and bureaucratic support and the formation of partnerships amongst community leaders. Furthermore, the importance of having the necessary level of financial resources and people with capabilities in place marketing has been shown. The city brand strategy should be based on sound research. Importantly, the brand campaign needs to have a medium to long-term focus, and be able to maintain continuity by the recruitment of new enthusiastic people when needed. Finally, managing the meaning of a place in the minds of the people who matter to its future should be an ongoing task and not one that is only given priority in response to a crisis.

References

Aaker, D. (1996), *Building Strong Brands*, The Free Press, New York, United States.

Aaker, D. and Joachimsthaler, E. (2000), *Brand Leadership*, The Free Press, New York, United States.

Accra Metropolitan Assembly (2007), *Medium Term Development Plan 2006–2009*.

Accra Metropolitan Assembly (2009), *A New Accra for a Better Ghana: Medium Term Development Plan 2010–2013*.

Advisory Council on the Environment (2008), "Brand Hong Kong Review", ACE Paper 20/2008, available at: http://www.epd.gov.hk/epd/english/boards/advisory_council/files/ACE_Paper_20_2008.pdf (accessed 6 February 2010).

Ahmedabad Mirror (2010), "A word worth thousand pictures: Amdavad", 3 January, p. 10.

AllMalaysia (2010), "Strictly Malaysian – Malaysia Boleh!", available at: http://allmalaysia.info/msiaknow/malaysiana/malaysia_boleh.asp (accessed 28 January 2010).

Andersen, V., Prentice, R. and Guerin, S. (1997), "Imagery of Denmark among visitors to Danish fine arts exhibitions in Scotland", *Tourism Management*, Vol. 18, No. 7, pp. 453–464.

Anholt, S. (2004), *Brand New Justice*, Second edition, Butterworth-Heinemann, Oxford, United Kingdom.

Anholt, S. (2006a), "The Anholt-GMI City Brands Index: How the world sees the world's cities", *Place Branding*, Vol. 2, No. 1, pp. 18–31.

Anholt, S. (2006b), "Public diplomacy and place branding: Where's the link?", *Place Branding*, Vol. 2, No. 4, pp. 271–275.

Anholt, S. (2007), *Competitive Identity: The New Brand Management for Nations, Cities and Regions*, Palgrave Macmillan, London, United Kingdom.

Anholt, S. (2008), "Place branding: Is it marketing, or isn't it?", *Place Branding and Public Diplomacy*, Vol. 4, No. 1, pp. 1–6.

Anholt-Gfk Roper City Brands Index (2009), www.gfkamerica.com

Anon (2010) "Absolutely, positively Wellington", *Business Today*, Issue 41 (Dec. 2009–Jan. 2010), p. 53.

Ariffin, A.A.M and Hasim, M.S. (2009), "Marketing Malaysia to the Middle East tourists: Towards a preferred inter-regional destinations", *International Journal of West Asian Studies*, Vol. 1, No. 1, pp. 43–58.

Ashworth, G. (2009), "The instruments of place branding: How is it done?", *European Spatial Research and Policy*, Vol. 16, No. 1, pp. 9–22.

Askegaard, S. and Ger, G. (1998), "Product-country images: Towards a contextualized approach", *European Advances in Consumer Research*, Vol. 3, pp. 50–58.

Astrup, S. (2009), Politiken.dk, "Københavns ry vinder på topmøde" [Copenhagen's reputation wins at summit], *Politiken.dk*, 19 December, available at: http://politiken.dk/klima/Topmode_i_Kobenhavn/ article864489.ece (accessed 5 February 2010).

Avraham, E. and Ketter, E. (2008), *Media Strategies for Marketing Places in Crisis: Improving the Image of Cities, Countries and Tourist Destinations*, Butterworth-Heinemann, Oxford, United Kingdom.

Baker, B. (2007), *Destination Branding for Small Cities: The Essentials for Successful Place Branding*, Creative Leap Books, Portland, Oregon, United States.

Balibrea, M. (2001), "Urbanism, culture and the post-industrial city: Challenging the 'Barcelona Model'", *Journal of Spanish Cultural Studies*, Vol. 2, No. 2, pp. 187–210.

Balmer, J.M.T. and Greyser, S.A. (2003), *Revealing the Corporation: Perspectives on Identity, Image, Reputation, Corporate Branding and Corporate Branding*, Routledge, London, United Kingdom.

Bayliss, D. (2007), "The rise of the creative city: Culture and creativity in Copenhagen", *European Planning Studies*, Vol. 15, No. 7, pp. 889–903.

Bell, D. and Valentine, G. (1997), *Consuming Geographies: We are Where We Eat*, Routledge, London, United Kingdom.

Bentil, N.L. (2010), "Accra declared Millennium City", *Daily Graphic (Metro News)*, 16 January, p. 18.

Berács, J. (2005), "Opinion pieces: How has place branding developed during the year that *Place Branding* has been in publication?", *Place Branding*, Vol. 2, No. 1, pp. 6–17.

Bickford-Smith, V. (2009), "Creating a city of the tourist imagination: The case of Cape Town, 'The Fairest Cape of Them All'", *Urban Studies*, Vol. 46, No. 9, pp. 1763–1785.

Biel, A.L. (1993), "Converting image into equity", in Aaker, D. and Biel, A.L. (eds), *Brand Equity and Advertising – Advertising's Role in Building Strong Brands*, Psychology Press, United States, pp. 67–82.

Black, R. (2009), "Why did Copenhagen fail to deliver a climate deal?", *BBC News*, 22 December 2009, available at: http://news.bbc.co.uk/2/hi/science/nature/8426835.stm (accessed 5 February 2010).

Boer, J.D. (2009), "Top 20 of the world's best city icons", *The Pop-Up City*, online, available at: http://popupcity.net/2009/05/top-20-of-the-worlds-best-city-icons/ (accessed 7 January 2010).

Boissevain, J. (1992), "Introduction", in Boissevain, J. (ed.), *Revitalizing European Rituals,* Routledge, London, United Kingdom, pp. 1–19.

Braiterman, J. and Takahashi, Y. (2010), "Urban biodiversity identification and tracking system", paper presented at Urban Biodiversity & Design – URBIO 2010 International Conference, 18–22 May, Nagoya, Japan.

Brown, A. (2010), *Just Enough: Lessons in Green Living from Traditional Japan*, Kodansha International, Tokyo, Japan.

Brown, G., Chalip, L., Jago, L. and Mules, T. (2002), "The Sydney Olympics and brand Australia", in Morgan, N., Pritchard, A. and Pride, R. (eds), *Destination Branding: Creating the Unique Destination Proposition*, Butterworth-Heinemann, Oxford, United Kingdom, pp. 163–185.

Buchan Consulting (2003), Wollongong Economic Development Road Map, available at: http://www.wollongong.nsw.gov.au/documents/Wollongong_Economic_Development_Roadmap.pdf (accessed 15 May 2010).

Burgan, B. and Mules, T. (1992), "Economic impact of sporting events", *Annals of Tourism Research*, Vol. 19, No. 4, pp. 700–710.

Business Week (2009a), "The Madrid region concentrated 82% of foreign direct investment into Spain during 2008. Do you want to know why?", 28 December, p. 23.

Business Week (2009b), "Japan regional initiative – Food industry Saitama-Shizuoka: A mouth-watering opportunity", 28 December, p. 77.

Business Week (2009c), "The Kyrgyz Republic looks ahead", 28 December, pp. 85–91.

Carr, J. and Servon, L. (2009), "Vernacular culture and urban economic development: Thinking outside the (big) box", *Journal of the American Planning Association*, Vol. 75, No. 1, pp. 28–40.

CEOs for Cities (2010), "New York city's $19b green dividend", April 21, available at: http://www.ceosforcities.org/ (accessed 30 May 2010).

Chalip, L. and Costa, C.A. (2005), "Sport event tourism and the destination brand: Towards a general theory", *Sport in Society*, Vol. 8, No. 2, pp. 218–237.

Chang, T.C. (2000), "Renaissance revisited: Singapore as a 'Global City for the Arts'", *International Journal of Urban and Regional Research*, Vol. 24, No. 4, pp. 818–831.

Chesshyre, T. (2009), "Copenhagen: Europe's greenest city", *The Times*, 5 December, available at: http://www.timesonline.co.uk/tol/travel/holiday_type/green_travel/article6941259.ece (accessed 5 February 2010).

Chinese Academy of Social Sciences (2009), *Blue Book of Cities in China*, Urban Development and Environment Research Center, Beijing, China.

Choe, S.-H. (2010), "In Seoul, green transit is mayor's pet project", *New York Times*, 27 March, p. 3.

Clark, G. (2007), *Report to the Economic Development Committee, City of Toronto, a Presentation to The City of Toronto*, January 24.

Cohen, E. (1988), "Authenticity and commoditization in tourism", *Annals of Tourism Research*, Vol. 15, No. 3, pp. 371–386.

Commission on Strategic Development (2000), "Bringing the vision to life: Hong Kong's long-term development needs and goals", available at: http://www.info.gov.hk/gia/general/200002/21/0221082.htm (accessed 12 January 2010).

Crandall, D., Backstrom, L., Huttenlocher, D. and Kleinberg, J. (2009), "Mapping the world's photos", Working Paper of the International World Wide Web Conference Committee, 20–24 April, Madrid, Spain, available at: http://www2009.eprints.org/77/1/p761.pdf (accessed 5 June 2010).

Cushman & Wakefield (2009), *European Cities Monitor 2009*, www.cushwake.com

Daily Express, East Malaysia (2009), "Najib explains 'One Malaysia' concept", 3 April, available at: http://www.dailyexpress.com.my/news.cfm?NewsID=63970 (accessed 7 January 2010).

DBKL (2008), "Research on creating various tourism products in Kuala Lumpur", prepared by the Consultation Unit of the University of Malaya for Kuala Lumpur City Hall.

De Carlo, M., Canali, S., Pritchard, A. and Morgan, N. (2009), "Moving Milan towards Expo 2015: Designing culture into a city brand", *Journal of Place Management and Development*, Vol. 2, No. 1, pp. 8–22.

de Chernatony, L. (1999), "Brand management through narrowing the gap between brand identity and brand reputation", *Journal of Marketing Management*, Vol. 15, Nos 1–3, pp. 157–179.

de Chernatony, L. and Christodoulides, G. (2004), "Taking the brand promise online: Challenges and opportunities", *Interactive Marketing*, Vol. 5, No. 3, pp. 238–251.

Delaney, K., and Eckstein, R. (2007), "Urban power structures and publicly financed stadiums", *Sociological Forum*, Vol. 22, No. 3, pp. 331–353.

Delanty, G. (1998), "Redefining political culture in Europe today: From ideology to the politics of identity and beyond", in Hedentoft, U. (ed.), *Political Symbols, Symbolic Politics: European Identities in Transformation*, Ashgate Publishing Company, Hampshire, United Kingdom, pp. 23–43.

Demos (2003), "Manchester is favourite with the 'new bohemians'", available at: http://www.demos.co.uk/press_releases/bohobritain (accessed 10 January 2010).

"Destination Edinburgh marketing alliance: A step change for Edinburgh", September 2009, DEMA (prepared on their behalf by Leithal Thinking). Available at: http://www.edinburgh-brand.com/PDF/DEMA%20General%20Presentation%20December.pdf (accessed 5 February 2010).

Devlin, J.F. and McKechnie, S. (2008), "Consumer perceptions of brand architecture in financial services", *European Journal of Marketing*, Vol. 42, No. 5/6, pp. 654–666.

Dickinson, S. (2006), "Urban regeneration: UK practice", in Diamond, J., Liddle, J., Southern, A. and Townsend, A. (eds), *Managing the City*, Routledge, United Kingdom, pp. 16–31.

Dinnie, K. (2008), *Nation Branding – Concepts, Issues, Practice*, Butterworth-Heinemann, Oxford, United Kingdom.

Dooley, G. and Bowie, D. (2005), "Place brand architecture: Strategic management of the brand portfolio", *Place Branding*, Vol. 1, No. 4, pp. 402–419.

dottourism.com (2010), "Case study – Monaco", available at: http://www.dottourism.com/case-study-monaco-tourism-email-marketing.php (accessed 5 January 2010).

Dutch Ministry of Foreign Affairs (2008), *Be Our Guests: Policy Review on Hosting International Organisations in the Netherlands*, No. 316, The Hague: Inspectie Ontwikkelingssamenwerking en Beleidsevaluatie.

Echtner, C.M. and Ritchie, J.R.B. (2003), "The meaning and measurement of destination image: [Reprint of original article published in v. 2, no. 2, 1991: 2–12.]", *Journal of Tourism Studies*, Vol. 14, No. 1, pp. 37–48.

Economist (2009), "Go north … or go south", 8 June, available at: http://www.economist.com/markets/rankings/displaystory.cfm?story_id=E1_TPRDJSSD (accessed 5 February 2010).

Ecorys Research and Consulting (2008), *The City and Region Success Carrier*, available at: http://www.ecorys.com/news-items-press-releases/the-ecorys-approach-to-place-marketing.html (accessed 2 May 2008).

Education Malaysia (2009), "International student statistics", available at: http://educationmalaysia.gov.my/studentpass2008.php (accessed 27 January 2010).

Edvinsson, L. (2006), "Aspects on the city as a knowledge tool", *Journal of Knowledge Management*, Vol. 10, No. 5, pp. 6–13.

Ernst & Young (2008), Baromed 2008, The Next European Frontier, www.ey.com

Ernst & Young (2009), *Globalization Index 2009*, available at: http://www.ey.com/GL/en/Issues/Business-environment/Redrawing-the-map--globalization-and-the-changing-world-of-business—The-Globalization-Index-2009 (accessed 2 June 2010).

Evans, G. (2003), "Hard-branding the cultural city – From Prado to Prada", *International Journal of Urban and Regional Research*, Vol. 27, No. 2, pp. 417–440.

Finfacts (2008), "Dublin fourth most expensive city of 71 global cites – Kuala Lumpur cheapest according to UBS report", available at: http://www.finfacts.com/irishfinancenews/article_1012932.shtml (accessed 21 January 2010).

Florek, M. and Conejo, F. (2007), "Export flagships in branding small developing countries: The cases of Costa Rica and Moldova", *Place Branding and Public Diplomacy*, Vol. 3, No. 1, pp. 53–72.

Florek, M., Insch, A. and Gnoth, J. (2006), "City Council websites as a means of place brand identity communication", *Place Branding*, Vol. 2, No. 4, pp. 276–296.

Florida, R. (2003), *The Rise of the Creative Class: And How It's Transforming Work, Leisure, Community and Everyday Life*, Basic Books, New York, United States.

Florida, R. (2005), *The Flight of the Creative Class: The New Global Competition for Talent*, HarperBusiness, New York, United States.

Fola, M. (2007), "The international image of Greece. An analysis on the occasion of the Athens 2004 Olympic Games", Hellenic Observatory 3rd PhD Symposium on Contemporary Greece, 14–15 June, available at: http://www.lse.ac.uk/collections/hellenicObservatory/pdf/3rd_Symposium/PAPERS/FOLA_MARIA.pdf (accessed 12 April 2010).

Forbes.com (2009), "City blogs", available at: http://autos.forbes.com/bow/b2c/category.jhtml?id=23 (accessed 3 January 2010).

Foreign Policy (2009), "The 2008 Global Cities Index", Nov./Dec., Issue 169, pp. 68–76.

Fortune (2009), 'Jalisco – Mexico's innovation capital', 21 December, p. 57.

Freire, J.R. (2005), "Geo-branding, are we talking nonsense? A theoretical reflection on brands applied to places", *Place Branding*, Vol. 1, No. 4, pp. 347–362.

Freire, J. (2009) "'Local People' a critical dimension for place brands", *Journal of Brand Management*, Vol. 16, No. 7, pp. 420–438.

Futurebuzz.com (2009), "49 amazing social media, Web 2.0 and Internet stats", available at: http://thefuturebuzz.com/2009/01/12/social-media-web-20-internet-numbers-stats/ (accessed 10 January 2010).

Gaggiotti, H., Cheng, P.L.C. and Yunak, O. (2008), "City brand management (CBM): The case of Khazakstan", *Place Branding and Public Diplomacy*, Vol. 4, No. 2, pp. 115–123.

Garrett-Jones, S., Gross, M., Kerr, G., Kotevski, S. and Zaeemdar, S. (2007), "Cities of innovation: Exploring the role of local community organisations in 'constructing advantage'", paper presented at the Australian and New Zealand Academy of Management Conference, 4–7 December, Sydney, Australia.

Gemeente Den Haag (Municipality of The Hague) (2008), *Economische betekenis internationale bedrijven en organisaties in Haaglanden (Economic impact of international corporations and organisations in Haaglanden region of Greater The Hague)*, The Hague: Decisio BV and Bureau Louter.

Gerhardt, W. (2008), "Prosumers: A new growth opportunity", Cisco Internet Business Solutions Group, available at: http://www.cisco.com/web/about/ac79/docs/wp/Prosumer_VS2_POV_0404_FINAL.pdf (accessed 5 January 2010).

Gilmore, F. (2002), "A country – Can it be repositioned? Spain – The success story of country branding", *Journal of Brand Management*, Vol. 9, Nos 4–5, pp. 281–293.

Govers, R. and Go, F.M. (2009), *Place Branding: Glocal, Virtual and Physical Identities, Constructed, Imagined and Experienced*, Palgrave Macmillan, Basingstoke, United Kingdom.

Grabow, B. (1998) *Stadtmarketing: Eine Kritische Zwischenbilanz*, Deutsches Institut für Urbanistik, Berlin, Germany.

Green, B.C. and Chalip, L. (1998), "Sport tourism as the celebration of subculture", *Annals of Tourism Research*, Vol. 25, No. 2, pp. 275–291.

Greenberg, M. (2000), "Branding cities: A social history of the urban lifestyle magazine", *Urban Affairs Review*, Vol. 36, No. 2, pp. 228–263.

Greenley, G.E. and Foxall, G.R. (1997), "Multiple stakeholder orientation in UK companies and the implications for company performance", *Journal of Management Studies*, Vol. 34, No. 2, pp. 259–284.

Guhathakurta, S. and Stimson, R.J. (2007), "What is driving the growth of new 'sunbelt' metropolises? Quality of life and urban regimes in Greater Phoenix and Brisbane-South East Queensland Region", *International Planning Studies*, Vol. 12, No. 2, pp. 129–152.

Hall, C.M., Sharples, L., Mitchell, R., Macionis, N. and Cambourne, B. (eds) (2003), *Food Tourism Around the World: Development, Management and Markets*, Butterworth-Heinemann, Oxford, United Kingdom.

Hankinson, G. (2001), "Location branding: A study of the branding practices of 12 English cities", *Journal of Brand Management*, Vol. 9, No. 2, pp. 127–142.

Hankinson, G. (2004), "Relational network brands: Towards a conceptual model of place brands", *Journal of Vacation Marketing*, Vol. 10, No. 2, pp. 109–121.

Hankinson, G. (2005), "Destination brand images: A business tourism perspective", *Journal of Services Marketing*, Vol. 19, No. 1, pp. 24–32.

Hankinson, G. (2007), "The management of destination brands: Five guiding principles based on recent developments in corporate branding theory", *Journal of Brand Management*, Vol. 14, No. 3, pp. 240–254.

Hankinson, G. (2009), "Managing destination brands: Establishing a theoretical foundation", *Journal of Marketing Management*, Vol. 25, Nos 1–2, pp. 97–115.

Hankinson, G. and Cowking, P. (1995), "What do you really mean by a brand?", *Journal of Brand Management*, Vol. 3, No. 1, pp. 43–50.

Harmaakorpi, V., Kari, K. and Parjanen, S. (2008), "City design management as a local competitiveness factor", *Place Branding and Public Diplomacy*, Vol. 4, No. 2, pp. 169–181.

Harrisinteractive.com (2009), "Internet users now spending an average of 13 hours a week online", available at: http://news.harrisinteractive.com/profiles/investor/ResLibraryView.asp?BzID=1963&Category=1777&ResLibraryID=35164 (accessed 2 January 2010).

Hatch, M. and Schultz, M. (1997), "Relations between organisational culture, identity and image", *European Journal of Marketing*, Vol. 31, No. 5, pp. 356–365.

Hayden, D. (1997), *The Power of Place: Urban Landscapes as Public History*, MIT Press, Cambridge, Massachusetts, United States.

Healey, P. (2004), "Creativity and urban governance", *Policy Studies*, Vol. 25, No. 2, pp. 87–102.

Heldt-Cassel, S. (2003), "Att tillaga en region" (In English: "The taste of the Archipelago. Representations and practises in regional food projects"), *Geografiska Regionstudier*, Vol. 56. Uppsala: Uppsala University.

Heritage Foundation (2010), *Index of Economic Freedom*, available at: http://www.heritage.org/Index/ (accessed 2 June 2010).

Hernandez, J. (2008), "Car-free streets, a Colombian export, inspire debate", *New York Times*, June 24, p. 6.

Hestor, R. (2006), *Design for Ecological Democracy*, MIT Press, Cambridge, United States.

Holman, N. (2008), "Community participation: Using social network analysis to improve developmental benefits", *Environment and Planning C: Government and Policy*, Vol. 26, No. 3, pp. 525–543.

Hong Kong General Chamber of Commerce (2003), "Developing Hong Kong's creative industries – An action-oriented strategy", available at: http://www.chamber.org.hk/member-area/chamber_view/others/Creative_industries.pdf (accessed 18 February 2010).

Hong Kong Information Services Department (2008), "Asia's world city", available at: http://www.info.gov.hk/info/sar5/easia.htm (accessed 3 February 2010).

Hong Kong Information Services Department (2009), "Hong Kong: The facts (tourism)", available at: http://www.gov.hk/en/about/abouthk/factsheets/docs/tourism.pdf (accessed 17 January 2010).

Hooi, N.S. (2009), "Air Asia named world's best low-cost carrier by Skytrax", 4 April, available at: http://thestar.com.my/news/story.asp?file=/2009/4/4/nation/20090404163724&sec=nation (accessed 27 January 2010).

Hospers, G.J. (2003), "Creative cities: Breeding places in the knowledge economy", *Knowledge, Technology, & Policy*, Vol. 16, No. 3, pp. 143–162.

Hospers, G.J. (2009a), *Citymarketing in Perspectief* (in Dutch), IVIO, Lelystad, The Netherlands.

Hospers, G.J. (2009b), "Lynch, Urry and city marketing: Taking advantage of the city as a built and graphic image", *Place Branding and Public Diplomacy*, Vol. 5, No. 3, pp. 226–233.

Hurme, P. (2001), "Online PR: Emerging organisational practice", *Corporate Communications: An International Journal*, Vol. 6, No. 2, pp. 71–75.

Ilbery, B. and Kneafsey, M. (2000), "Producer construction of quality in regional speciality food production: A case study from South West England", *Journal of Rural Studies*, Vol. 16, No. 2, pp. 217–230.

Illroots (2008), "Sean 'Diddy' Combs featured in NYC's Tourism Campaign 'Just Ask The Locals'", available at: http://illroots.com/2008/04/28/sean-diddy-combs-featured-in-nycs-tourism-campaign-just-ask-the-locals (accessed 24 January 2010).

Ind, N. and Riondino, C.M. (2001), "Branding on the web: A real revolution?", *Journal of Brand Management*, Vol. 9, No. 1, pp. 8–19.

Insch, A. (in press), "Managing residents' expectations and satisfaction with city life: Application of importance-satisfaction analysis", *Journal of Town and City Management*, Vol. 1, No. 2.

Insch, A. and Florek, M. (2008), "A great place to live, work and play: Conceptualising place satisfaction in the case of a city's residents", *Journal of Place Management and Development*, Vol. 1, No. 2, pp. 138–149.

Insch, A. and Florek, M. (2010), "Place satisfaction of city residents: Findings and implications for city branding", in Ashworth, G. and Kavaratzis, M. (eds), *Towards Effective Place Brand Management: Branding European Cities and Regions*, Edward Elgar, Cheltenham, United Kingdom.

Interbrand (2009), *Most Valuable Global Brands*, available at: http://www.interbrand.com (accessed 30 September 2009).

International Congress and Convention Association (2008), www.iccaworld.com

IRIS Research (2004), *Wollongong Image Study, 2004: Measuring External Perceptions of Wollongong*, Innovation Campus, University of Wollongong, Australia.

Jain, K. (1988), "Wooden houses", in Michell, G. and Shah, S. (eds), *Ahmadabad*, Marg Publications, Mumbai, India.

Jansson, J. and Power, D. (2006), *Image of the City: Urban Branding as Constructed Capabilities in Nordic City Regions*, Research Report, Nordic Innovation Centre, Oslo, Norway, available at: http://www.nordicinnovation.net/_img/image_of_the_city_-_web.pdf (accessed 2 June 2010).

Jinnai, H. (1995), *Tokyo: A Spatial Anthropology*, University of California Press, Berkeley, United States.

Kajikawa, A., Masuda, Y., Sato, M., Takahashi, N. and Ojima, T. (2005), "A field study on revival conditions of covered rivers in Tokyo's 23 wards", *Journal of Asian Architecture and Building Engineering*, Vol. 4, No. 2, pp. 489–494.

Kapferer, J.-N. (2008), *The New Strategic Brand Management: Creating and Sustaining Brand Equity Long Term*, Fourth edition, Kogan Page, London, United Kingdom.

Kavaratzis, M. (2004), "From city marketing to city branding: Towards a theoretical framework for developing city brands", *Place Branding*, Vol. 1, No. 1, pp. 58–73.

Kavaratzis, M. (2009a), "Cities and their brands: Lessons from corporate branding", *Place Branding and Public Diplomacy*, Vol. 5, No. 1, pp. 26–37.

Kavaratzis, M. (2009b), "What can we learn from city marketing practice?", *European Spatial Research and Policy*, Vol. 16, No. 1, pp. 41–58.

Kavaratzis, M. and Ashworth, G.J. (2006), "City branding: An effective assertion of identity or a transitory marketing trick?", *Place Branding*, Vol. 2, No. 3, pp. 183–194.

Kavaratzis, M. and Ashworth, G.J. (2007), "Partners in coffeeshops, canals and commerce: Marketing the city of Amsterdam", *Cities*, Vol. 24, No. 1, pp. 16–25.

Kazis, N. (2010), "Picturing a car-free seine: The new vision for the Paris waterfront", Streetsblog, 7 May, available at: http://www.streetsblog.org/2010/05/07/picturing-a-car-free-seine-the-new-vision-for-the-paris-waterfront/ (accessed 24 May 2010).

Keith, V. (2010), "Clip-on architecture: Reforesting cities", *Urban Omnibus*, 13 January, available at: http://urbanomnibus.net/2010/01/clip-on-architecture-reforesting-cities/ (accessed 28 May 2010).

Kelts, R. (1999), 'Hiropon my heroine', *Zoetrope All-Story*, Vol. 3, No. 4, available at: http://www.all-story.com/issues.cgi?action=show_story&story_id=55 (accessed 5 June 2010).

Kelts, R. (2007), *Japanamerica: How Japanese Pop Culture Has Invaded The U.S.*, Palgrave Macmillan, New York, United States.

Khera, M. (2009), "Ahmedabad: The entrepreneurship capital of India", *The Times of India*, Ahmedabad edition, 13 August, Special Supplement, p. 6.

Kleppe, I.A., Iversen, N.M. and Stensaker, I.G. (2002), "Country images in marketing strategies: Conceptual issues and an empirical Asian illustration", *Journal of Brand Management*, Vol. 10, No. 1, pp. 61–74.

Kneafsey, M. (2000), "Tourism, place identities and social relations in the European rural periphery", *European Urban and Regional Studies*, Vol. 7, No. 1, pp. 19–33.

Kotler, P., Asplund, C., Rein, I. and Haider, D.H. (1999), *Marketing Places Europe: How to Attract Investments, Industries, Residents and Visitors to Cities, Communities, Regions and Nations in Europe*, Financial Times Management, London, United Kingdom.

Kotler, P., Haider, D. and Rein, I. (1993), *Marketing Places: Attracting Investment, Industry, and Tourism to Cities, States, and Nations*, Free Press, New York, United States.

Kuala Lumpur City Hall (2008), *Draft Kuala Lumpur City Plan 2020*, available at: http://klcity-plan2020.dbkl.gov.my/eis/?page_id=280 (accessed 7 January 2010).

Kumagai, Y. and Yamada, Y. (2008), "Green space relations with residential values in downtown Tokyo: Implications for urban biodiversity conservation", *Local Environment: The International Journal of Justice and Sustainability*, Vol. 13, No. 2, pp. 141–157.

Lanfant, M.-F. (1995), "International tourism, internalization and the challenge to identity", in Lanfant, M.-F., Allcock, J.B. and Bruner, E.M. (eds), *International Tourism: Identity and Change*, Sage Publications, London, United Kingdom, pp. 24–43.

Leonard, M. (1997), *Britain ᵀᴹ Renewing Our Identity*, Demos, London, United Kingdom.

Lindstrom, M. (2001), "Corporate branding and the Web: A global/local challenge", *Journal of Brand Management*, Vol. 8, No. 4/5, pp. 365–368.

Long, L. (ed.) (2004), *Culinary Tourism*, University Press of Kentucky, Lexington, Kentucky, United States.

Lynch, K. (1960), *The Image of the City*, The MIT Press, Cambridge, United States.

MacCannell, D. (1999), *The Tourist: A New Theory of the Leisure Class*, University of California Press, Berkeley, United States.

Markusen, A. (2006), "Urban development and the politics of a creative class: Evidence from a study of artists", *Environment and Planning*, Vol. 38, No. 10, pp. 1921–1940.

Markusen, A. and Schrock, G. (2006), "The distinctive city: Divergent patterns in growth, hierarchy and specialization", *Urban Studies*, Vol. 43, No. 8, pp. 1301–1323.

Marshall, T. (ed.) (2004), *Transforming Barcelona*, Routledge, London, United Kingdom.

Martinez, J.G. (2007), "Selling avant-garde: How Antwerp became a fashion capital (1990–2002)", *Urban Studies*, Vol. 44, No. 12, pp. 2449–2464.

McCleary, K.W. and Whitney, D.L. (1994), "Projecting Western consumer attitudes toward travel to six Eastern European countries", in Uysal, M. (ed.), *Global Tourist Behaviour*, International Business Press, New York, United States, pp. 239–256.

McWilliam, G. (2000), "Building stronger brands through online communities", *Sloan Management Review*, Vol. 41, No. 3, pp. 43–54.

Mehta, H. (2010), "Vibrant Gujarat 2011 attempts a Davos", *The Times of India*, Ahmedabad edition, 5 February, p. 1.

Mehta, R.N. and Jamindar, R. (1988), "Urban context", in Michell, G. and Shah, S. (eds), *Ahmadabad*, Marg Publications, Mumbai, India.

Melissen, J. (2005), "Wielding soft power: The new public diplomacy", Netherlands Institute of International Relations "Clingendael", available at: http://www.clingendael.nl/publications/2005/20050500_cdsp_paper_diplomacy_2_melissen.pdf (accessed 5 June 2010).

Mercer Human Resource Consulting (2008), *Quality of Living Global City Rankings 2008*, available at: http://www.mercer.com/summary.htm?idContent=1307990 (accessed 25 May 2010).

Merton, R. (1968), "The Matthew effect in science", *Science*, Vol. 159, No. 3810, pp. 56–63.

Metzger, J. (2005), "I Köttbullslandet: Konstruktionen av svenskt och utländskt på det kulinariska fältet" (In the land of meatballs: The historical construction of Swedishness and foreignness in the culinary field), *Stockholm Studies in Economic History 42*, Stockholm University, Sweden.

Miele, M. and Murdoch, J. (2002), "The practical aesthetics of traditional cuisines: Slow food in Tuscany", *Sociologia Ruralis*, Vol. 42, No. 4, pp. 312–328.

Miguéns, J., Baggio, R. and Costa, C. (2008), "Social media and tourism destinations: TripAdvisor case study", *Advances in Tourism Research*, Aveiro, Portugal, 26–28 May.

Mishima, Y., Shikanai, K., Hayashi, M. and Ishikawa, M. (2010), "Revitalization of the Kyobashi River in Tokyo", paper presented at 15th Inter-University Symposium on Asian Mega-Cities (IUSAM), 11–12 March, University of Tokyo, Japan.

Mitchell, R.K., Agle, B.R. and Wood, D.J. (1997), "Toward a theory of stakeholder identification and salience: Defining the principle of who and what really counts", *Academy of Management Review*, Vol. 22, No. 4, pp. 853–886.

Miyazaki, H. (1991), *Totoro no sumu ie* [The place where Totoro lives], Asahi Shinbunsha, Tokyo, Japan.

Moilanen, T. and Rainisto, S. (2008), *How to Brand Nations, Cities and Destinations: A Planning Book for Place Branding*, Palgrave Macmillan, London, United Kingdom.

Morgan, N. (2004), "Problematizing place promotion", in Lew, A., Hall, C. and Williams, A. (eds), *A Companion to Tourism*, Blackwell, Oxford, United Kingdom, pp. 173–183.

Morgan, N., Pritchard, A. and Pride, R. (2002), *Destination Branding – Creating the Unique Destination Proposition*, Butterworth-Heinemann, Oxford, United Kingdom.

Morgan, N., Pritchard, A. and Pride, R. (2004), *Destination Branding: Creating the Unique Destination Proposition*, Second edition, Elsevier, Butterworth-Heinemann, Oxford, United Kingdom.

Morton, L.W., Chen, Y.C. and Morse, R. (2008), "Small town civic structure and interlocal collaboration for public services", *City & Community*, Vol. 7, No. 1, pp. 45–60.

Moscardo, G. (1996), "Mindful visitors: Heritage and tourism", *Annals of Tourism Research*, Vol. 23, No. 2, pp. 376–397.

Mossberg, L. and Getz, D. (2006), "Stakeholder influences on the ownership and management of festival brands", *Scandinavian Journal of Hospitality and Tourism*, Vol. 6, No. 4, pp. 308–326.

Muniz, A.M. and O'Guinn, T.C. (2001), "Brand community", *Journal of Consumer Research*, Vol. 27, No. 4, pp. 412–432.

Muntal, J. (2009), "Propuesta de Plan Estratégico Conglomerado de Turismo en Montevideo" [Competitiveness reinforcement plan], available at: http://www.diprode.opp.gub.uy/pacc/mvd/planestrategico.pdf (accessed 2 June 2010).

Musa, G. (2000), "Tourism in Malaysia", in Hall, C.M. and Page, S. (eds), *Tourism in South and South East Asia: Issues and Cases*, Butterworth-Heinemann, Oxford, United Kingdom, pp. 144–156.

New Economics Foundation (NEF) (2004), "Clone town Britain", New Economics Foundation, United Kingdom.

New Straits Times (2010), "Putrajaya, Cyberberjaya aim low", 22 January, p. 12.

Nilsson, P.Å. (2007), "Stakeholder theory: The need for a convenor. The case of Billund", *Scandinavian Journal of Hospitality and Tourism*, Vol. 7, No. 2, pp. 171–184.

Nordic Council (2005), *The Nordic Council Declaration in Aarhus on a New Nordic Cuisine*, signed 30 June 2005, Nordic Council, Copenhagen, Denmark.

O'Flaherty, B. (2005), *City Economics*, Harvard University Press, Cambridge, United States.

O'Keefe, K. (2008), "75% of journalists use blogs for story ideas: New survey", available at: http://kevin.lexblog.com/2008/01/articles/public-relations/75-of-journalists-use-blogs-for-story-ideas-new-survey/ (accessed 15 January 2010).

Oakes, T.S. (1993), "The cultural space of modernity: Ethnic tourism and place identity in China", *Society and Space*, Vol. 11, No. 1, pp. 47–66.

Obama, B. (2009), *Speech to the Parliament of Republic of Ghana*, 11 July.

OECD (1995), *Niche Markets as a Rural Development Strategy*, Organisation for Economic Co-operation and Development, Paris, France.

OECD (2005), *Culture and Local Development*, OECD, Paris, France.

Ooi, C.-S. (2005), "State-civil society relations and tourism: Singaporeanizing tourists, touristifying Singapore", *Sojourn – Journal of Social Issues in Southeast Asia*, Vol. 20, No. 2, pp. 249–272.

Ooi, C.-S. (2007), "The creative industries and tourism in Singapore", in Richards, G. and Wilson, J. (eds), *Tourism, Creativity and Development*, Routledge, London, United Kingdom, pp. 240–251.

Ooi, C.-S. (2008), "Reimagining Singapore as a creative nation: The politics of place branding", *Place Branding and Public Diplomacy*, Vol. 4, No. 4, pp. 287–302.

Ooi, C.-S. and Stöber, B. (2010), "Authenticity and place branding: The arts and culture in branding Berlin and Singapore", in *Re-Investing Authenticity: Tourism, Places and Emotions*, Knudsen, B.T. and Waade, A.M. (eds), Channel View Publications, Bristol, United Kingdom, pp. 66–79.

Osborne, P. (2000), *Travelling Light: Photography, Travel and Visual Culture*, Manchester University Press, Manchester, United Kingdom.

Paddison, R. (1993), "City marketing, image reconstruction and urban regeneration", *Urban Studies*, Vol. 30, No. 2, pp. 339–350.

Palmer, A. (2002), "Destination branding and the Web", in Morgan, N., Pritchard, A. and Pride, R. (eds), *Destination Branding: Creating the Unique Destination Proposition*, Butterworth-Heinemann, Oxford, United Kingdom, pp. 186–197.

Papadopoulos, N. and Heslop, L.A. (1993), *Product-Country Images: Impact and Role in International Marketing*, International Business Press, New York, United States.

Parent, M.M. and Deephouse, D.L. (2007), "A case study of stakeholder identification and prioritization by managers", *Journal of Business Ethics*, Vol. 75, No. 1, pp. 1–23.

Parkerson, B. and Saunders, J. (2005), "City branding: Can goods and services branding models be used to brand cities?", *Place Branding*, Vol. 1, No. 3, pp. 242–264.

Parmar, V. (2008), "Here, farmers welcome Nano", *Sunday Times*, Ahmedabad edition, 5 October, p. 1.

Peck, J. (2005), "Struggling with the creative class", *International Journal of Urban and Regional Research*, Vol. 29, No. 4, pp. 740–770.

Peel, D. and Lloyd, G. (2008), "New communicative challenges: Dundee, place branding and the reconstruction of a city image", *Town Planning Review*, Vol. 79, No. 5, pp. 507–532.

Pesek, W. (2006), "Our future up in the air", *The Standard*, 8 December, available at: http://www.thestandard.com.hk/news_detail.asp?pp_cat=15&art_id=33647&sid=11224813&con_type=1&d_str=20061208&sear_year=2006 (accessed 20 May 2010).

Peterson, R.A. and Jolibert, A.J.P. (1995), "A meta-analysis of country-of-origin effects", *Journal of International Business Studies*, Vol. 26, No. 4, pp. 883–900.

Pine, J. and Gilmore, J. (1999), *The Experience Economy: Work is Theatre & Every Business a Stage*, Harvard Business School Press, Boston, United States.

Prashanth, B. (2009), "Ahmedabad: The city of the future", *The Times of India*, Ahmedabad edition, 10 October, Special Supplement, p. 1.

Prentice, R. and Andersen, V. (2007), "Interpreting heritage essentialisms: Familiarity and felt history", *Tourism Management*, Vol. 28, No. 3, pp. 661–676.

"Promoting Edinburgh as a destination: Investigating the future promotion of Edinburgh as a place to live, invest and visit". February 2008, The Communication Group. Available at: http://www.edinburgh.gov.uk/internet/Attachments/Internet/Business/Economic_development/Promoting_Edinburgh_as_a_Destination.pdf (accessed 12 February 2010).

Puczko, L., Ratz, T. and Smith, M. (2007), "Old city, new image: Perception, positioning and promotion of Budapest", *Journal of Travel and Tourism Marketing*, Vol. 22, No. 3, pp. 21–34.

Puntigam, M., Braiterman, J. and Suzuki, M. (2010), "Biodiversity and new urbanism in Tokyo: The role of the Kanda River", paper presented at the International Federation of Landscape Architects 47th World Congress, 28–30 May, Suzhou, China.

Reader, J. (2004), *Cities*, Atlantic Monthly Press, New York, United States.

Richards, B. (1992), *How to Market Tourist Attractions, Festivals, and Special Events*, Longman, Essex.

Robertson, S. (2008), "Malaysia education: Strategic branding leads to growth in international student numbers 2006–8", *GlobalHigherEd*, available at: http://globalhighered.wordpress.com/ 2008/03/16/malaysias-international-student-numbers-increase-by-30-between-2006-8/ (accessed 27 January 2010).

Rowley, J. (2004), "Online branding", *Online Information Review*, Vol. 28, No. 2, pp. 131–138.

Russell, D., Mort, G.S. and Hume, M. (2009), "Analysis of management narrative to understand social marketing strategy: The case of 'Branding Logan City'", *Australasian Marketing Journal*, Vol. 17, No. 4, pp. 232–237.

Saffron Brand Consultants (2008), *The City Brand Barometer 2008*, www.saffron-consultants. com

Salomonsson, A. (1984), "Some thoughts on the concept of revitalization", *Ethnologia Scandinavica*, Vol. 1, pp. 34–47.

Sauer, A. (2006), "Las Vegas cashes in", Brandchannel, available at: http://www.brandchannel.com/ features_profile.asp?pr_id=292 (accessed 10 July 2009).

Scott, A.J. (2006), "Creative cities: Conceptual issues and policy questions", *Journal of Urban Affairs*, Vol. 28, No. 1, pp. 1–17.

Selby, M. (2004), *Understanding Urban Tourism: Image, Culture and Experience*, I.B. Taurus & Co., London, United Kingdom.

Seno, A. (2009), "Art wars: Hong Kong vs Singapore", *Wall Street Journal* [online], 30 October, available at: http://online.wsj.com/article/SB125678376301415081.html (accessed 24 November 2009).

Sesser, S. (2006), "The cheapest city on earth", *The Wall Street Journal* [online], 21 October, available at: http://online.wsj.com/article/SB116137824861399313.html (accessed 21 January 2010).

Shah, R. (2008), "Nano will be made in Ahmedabad", *Sunday Times*, Ahmedabad edition, 5 October, p. 1.

Shah, R. and Shukla, N. (2009), "Liquidity flows into 'dry' Gujarat", *The Times of India*, Ahmedabad edition, 12 January, p. 1.

Sharp, L. (2001), "Positive response action: The ultimate goal of website communication", *Journal of Communication Management*, Vol. 6, No. 1, pp. 41–52.

Sheth, J. and Sisodia, R. (2005), "A dangerous divergence: Marketing and society", *Journal of Public Policy and Marketing*, Vol. 24, No. 1, pp. 160–162.

Skinner, H. (2005), "Wish you were here? Some problems associated with integrating marketing communications when promoting place brands", *Place Branding*, Vol. 1, No. 3, pp. 299–315.

Smith, A. (2005), "Conceptualizing city image change: The 're-imaging' of Barcelona", *Tourism Geographies*, Vol. 7, No. 4, pp. 398–423.

Smith, M.F. (2004), "Brand Philadelphia: The power of spotlight events", in Morgan, N., Pritchard, A. and Pride, R. (eds), *Destination Branding: Creating the Unique Destination Proposition*, Second edition, Butterworth-Heinemann, Oxford, United Kingdom, pp. 261–278.

Sterne, J. (1999), *World Wide Web Marketing*, Second edition, Wiley, New York, United States.

Svenska Livsmedel (2009), "Det nya matlandet: Att göra näringspolitik av gastronomi" (In English: The new food land: Making economic policies of gastronomy), *Svenska Livsmedel*, No. 6, pp. 20–22.

Sya, L.S. (2005), *Branding Malaysia*, Oak Enterprise, Petaling Jaya, Malaysia.

Tatevossian, A.R. (2008), "Domestic society's (often-neglected) role in nation branding", *Place Branding and Public Diplomacy*, Vol. 4, No. 2, pp. 182–190.

Tellström, R., Gustafsson, I.B. and Mossberg, L. (2005), "Local food cultures in the Swedish rural economy", *Sociologia Ruralis*, Vol. 45, No. 4, pp. 346–360.

Tellström, R., Gustafsson, I.B. and Mossberg, L. (2006), "Origin as brand: Converting anonymous food products into symbols of place using regional food cultural heritage", *Place Branding*, Vol. 2, No. 2, pp. 130–143.

Temporal, P. (2001), *Branding in Asia*, John Wiley and Sons, Singapore.

The Economist (2008), "The rivals – London and Paris", 15 March, p. 35.

The Globe and Mail (1987), Peter Ustinov Interview with John Bentley Mays, 1 August 1987.

The Governor's Residence Cookery Book – Food from the West for Everyday and Festive Meals (1999). (In Swedish: Residensets kokbok: Mat från väst till vardag och fest., Nordbok International, Gothenburg, Sweden.

The Star Online (2008), "Highlights of Budget 2009", 29 August, available at: http://thestar.com. my/news/story.asp?file=/2008/8/29/budget2009/20080829161149&sec=budget2009 (accessed 11 January 2010).

The Times of India (2009), "Apco to market Vibrant Guj", Ahmedabad edition, 15 October, p. 1.

The Times of India (2010a), "One more feather in the cap for city BRTS", 29 May, p. 2.

The Times of India (2010b), "At 50, ready to rival Mumbai", Ahmedabad edition, 1 May, p. 1.

Therkelsen, A. and Halkier, H. (2008), "Contemplating place branding umbrellas. The case of coordinated national tourism and business promotion in Denmark", *Scandinavian Journal of Hospitality and Tourism*, Vol. 8, No. 2, pp. 159–175.

Thetourismcompany.com (2009), "Twitter and its use by tourism destinations", available at: http://www.thetourismcompany.com/topic.asp?topicid=21 (accessed 12 January 2010).

Tourismireland.com (2007), "Tourism Ireland launches the world's first tourism marketing drive in 'Second Life'", available at: http://www.tourismireland.com/Home/about-us/press-releases/2007/Tourism-Ireland-Launches-the-World%E2%80%99s-First-Tourism.aspx (accessed 6 January 2010).

Travolution.co.uk (2009), "Case study – WAYN-Joburg tourism", available at: http://www.travolution.co.uk/articles/2009/02/23/2258/case-study-wayn-joburg-tourism.html (accessed 5 January 2010).

Tregear, A. (1998), "Artisan producers in the UK food system: Attributes and implications", paper presented at the Agricultural Economics Society Annual Conference, University of Reading, 26 March 1998.

Tregear, A. (2003), "From Stilton to Vimto: Using food history to re-think typical products in rural development", *Sociologia Ruralis*, Vol. 43, No. 2, pp. 91–108.

Trubek, A. (2008), *The Taste of a Place: A Cultural Journey into Terror*, University of California Press, Berkeley, United States.

Trueman, M., Cook, D. and Cornelius, N. (2008), "Creative dimensions for branding and regeneration: Overcoming negative perceptions of a city", *Place Branding and Public Diplomacy*, Vol. 4, No. 1, pp. 29–44.

Trueman, M., Klemm, M. and Giroud, A. (2004), "Can a city communicate? Bradford as a corporate brand", *Corporate Communications: An International Journal*, Vol. 9, No. 4, pp. 317–330.

United Nations (2005), *World Urbanization Prospects: The 2005 Revision*, Population Division, Department of Economic and Social Affairs, United Nations, available at: http://www.un.org/esa/population/publications/WUP2005/2005wup.htm.

United Nations Population Fund (2007), *State of World Population 2007: Unleashing the Potential of Urban Growth*, available at: http://www.unfpa.org/swp/2007/english/introduction.html (accessed 15 May 2010).

Urry, J. (1990), *The Tourist Gaze: Leisure and Travel in Contemporary Societies*, Sage, London, United Kingdom.

Urry, J. (1995), *Consuming Places*, Routledge, London, United Kingdom.

Urry, J. (2002[1990]), *The Tourist Gaze: Leisure and Travel in Contemporary Societies*, Second edition, Sage Publications, London, United Kingdom.

Valerio, P., Baker, B. and Gulloch, G. (1999), *Wollongong Image Strategy*, Report to Wollongong City Council, Wollongong, Australia.

Vallaster, C. and de Chernatony, L. (2006), "Internal brand building and structuration: The role of leadership", *European Journal of Marketing*, Vol. 40, No. 7/8, pp. 761–784.

van Gelder, S. (2008), "An introduction to city branding", available at; www.placebrands.net/_files/An_Introduction_to_City_Branding.pdf (accessed 20 January 2010).

Vanolo, A. (2008), "Internationalization in the Helsinki metropolitan area: Images, discourses and metaphors", *European Planning Studies*, Vol. 16, No. 2, pp. 229–252.

Vastu-Shilpa Foundation (2002), *The Ahmedabad Chronicle: Imprints of a Millennium*, Vastu Shilpa Foundation for Studies and Research in Environmental Design, Ahmedabad, India.

Vasudevan, S. (2008), "The role of internal stakeholders in destination branding: Observations from Kerala tourism", *Place Branding and Public Diplomacy*, Vol. 4, No. 4, pp. 331–335.

Verlegh, P.W.J. and Steenkamp, J-B.E.M. (1999), "A review and meta-analysis of country-of-origin research", *Journal of Economic Psychology*, Vol. 20, No. 5, pp. 521–546.

Visit Aarhus (2010), *Frontpage*, available at; http://www.visitaarhus.com/international/en-gb/menu/turist/turist-maalgruppe-forside.htm (accessed 5 February 2010).

Waller, J. and Lea, S.E.G. (1999), "Seeking the real Spain? Authenticity in Motivation", *Annals of Tourism Research*, Vol. 26, No. 1, pp. 110–129.

Watson, S. (1991), "Gilding the smokestacks: The new symbolic representations of de-industrialised regions", *Environment and Planning D: Society and Space*, Vol. 9, No. 1, pp. 59–70.

Weisman, A. (2007), *The World Without Us*, St Martin Press, New York, United States.

White, C. and Raman, N. (1999), "The World Wide Web as a public relations medium: The use of research, planning and evaluation in website development", *Public Relations Review*, Vol. 25, No. 4, pp. 405–513.

Williams, A., Kitchen, P., Randall, J. and Muhajarine, N. (2008), "Changes in quality of life perceptions in Saskatoon, Saskatchewan: Comparing survey results from 2001 and 2004", *Social Indicators Research*, Vol. 85, No. 1, pp. 5–22.

Winn, M. (2008), *Central Park in the Dark: More Mysteries of Urban Wildlife*, Farrar, Straus and Giroux, New York, United States.

Winter, C. (2009), *Branding Finland on the Internet: Images and Stereotypes in Finland's Tourism Marketing*, Master's Thesis, University of Jyväskylä, Jyväskylä, Finland, available at: https://jyx.jyu.fi/dspace/bitstream/handle/123456789/21829/URN_NBN_fi_jyu-200910073971.pdf?sequence=1 (accessed 28 May 2010).

Wolf, E. (2006), *Culinary Tourism: The Hidden Harvest*, Kendall/Hunt Publishing Company, United States.

Wollongong City Council (2010a), *Community Profile*, available at: http://profile.id.com.au/Default.aspx?id=302 (accessed 15 January 2010).

Wollongong City Council (2010b), *City of Innovation*, available at: http://www.wollongong.nsw.gov.au/ (accessed 15 January 2010).

Wong, A. (2008), "Heritage and ecology may become part of Hong Kong branding", *South China Morning Post*, 29 September, p. 5.

Yale Center for Environmental Law and Policy, and Center for International Earth Science Information Network, Columbia University (2010), *2010 Environmental Performance Index*, Yale University, Yale, available at: http://epi.yale.edu/file_columns/0000/0008/epi-2010.pdf (accessed 5 February 2010).

Yoder, D. (1981), "The sausage culture of the Pennsylvania Germans", in Fenton, A. and Owen, T.M. (eds), *Food in Perspective: Proceedings of the Third International Conference on Ethnological Food Research, Cardiff, Wales, 1977*, J. Donald Publishers Ltd, Edinburgh, United Kingdom, pp. 409–425.

Zanina, P. (2010), "We're tops in tourism", *Travel Times/New Straits Times* [online], available at: http://travel.nst.com.my/article/FeatureStory/20100105100226/Article/print_html (accessed 29 January 2010).

Zeller, Jr, T. (2009), "Bloomberg eyes Danish offshore wind farm and sees New York's future", *New York Times*, 14 December, available at: http://greeninc.blogs.nytimes.com/2009/12/14/bloomberg-eyes-danish-offshore-wind-farm-and-sees-new-yorks-future/?scp=3&sq=copenhagen%20wind&st=cse (accessed 5 February 2010).

Zenker, S. (2009), "Who's your target? The creative class as a target group for place branding", *Journal of Place Management and Development*, Vol. 2, No. 1, pp. 23–32.

Zhang, L. and Zhao, S.X. (2009), "City branding and the Olympic effect: A case study of Beijing", *Cities*, Vol. 26, No. 5, pp. 245–254.

RECOMMENDED READING

Baker, B. (2007), *Destination Branding for Small Cities: The Essentials for Successful Place Branding*, Creative Leap Books, Portland Oregon, USA. Succinct and compelling, an easy-read recipe for branding success from one of today's top destination marketers and an architect of the Australian Tourism Commission's 'Shrimp on the Barbie' campaign.

Greenberg, M. (2008), *Branding New York City: How a City in Crisis Was Sold to the World*, Routledge, London and New York. Meticulously researched, this study is written by a sociologist rather than a marketer, and provides an interesting perspective on New York City's woes during the 1970s as the campaign was developing.

INDEX